THE SCIENCE OF HOUSEWORK
The Home and Public Health, 1880–1940

Ann Oakley

P

First published in Great Britain in 2024 by

Policy Press, an imprint of
Bristol University Press
University of Bristol
1–9 Old Park Hill
Bristol
BS2 8BB
UK
t: +44 (0)117 374 6645
e: bup-info@bristol.ac.uk

Details of international sales and distribution partners are available at policy.bristoluniversitypress.co.uk

© Bristol University Press 2024

British Library Cataloguing in Publication Data
A catalogue record for this book is available from the British Library

ISBN 978-1-4473-6961-5 hardcover
ISBN 978-1-4473-6962-2 paperback
ISBN 978-1-4473-6963-9 ePub
ISBN 978-1-4473-6964-6 ePdf

The right of Ann Oakley to be identified as author of this work has been asserted by her in accordance with the Copyright, Designs and Patents Act 1988.

All rights reserved: no part of this publication may be reproduced, stored in a retrieval system, or transmitted in any form or by any means, electronic, mechanical, photocopying, recording, or otherwise without the prior permission of Bristol University Press.

Every reasonable effort has been made to obtain permission to reproduce copyrighted material. If, however, anyone knows of an oversight, please contact the publisher.

The statements and opinions contained within this publication are solely those of the author and not of the University of Bristol or Bristol University Press. The University of Bristol and Bristol University Press disclaim responsibility for any injury to persons or property resulting from any material published in this publication.

Bristol University Press and Policy Press work to counter discrimination on grounds of gender, race, disability, age and sexuality.

Cover design: Robin Hawes
Front cover image: Q/PH3/12 King's College London Archives

Readers should be aware that Chapter 10 contains
a racist image and a discussion of that image.

The province of Domestic Science in its application to the normal life, may be conceived as in one respect parallel to that of medicine in its application to diseased life. Both are applying knowledge, the splendid instruments of science, the one to the maintenance of life in efficiency and health, the other to the restoration of life after it has fallen from that condition.

> *Hilda Oakeley (1911) Speech at the Opening of the Extension of the Gloucester School of Domestic Science, King's College, London, Archives, KWA/GPF/11*

Household economics is the connecting link between the physical economics of the individual and the social economics of the state. Its relation to human life is of the most intimate and vital nature. ... Whether we live or die, and how we live or die, are largely determined by our household condition.

> *Helen Campbell (1897) Household Economics: A Course of Lectures in the School of Economics of the University of Wisconsin, New York: G.P. Putnam's Sons, p 2*

Contents

List of figures and tables		vi
Acknowledgements		viii
Prologue: My life in housework		x
1	Introduction: From the sociology to the science of housework	1
2	Gender and germs: housework today	12
3	Teaching girls about housework	23
4	Sweeping science into the home	44
5	This man-made world	65
6	Lectures for ladies	87
7	Alice through the cooking class	107
8	Transatlantic experiments	130
9	Sources of power	151
10	White subjects: domestic science in the colonies and other places	173
11	Legacies and meanings	191
Appendix: List of characters		207
Notes		210
Additional sources		228
Index		237

List of figures and tables

Figures

P.1	Cotton patch. Domestic science lesson, Haberdashers' Aske's School, Acton, 1955	xiii
P.2	Design for my apron. Domestic science lesson, Haberdashers' Aske's School, Acton, 1955	xiv
2.1	Cleaning utensils for dishwashing in ten European countries	16
2.2	Silverfish foraging in the nightly hours	18
2.3	What housework do Britons say only they do at home?	20
3.1	Catherine Beecher aged 77	25
3.2	Girls learning cookery at school in Leeds	26
3.3	Girls in cooking class with instructor	36
4.1	'The antique "pan-closet" – the sanitarian's horror'	46
4.2	Housework in the old days	48
4.3	Bacteria in the 'eyes' of potatoes	52
4.4	A dust garden	53
4.5	Ellen Swallow Richards, portrait with cat, 1860–1867	62
5.1	Paulette Bernège in her rationally organised kitchen in 1930	70
5.2	'Inside the gas meter'	72
5.3	'Select knives carefully to meet a definite need'	73
5.4	Margarete Schütte-Lihotzky at the age of 100 in 1997	78
5.5	A Frankfurt Kitchen in Frankfurt, 1927–1928	79
6.1	'Vestry Hall' in Kensington, 2023, where Lectures for Ladies began	89
6.2	Conspirators for academic household science at King's College: Lilian Faithfull, Adèle Meyer, Alice Ravenhill and Thereza Rücker	95
6.3	King's College for Women, June 1911	106
7.1	The periodic table in cupcakes	111
7.2	The gates of the Campden Hill building	113
7.3	Quadrangle view towards the cookery class window	114
7.4	Staff and students of King's College for Women in 1920	118
7.5	Working in the science laboratories, 1924	120
7.6	The ironing room	121
8.1	The domestic pipe system	133
8.2	Marion Talbot in 1892	136
8.3	Respiration Calorimeter, Washington, DC, circa 1915	140
8.4	Sophonisba Breckinridge and Edith Abbott, 'A & B', undated	141
8.5	The effect on bread of different amounts of salt	145
9.1	The new electric hairdryer	155
9.2	Woman with vacuum cleaner smiling	156

9.3	Annie confused	157
9.4	'The most wonderful health safeguard'	163
9.5	Woman mending fuse	165
9.6	The Bristol All-Electric House, 1935	170
10.1	Dingman's Electric Soap, advertisement, c 1880–1889	175
10.2	Marian Irwin and Hideko Inoue at a peace conference in 1921	178
10.3	Ann Gilchrist Strong with household arts students in Baroda, India, 1917	188

Table

5.1	Daily schedule for family of three	75

Acknowledgements

I've been thinking about the science of housework for far longer than I've been writing it – not all my life, because children aren't much interested in housework unless they have to be – but for at least the last 60 years. Housework is embedded in our daily lives. We give the matter of its mechanics minor attention, and some of us rail against its very existence, yet why housework exists in the way it does and why it matters are questions of great import that mostly shelter unconsidered in the locked over-stuffed cupboards of our minds. A lifetime of thinking and not thinking about housework is the background to this book. Thus, my acknowledgements must begin with a general recognition that *The Science of Housework* wouldn't be the book it is without the multiple prompts and insights of a lived domesticity. The mother who wrung her flour-encrusted hands with despair at the daughter's disdain for the enterprise of cake-making; the husband's (mostly vain) entreaties for steak-and-kidney pudding; the children's fractious complaints about wrinkled, off-white clothes; the way dust marred the surfaces on which books about this and that were written while cobwebs dangled mockingly overhead: all these have been a kind of inspiration.

Other more precise debts must be acknowledged. First, I'm very grateful to all the archivists and librarians who have helped me locate the books and papers that have contributed to the story I tell in *The Science of Housework* about the movement to rehabilitate housework that spanned the latter part of the 19th and the early 20th centuries. Staff at the Women's Library at the London School of Economics, at the Norfolk Records Office in Norwich and at the West Yorkshire Archive Service in Leeds were valuable aids. I spent many weeks in the archives of King's College, London, exploring the history of King's College of Household and Social Science, that maverick institution whose existence, drawing together the two great occupations of my life, first convinced me that there was a larger narrative here that needed to see the light of day. Without the specialist help of the archival staff there it would have been impossible for me to find out what I wanted to know. The conversations I had with Dawn Bonfield about electricity, engineering and women as a result of the staff's introduction of two women who appeared to be poring over the same set of papers was inspiring, so big thanks all round.

I have the good fortune still (at the age of 80) to have maintained a university research contract. This is funded in part by a grant from the Titmuss-Meinhardt Fund at London School of Economics which has supported my work on forgotten women and neglected histories for many years. In thanking the Fund Committee, I'm aware that house dust mites, bacteria in the eyes of potatoes and electric moth-destroyers do somewhat strain the Fund's brief to cover social policy work, but I hope the Committee agrees

Acknowledgements

with the logic I've tried to spell out in the book that a primary requirement for social welfare is scientifically driven, health-enhancing homes.

In writing *The Science of Housework* I've relied heavily on the advice and support of a group of dedicated readers: Graham Crow, Karen Dunnell, Robin Oakley and Joy Schaverien. What would I have done without all your comments and questions? These have ranged all the way from the major (the last chapter should come first; how do you define a movement? why don't you mention what Max Weber says about households?) to the less so (these sentences are too long; you've misplaced 'only' yet again). I am immensely grateful for all this help. I apologise to Graham Crow for not doing as he asked and including the telling comment he chanced upon in his mother's copy of *Little Women*, but here it is: 'I do think washing dishes and keeping things tidy is the worst work in the world.' This observation comes from the most compliant of Louisa M. Alcott's quartet, Beth (on page 2), and if Beth thinks that, well, it must be true. My dear bilingual friend Catherine Cullen checked my French spellings and kindly translated a French text on housework for me.

The Science of Housework was written in my home in Rutland where I was able to take to my bicycle or lie under the apple tree when I couldn't see the wood for the trees. There I benefited from many acts of neighbourly kindness (figs, eggs, friendly chats, the repairing of a broken window, access to the internet when BT ruined mine). Thanks especially for the gift of respecting and protecting my solitude. Similarly, the wonderful team at Policy Press left me alone to get on with it, and it has been a pleasure to work through the production process with them again.

My own family have contributed in diverse ways. My very hygienic daughter-in-law, Sanja Oakley, with whom I have sparred happily for years about standards of household cleanliness, was delighted to point out that I had missed the disinfecting capacity of sunlight. My grandson, Reuben Oakley-Brown, achieved technical wonders with the pictures, noting with particular amusement the map of dishwashing techniques around the world which turns up in Chapter 2. My son Adam Oakley, daughters Emily Caston and Laura Oakley, and grand-daughters Zoe Oakley, Tabitha Oakley-Brown, Adrienne Caston and Sylvie Oakley-Brown, have graciously (most of the time) put up with the mental and social absences from their lives my obsession with the science of housework has entailed. And as always – but I never take this for granted – I have been sustained, encouraged and resourced in every possible way by Robin, who still doesn't know what a duster is for.

Prologue: My life in housework

This book is about housework as *science*: bacteria, germs, dirt, tools, machines, water, coal, gas, electricity and architecture are among its main characters. So are the people, mostly women, who had the vision needed to understand the importance of household science in making the world a healthier place. To this end, they engaged in huge amounts of scientific and educational work, much of which has been eclipsed from our cultural memory, and some of which appears in the following chapters of this book. But housework is a matter of personal experience as well as of scientific analysis and public policy. The observations that follow originally formed an Appendix to *The Science of Housework*, but I came to see that they were misplaced, that I had succumbed to the academic convention which hides from view the origins of our intellectual engagement with the world.

★★★

I began this morning by watching a YouTube video about how to mend a dishwasher. One of the machine's little red lights was flashing. I had no idea why: the light said the machine needed more salt to be added, but I'd done that, and still the light blinked fiercely at me. This whole episode is a huge inconvenience to me, a pensioner (which is not how I think of myself) living on her own with no one else to blame, most of the time, for the burnt porridge saucepans and the congealed remains of odd delicious meals.

I've never liked washing up. I do it so badly that my family refuse to let me do it in their houses. Often I don't put my glasses on, so much of the detritus just has a swim and is still there afterwards. I read somewhere the useful piece of advice that housework is easier if you can't see the dust and the bits of rubbish which this book is so excruciatingly about; thus, leave your glasses off when you do it. None of those wise matrons whose sensible scientific tracts feature in this book would have approved of me. This morning I have to take all the dirty dishes out of the dishwasher and subject them to my version of hand-cleaning. The water is barely hot, and I am cross. After I've done it all I apply a YouTube remedy to the blinking dishwasher (two litres of boiling water in the salt hole) and feel a ridiculous sense of achievement when the red light consents to turn itself off.

Housework is a deeply emotional subject: it involves feelings, hopes, disappointments, histories, desires, memories. As I 'wash' the dishes I remember my parents standing at the kitchen sink, a tiny sink in a tiny cramped kitchen: my mother washed, wearing one of her many aprons, and placed the clean dishes on the small draining board from where my father, tea-towel in hand, lifted and wiped them, returning them to the

Prologue

plate cupboard that stood just behind him. The cupboard was two steps up in the dining room; he was a tall man, and in my memory his head is touching the ceiling.

This is a memory from the 1950s. Attached to it is the image of a small cream and brown jug which lived at the front of the plate cupboard and which carried the legend in pretend copperplate writing, 'Never burden today's strength with tomorrow's loads'. As a small child I found this strangely fascinating. My parents' dishwashing dance also interested me, because it was one of the few things I saw them do together. Cleaning the dishes united them in a ceremony of domestic difference: she washed, he dried, never the other way round. Moreover, and I only realised this just now, when they dishwashed they couldn't smoke their cigarettes, which they were otherwise suffocatingly fond of doing.

Housework – the whole physical apparatus of the house, the provision, preparation and serving of food, the caring for clothes and house linen – was my mother's domain. My father went out to work and brought home the money, like millions of other men. The only other domestic duty my father performed was peeling the potatoes. We seemed to have them at most meals. He would stand in front of the sink, in my mother's dishwashing position, and the curls of peel, as long as he could make them, would fall into the whiteness of the sink, discolouring it with crumbs of earth.

It was altogether a ridiculous kitchen. The British researcher and novelist Clementina Black, who appears in Chapter 5, would certainly have considered it an idiocy. I don't remember when I first thought that, but it's an opinion I've held for a very long time, and even written about before. The kitchen was narrow, barely two metres wide, and perhaps four metres long. At one end was a gas-powered fridge which my mother was very proud of (she said it was more economical than the electric sort – and she was right [see Chapter 9]). Next to that was a 1930s contraption which she loved even more than the fridge: a two-doored cupboard below and another above, and in-between a vitreous enamel shelf that pulled out to form the kitchen's only work surface. The British television cook Zena Skinner, interviewed in the late 1940s, recalled that 'everybody seemed to have one of those cabinets'.[1] Inside the top cupboard of the cabinet was a device for measuring flour. My mother would stand in front of this in another of her aprons, her hands coated in flour, concocting pastry or cakes and puddings, into which went a good deal of fine white sugar from the upper cupboard. This piece of furniture was the heart of the kitchen. Next to it was an antiquated gas stove, its frame fashioned out of some blue speckled material. The stove was opposite the back door and therefore its flames were subject to the constant opening of the door and the weather. It frightened me: the hiss and smell of the gas, the intensity of the blue-flamed jets, the frequent dangerous disasters of blown-out flames.

And that, apart from the sink, was the kitchen. When, some years ago, English Heritage affixed a blue plaque to the house declaring that my father (but not my mother) had lived there, its current owners showed us round the house. I was glad to see that the kitchen had gone. Well, *that* kitchen had gone, and a new one had sprung up in what had been my father's study, in his time a serious book-lined room overlooking the paved front garden with its faded blue hydrangeas. The new kitchen was now transformed into a monument of black marble worktops and space-age kitchen design. I seem able to hold both images in my head at the same time; the new one isn't simply superimposed on the old. I can switch between them; they coexist. Memory can be very ingenious and precise as well as duplicitous and misleading.

In the 1950s good middle-class wives and mothers in countries like Britain stayed at home to look after their families and get depressed about the self-defeating repetitive nature of the duty life had assigned to them. In my memory my mother is totally occupied by housework to the exclusion of almost everything else, except listening to my father's accounts of his struggles with academic life, accompanying him to official celebrations, buying my school uniform and checking my school reports. I'm quite sure that this is a misremembered memory – she must have done and been other things apart from Mrs Good Housewife. Yet this is how I think of my childhood: my mother bustling round the house carrying out intensive enquiries into the possibility of dust and dirt in the crevices of the lino-covered floor or the angles of chair legs, and especially on the highly polished surfaces of various mahogany tables and cupboards in the sitting-room. I wondered then why anyone would choose to buy something that cried out for so much labour, especially when my mother otherwise welcomed labour-saving approaches such as baths and banisters enclosed in dust-free hardwood sides. I remember her delight, I think I can even see her clapping her hands, at arranging the disappearance of the ornate banisters and the curved bath sides inside their white-painted coverings. It seemed very idiosyncratic to me then, even rather silly and certainly unaesthetic, but, having done the research for this book, I see that she may simply have been responding to a cultural moment in the history of housework that ordained such labour-reducing minimalist techniques.

My mother didn't actually do most of the labour herself: that was performed by a succession of women who came in pink nylon overalls from the housing estates of East Acton in order to be berated by my mother for not doing the housework correctly. She had almost as much trouble with these untrained domestic helpers as my father did with the trained social workers who staffed the department he ran at the university. Both groups of women were querulous and self-interested, although one was paid much more highly than the other. I wasn't into gender and economics then, and wages for housework was decades into the future as a liberationist campaign. I don't know what my mother paid the women from East Acton, but I do hope she paid them well.

As a child I displayed no interest in housework, but this didn't mean that I had no feelings or thoughts about it. We did have some sort of lessons in domesticity at my girls' school, mostly concerning jam tarts and sewing intricate patches on things. Figure P.1 comes from my 1955 school domestic science book (I was 11); it shows a badly executed patch for which the teacher awarded me a C+. 'Design for my apron', Figure P.2, is even more oppressive. But what was the point of these exercises? I don't remember any science in the domestic lessons, no attempt to lead us into an understanding of why well-done housework was important for personal and public health. The school I attended, Haberdashers' Aske's in Acton, London, taught so-called domestic science to all its girls, following the dictates of an earlier

Figure P.1: Cotton patch. Domestic science lesson, Haberdashers' Aske's School, Acton, 1955

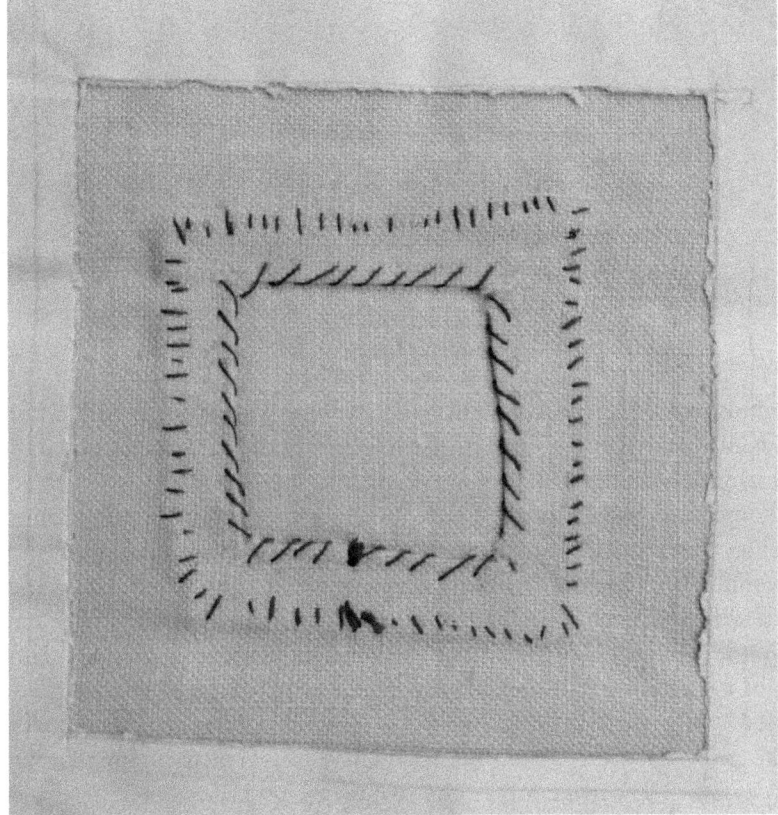

Source: Author's photo

Figure P.2: Design for my apron. Domestic science lesson, Haberdashers' Aske's School, Acton, 1955

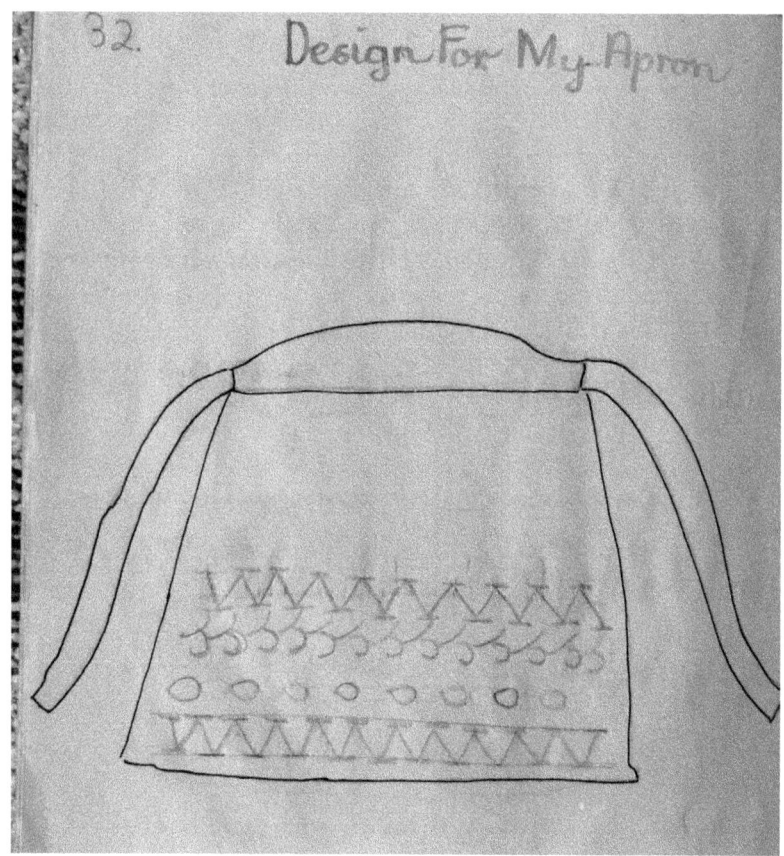

Source: Author's photo

headmistress, Margaret Gilliland, who said that girls' schools with a purely academic bias might produce fine scholars, 'But they are doing little to help our national life, because they are doing nothing to make our girls builders of homes and makers of men.'[2] In my early exposure to school domestic science, there was, of course, no reference to the gender division of labour. It would never have occurred to me, in any case, to dispute the arrangements with which I and my friends grew up. All of us had mothers who stayed at home, and we wouldn't have dreamed of suggesting that our fathers ought to have done more housework, because obviously nothing could be less important than housework (or more important than men's work). I also grew up with a firm, but completely unarticulated, conviction that housework didn't make my mother happy. As a social scientist, I do accept that the relationship between her housework and her misery could have been correlational rather than causal. Yet I am persuaded by the evidence of much research carried out into women's situation that she was one of a kind.

When I was a teenager my mother tried to enrol me in what I had by then decided was this global conspiracy of women who assume home-making is something they have to do. (My decision was based more on a wish not to tidy my bedroom than on any competent intellectual analysis.) She wanted to teach me how to make pies and cakes on her 1930s contraption or stew meat on her exploding gas stove. I was unresponsive, a disappointment to her. But when I got married at the age of 20 and some months later set up home in a small flat in Islington, she brought her next-door neighbour, who had given us a set of red-handled saucepans as a wedding present, to have lunch with me, so she could show off her now finally domesticated daughter. I gave them tinned chicken in white sauce from Marks & Spencer, which I elaborated with frozen peas and rice. They seemed satisfied.

This was 1965. I had learnt how to open tins from my time as a student living in the house of Oxford's Medical Officer of Health. A friend and I rented rooms in Norman and Jessie Parfitt's cold draughty house. We each had a gas ring in our rooms. Mine was right by my bed and of course it worried me, since it reminded me of other dysfunctional gas appliances. The friend I lived with in that house, Sally Hunt, became an economist and a world expert on electricity. Twenty years ago she gave me a copy of her hefty book, *Making Competition Work in Electricity*, which sits on my bookshelves, uneasily between history and gender studies. In the last six months of my student career, when I became a married woman, I moved into a three-room basement flat in North Oxford which required a lot of looking after, as it was damp, cold and ill-furnished, and had an incomprehensible boiler. I was in no doubt that it was my job to sort all this out; I even felt a little proud of my new role, inviting my unmarried student friends (in the spring, when the boiler wasn't needed) to witness the spectacular level of domestic skill I had acquired in such a short time.

I did say this was all a long time ago. For about five years I carried on in the same vein, doing it all and minding periodically, but closing the door on my irritation as unworthy and pointless. One sign of my commitment was that I managed to go into butchers' shops, holding my nose against the terrible smell, because I thought a good woman should be able to cook meat, although I was/am a lifelong non-meat-eater. I beat the liver hard with a wooden rolling-pin to flatten it, and this helped somewhat. I think I was proud of doing it all. It felt as though it had something to do with love. By planning and cooking the meals (I think my husband, Robin, did help with the washing up, or do I think that because my father did?), by taking the washing to the launderette, by trying to make hopeless mechanical aids work, I was somehow showing how much I cared for and about the man I'd married, and then about the babies that were born to us and who never behaved like the ones in the schedules of time-and-motion expert Christine Frederick we'll read about in Chapter 5.

I wrote it all down in little red notebooks. They survive as mementoes of my attempt to understand what I was doing with my life (and as unnerving prophecies of what was to come). This is Friday, 10 March 1967, when I was the mother of an eight-week-old baby, Adam:

> 5 am–6 am, Feed and change Adam. Cup of tea.
> 6.30 am–8.45 am, Sleep.
> 8.45 am–9.40 am, Feed Adam. Change him and wash his face.
> 9.40 am–10.05 am, Have breakfast, get dressed.
> 10.05 am–10.20 am, Make bed. Clear up bedroom. Collect dirty washing together.
> 10.20 am–11.50 am, Clean kitchen. Clean oven. Scrub floor. Wash up breakfast things.
> 11.50 am–11.55 am, Eat apple.
> 11.55 am–12.50 pm, Wash 4 nappies, 3 sheets, 2 nighties, 1 cardigan, 1 dress, 1 skirt, 8 prs stockings, 7 pants, 1 shirt, 3 prs socks. Hang on line. Finish cleaning kitchen (sink unit, rubbish bin, dish rack).
> 12.50 pm–1.10 pm, Have my lunch.
> 1.10 pm–2.00 pm, Feed and change Adam. Put in pram.
> 2.00 pm–2.30 pm, Wash up and tidy up.
> 2.30 pm–3.15 pm, Go to launderette. Do shopping.
> 3.15 pm–3.30 pm, Put Adam in cot, unpack shopping, sort out washing, make cup of tea. Start defrosting fridge.
> 3.30 pm–5.00 pm, Scrub breakfast room floor. Dust and clean. Polish table. Vacuum, dust, polish sitting room. Tidy up.
> 5.00 pm–6.00 pm, Bath, feed and change Adam
> 6.00 pm–7 pm, Clear up bath things. Vacuum hall. Cook cat's fish. Clean out fridge. Cook supper.
> 7.00 pm–8.30 pm, Have supper. Watch television.
> 7.30 pm–9.15 pm, Wash and dry hair. Wash up.
> 9.15 pm–10.30 pm, Feed and change Adam.
> 10.30 pm–11 pm, Have bath. Get into bed.

Dreary, isn't it? The fridge seems to have got a lot of attention. Note that I did washing by hand as well as going to the launderette. Note also the absence from this recitation of any other adult. Housework was something that had to be done, like paying the bills, which, in a conventional division of labour, was a duty that belonged to men. That was it, it was called *the division of labour*. Giving it a name (which I learnt as a sociology student) somehow made it more acceptable. Housework was swallowed up into a whole glorious pattern whereby the advance of civilisation was marked by the increasing differentiation of tasks, because this was clearly more efficient and comfortable for everybody. But was it? And who is 'everybody'? I've just looked at the Wikipedia entry on 'division of labour', and all the 16 authorities on the subject quoted are men. The most famous of these, the French sociologist Émile Durkheim, thought that the division of labour produced a kind of *moral* solidarity in society. He wasn't thinking about housework here, but, were the assignment of housework to women not disguised in moral clothes, we wouldn't be doing it. We can never get away from the fact that housework is women's fate in a patriarchal capitalist society. In the end there's no escaping this weighty terminology because it just tells the truth.

It took me a long time to work this out, partly because I had so much housework to do. After the two flats came four houses, all of which I made the curtains for, on my grandmother's 1879 mother-of-pearl-encrusted sewing machine. I can remember all the curtains. In the first house, the kitchen ones were black-and-white pillow ticking, which was quite easy (the lines on them meant I could cut them straight). The sitting room curtains were made out of some beige material that never hung properly, because I'd sewn the lining in crooked. The children's room had thick purple serge, with purple linings, against the light (and a matching purple toy cupboard – yes, I also painted furniture). The room off the kitchen where we ate had an orange daisy pattern from John Lewis, and round cushions on the chairs with differently coloured cushions and ties that periodically detached themselves and had to be resewn. Upstairs was the blue version of the daisy pattern in our bedroom; the yellow one in the bathroom; the black and pink one in another small room (the material must have been on some special offer); and then in my study (which jutted out over the kitchen and where I rarely studied) there was a pair of red denim curtains, which faded in the sunshine because they'd been made out of cheap dress material; and, finally, floor-to-ceiling grey-and-white striped ones in the room where Robin wrote his PhD on Cypriot immigration to Britain and prepared his lectures on the sociology of the family for his students. It may sound like a huge grand house but it wasn't. The rooms were squashed, as was the house itself in a terrace between two others. The previous incumbents had left cheap red carpets on the floors which wore thin and showed every bit of debris, but we couldn't afford to replace them (we lived in a condition of permanent debt which I tried not to think about). The vacuum cleaner was eaten by mice in the cupboard under the stairs.

I don't remember having a routine of the kind advised in all the housework books I read in order to write this one. No amount of inscribing in little red notebooks what I was up to constituted a proper, scientific system. With two babies 16 months apart in an era before disposable nappies, the washing was particularly burdensome. There *was* something, though, about that line of white nappies blowing in the wind … I bought *Woman* and *Woman's Own* most weeks out of the housekeeping money, arguing that as a sociologist I had to know about the culture to which other women were exposed. There was much more about housework in those magazines then than there is now: now microbes have been superseded by media stars and only a very brazen or insane editor would print tips about the best way to remove dust from crevices or sew curtains that hang properly. I went out and bought copies of these magazines today and could find nothing about housework in either of them apart from one small item in each about feeding your family for less: the rest is about celebrities ('You did what? Stars reveal their embarrassing moments'); so-called 'lifestyle' ('Second chance love thanks to my toyboy', '10 of the best bras'); and health ('Diet myths debunked', 'Supermarket skincare wrinkle-free fixes from £1.49').[3] Back in the 1960s I cut recipes out of the magazines and stuck them in a little book with an alphabetical index: *apple cake, cauliflower cheese, oven chips, sausage hotpot*. I bought a little book by the journalist Claire Rayner called *Housework the Easy Way*. It was truly little, a Corgi Mini Book, just the size to fit in a housewife's pocket (rather like the manuals witch-hunters used to have in the 16th century which they could tuck into their clothes). Rayner began with prehistoric man and his allocation of woman to the cave and went on to provide all sorts of tips about how not to waste one's life doing housework: 'Equipping with ease', 'Laundry is ludicrous', 'Kitchen kit' and – yes!! 'Scrubbing with science'. Two of her tips which I couldn't make work were how to peel potatoes while reading a book (impossible) and having a bath with laundry detergent in it to soften the water.

I also own a small hardback called *Housework Without Tears* that was published in 1945 by a woman called Priscilla Novy. This is a book with a history which I didn't know when I bought it years ago from one of my rummages in second-hand bookshops. Janet Beveridge, Lady Beveridge, who was married to welfare-state founder Sir William Beveridge, wrote the foreword to the book, which is a plea for more housework-friendly houses and the intelligent purchase of housekeeping aids. Novy's text repeats the approach of many of the earlier, especially American, housework manuals, in exhorting women to embrace the science behind it all. 'Perhaps you've always wondered how a refrigerator works?' she asks, answering her own question with two pages of explanation.[4] One point about *Housework Without Tears* is that Lady Beveridge's son thought that his mother had written the whole book using 'Priscilla Novy' as a pseudonym, and other people have repeated this mistake. In fact Priscilla Novy was a real person who worked for an organisation called Mass Observation; she wrote children's books as well as her engagingly scientific guide to housework. I doubt whether anyone who cited this book ever read it, since who would bother with a little book about housework?

The date is now 1969. I am being treated for depression. I knew something was wrong but I didn't think it was depression. That was the only technical language we had for describing what happens to people who are encouraged to regard the world as an interesting and educative place for 20-odd years, and who then find themselves confined to housework. That year was a very important one for me as it brought a major *éclaircissement*, that possibly the most awful aspect of housework was that no one thought it was real work at all. We women got exhausted doing it and thinking about it – what food to buy and cook, whether there was enough toilet paper, could the children's feet be squeezed into those shoes for a few more weeks – and our exhaustion was attributed to our hormones or our heads. I used to watch a lot of old black-and-white films on TV in the evenings, flat on the sofa, escaping into another unreal world. The actual moment of *éclaircissement* has been inscribed (by me) into a narrative about how I became a sociologist, and it occupies a very definite place in my memory, which makes it suspicious, because memories are coded and recoded over time to fit the purposes for which they're being used.

We're in house number two now, in Robin's study where the grey-and-white striped curtains have been rehung (quite successfully), and I am standing in front of his bookshelves, duster and can of spray polish in hand, and my eyes fall on a section of his books concerning the sociology of work, and, lo and behold, when I lift them off the shelves, I find that housework is barely mentioned in these books – well, it features as a minor off-stage character, an afterthought, a female peccadillo, a bit of the occupational world that is known to be there, but which doesn't really fit in, so let's forget about it. I wish I'd known then about Mabel Atkinson and Margaret McKillop's work on household economics, or about Charlotte Perkins Gilman's on the man-made world, or about whole sheaths of literature I've drawn on for this book, but this was a world of fugitive understandings for me and others then. There was no internet, and no time to go to libraries. I wouldn't have known what to look for anyway. I never dreamed the world I've written about in this and other of my books existed, and it's really only now, looking back at my life, that I can recognise how angry I am that my education so signally failed to alert me to its existence.

Back to that moment in front of the bookshelves. I found a determination among the clouds of dust raised by turning the pages of those books to do something about the mistreatment of housework and women in them. The rest is history: I interviewed other women about housework, wrote a PhD and three books about it, all while under the marvellous influence of the women's liberation movement that swept through Europe and North America in the late 1960s and early 1970s. To understand the sociology of housework you have to appreciate how gender works as a social system. To understand the science of housework you have to ungender housework and treat it as a form of human labour.

For 33 years, from my marriage in 1964 to 1997 when my last child left home (although there was a certain amount of coming back for all three of them), I was doing housework for other people as well as myself. It's not an entirely different matter to do it just for oneself, but there are freedoms. For example, you can do housework at peculiar times of the day (or night). Some years ago I decided it was a waste of time to use the 'good' hours in the day (which vary between people, but for me are the mornings) to hoover, dust, shop, cook, wash, and so on. All this is now done when I can't do any more creative/intellectual work that day. Also, I do it in sections: I never hoover the whole house in one session, but divide it into three or four. This is less tiring and can be fitted in between other activities (one set of TV advertisements covers a whole floor). This regime became easier after I became acquainted with the life of the wonderful Baroness Wootton of Abinger through writing a biography about her: Barbara Wootton was a woman who knew about both sociology and science, who did her own housework and who kept a hoover on every floor of her house (I buy cheap lightweight ones, not the heavy complicated sort).

Another housework-related benefit of living on one's own is that you don't have to have arguments with anyone else about what they have (or more usually haven't) done. Pat Mainardi's famous, and still constantly cited, *The Politics of Housework*, written in 1969 (which I read shortly after), lays out the main themes that featured in discussions with her husband when she suggested sharing the chores. His responses included insisting that he doesn't do housework very well, she does it better, and they both ought to do what they're best at (the division of labour argument rears its ugly head again); that they have different standards and he doesn't see why he should have to stick to hers; housework is too trivial to even talk about, it's beneath his status: 'My purpose in life is to deal with matters of significance. Yours is to deal with matters of insignificance. You should do the housework.'[5] Anyone who has ever had such conversations will recognise how extremely tedious they are. It's very rare to reach any definitive conclusion. The argument I remember best having repeatedly when Robin and I agreed in principle to share the chores, like Pat Mainardi and her husband, was the one about clearing up the kitchen. To me this meant putting everything that was out on the surfaces away. To him it meant pushing everything to the back against the wall where he could pretend he couldn't see it.

For readers who are interested in the kinds of practical tips writers of books about scientific housework have offered, here are a few of mine.

Washing and ironing

1. Put clothes straight out of the washing machine onto hangers and hang them outside in fine weather or off door frames inside when the weather is bad – this way you'll never have to iron them (or use an energy-intensive tumbler dryer).

2. Don't buy clothes that need ironing in the first place (*The Sociology of Housework* study found that ironing was the task women disliked most – I haven't ironed anything for at least 20 years).
3. Most of what goes in the washing machine can be washed quite well in cold water.

Food

1. Don't peel potatoes – the peel is good for you.
2. You can make soup out of anything, including the outer leaves of cauliflowers, chard stalks and radish- and carrot-tops.
3. If you're a vegetarian and the food smells and looks OK, ignore the dates on it.
4. Put the lid on saucepans and turn the heat off before the food is done, and you'll get some free cooking time.

Cleaning

1. If a floor needs to be washed, get down on your hands and knees to do it. It's good exercise: you look after your pelvic floor as well as the real one. This was well-recognised by household scientists at least 125 years ago. Using this method you'll also be able to get into the corners and the edges of the floor which none of the expensive floor-cleaning equipment can do.
2. Most household cleaning can be done using vinegar, bicarbonate of soda and borax. Add essential oils so that your house doesn't smell like a fish and chip shop. Another way to do this is to put a few drops of a nice oil in water in a spray bottle to deceive people into thinking you have a fresh, sweet-smelling home.

Housework is a commercial industry, and a lot of money is made out of the understandable desire to find a nicer or easier way of doing it. Some years ago I launched my own range of cleaning products, together with a little manual I produced for family and friends. They found it amusing. But I am quite serious about it. The only commercial products I still buy are scouring powder (I made my own but it got damp and clogged up the holes in the container); washing up and dishwashing detergent; the occasional bottle of bleach; and limescale remover (the ecological alternative of lemon juice and vinegar takes a long time to work). I enjoy reading practical aids to housework, which is one reason why I felt enthusiastic about embarking on the research for this book. My kitchen library includes a few favourites: Mary Rose Quigg's *1001 Country Household Hints*, Annie Berthold-Bond's *Better Basics for the Home* and *The Green Witch* by Barbara Griggs. Many of Quigg's hints have proved very helpful (for example, use wet cotton wool to pick up broken glass, wash woollen garments in shampoo), but some less so (keep a pair of cut-off shirt sleeves in the car in case you have to tinker with the engine). I did do a herbal medicine course a few years ago, and successfully managed to grow a vinegar mother in my airing cupboard. I made a hair rinse out of nettles when my younger daughter was having chemotherapy for breast cancer, but I don't think she used it (it wasn't a very pleasant colour). I also own a book called *Liquid Gold* which is about using urine to grow plants. Most people seem to find this disgusting, but my grandson was happy when I advised him to pee on the compost heap. (I didn't tell him that urine can also be used to make explosives: during the American Civil War, women saved theirs for this purpose.)

In 2010 when the documentary film-maker Vanessa Engle made a series of BBC documentaries about women, she wanted some non-intellectual shots of me so she filmed me making my 'gloop', or washing machine detergent (grate a bar of white soap into four litres of boiling water, stir until dissolved, add half a cup of washing soda when cool, and whatever essential oil you fancy). But this sequence was omitted from the finished film which showed me uncontroversially cycling down a local hill instead. Perhaps my scientific housework is just too eccentric. Perhaps this book will make it seem a little less so. At any rate, I feel I have completed some sort of important personal circle in bringing the sociology and science of housework together. This is apart from any small service I may have done to both subjects by recording and illuminating their interconnections.

The small cream and brown jug inscribed with a message about today and tomorrow has survived all these shenanigans and now lives in East London with one of my daughters. The blinking red light on the dishwasher has come on again.

1

Introduction: From the sociology to the science of housework

Most of the world's labour isn't manufacturing articles in factories, farming the land or the sea for food, providing financial, social or health care services, engaging in technological flights of fantasy, or thinking and analysing all of this. Most of human labour is housework. How do we define housework? Most obviously, housework is concerned with the care of people's bodies and the material environments in which they live. Feeding, washing, cleaning are its core. But then, as societies become more complex, other items get attached to the core: housework struggles under the weight of an assigned additional responsibility for moral values, social relationships and psychological health.

In her historical study of housework in Ireland, Joanna Bourke raises the complication that:

> '[H]ousework' suggests work inside the 'house', although not necessarily one's own house, but what are the boundaries of the 'house'? ... In rural households, what is farm work and what is housework? ... Is an Irish woman who feeds chickens from her front door performing housework if the eggs are to be consumed by the household rather than sold?

For the purposes of her book, Bourke decides to define housework as 'those uses of household time, outside the arrangements of paid markets, which are aimed at the production of goods and services that might be replaced by market goods and services'.[1] This line, that housework is a form of unwaged labour providing services that otherwise could be paid for, has been adopted by those few economists who have taken housework seriously. The same case was central to the wages for housework movement which emerged in tandem with the women's movement in Europe and North America in the late 1960s. These two movements, for paid housework and women's liberation, were associated because one can never get very far discussing housework (in this case, two paragraphs) without landing on what ought to be an earth-shattering statistical fact, that more than three-quarters of the world's unpaid domestic work is done by *women*.

What this book is about

The particular story that drew me to attempt this book is how various bevies of keen individuals in many countries tried to get *universities* to understand that the science of housework is just as worthy of study as any other science, because it is, in fact, itself a scientific subject: bacteriology, microbiology, physics, chemistry, botany, biology, sociology, psychology, economics – these are some of its ingredients. The composite science of the household was described by its campaigners using a variety of terms: household/domestic science, household/domestic economy, home/household economics, household arts, and so forth. (There was a lot of argument about what exactly to call it.) I switch between these terms in the chapters that follow, in the interests of a text that isn't, hopefully, too repetitive to stop people reading it.

For the purposes of this book, housework is the work done, mainly by women, in people's homes that promotes their survival, well-being and wider social participation. Housework overlaps with motherhood, in the sense that rearing children involves a great deal of feeding, washing and cleaning. But they aren't the same: ideas and prescriptions about housework and about motherhood have their own distinct histories. *The Science of Housework* isn't about motherhood or about childcare, although I had to make a small exception for the disturbing convention that developed in North America around 1920 (and lasted for more than 40 years) of installing babies in educational institutions so that students could practice domestic science on them. This arrangement was an attempt to extend the lessons of scientific housework to the new moral discipline of scientific motherhood.

Scientific housework is what this book is about. Its focus is the social and educational movement for importing into housework the tools of modern science that developed in many countries in the period between about 1880 and 1940. Some of its precedents referred to in the book were earlier, and I haven't tried to cover the impact of the Second World War and its aftermath. Other histories and commentaries on the household science movement exist, and are listed in the references to this chapter: much of this literature is restricted to the American scene, and little of it attempts any kind of systematic analysis or contextualisation of how household science fitted into the general picture of social/economic change.

My usage of the term 'science' refers to a systematic and rigorous endeavour that creates and organises knowledge in the form of testable explanations of both natural and social worlds. Key to science are the methodologies of systematic measurement, observation and experimentation; the use of inductive reasoning to derive general rules; and repetition and verification. These were all trademarks of the household science movement. One of its staunchest proponents, the American Professor of Household Economics and Hygiene at Kansas State University, Nellie Kedzie, asked in 1885:

Introduction

> Just what is domestic science? We can only answer, it is classified domestic knowledge. ... It means that cooking is to be done in such a way that good food will always be the result; that good materials are never to be ruined for lack of knowledge; that systematic work will bring good results in the kitchen as well as the factory; and that the head of a house needs system and training in her work as well as does the head of a bank.[2]

I call the campaign in which Nellie Kedzie and hundreds like her were involved a 'movement', because it did have distinctive institutional/organisational manifestations, and a common set of concerns that united its proponents nationally and internationally. But within this framework, there were, of course, differences, some of which are discussed in the rest of this book.

Partly because housework is the most dominant form of labour in the world, the potential landscape for such a book is huge. I've tried, not always successfully, to limit it. I begin with the present: Chapter 2 takes gender and germs as two reasons why any sane socially responsible person today should be interested in the systematic study of domestic labour. Issues in 2024 about cleanliness in the home may be not quite what they were in the 1880s (when, according to many accounts, even wealthy middle-class homes could be quite disgusting places), but being clean is still a salient personal and public goal, and one for which science is a great help. And for many people, the topic of housework generates what it did not do (very much) in the 1880s: an engulfing puzzlement about why more men don't do more of it. Chapter 3 tangles with the dense history of teaching girls about housework – that history at the end of which my own efforts at sewing and designing aprons put in a short dismal appearance. Chapter 4 moves onto the early sanitary science texts and the authorised birth of the academic household science movement at a place inappropriately called Lake Placid (the discussions were anything but placid) in the Adirondack Mountains of the United States in 1899. Because housework is done in homes, how homes are designed must be part of our effort to understand the extent to which science is possible: hence Chapter 5. This chapter also considers the case for scientific efficiency in the home as developed between the early 1910s and the 1930s, particularly by the frighteningly efficient American ideologues Christine Frederick and Lillian Gilbreth. Frederick's schedule for how the mother of a small baby spent one day in 1915 is remarkably like the one I retrieved from my own past in the Prologue (before I knew anything about any of these science and efficiency notions). Chapters 6, 7 and 8 hone in on the case-histories of the academic household science movement at King's College, London, which began in the early 1900s, and at the University of Chicago in the 1920s and 1930s. These tales of spirit, determination and rebuff allow us to inspect more closely the dynamics of both what is required for housework to be taken seriously in academic circles, and the strategies that are deployed to ensure that this doesn't happen for very long.

Material resources are crucial to any (scientific or unscientific) form of housework: thus Chapter 9 looks at gas and electricity as sources of power and at how the development of these industries opened the doors to new technical occupations for women. That overpowering image of a line of white washing drying in the wind evokes the title of Chapter 10: 'White subjects'. The story of housework is punctuated by 'isms': sexism, classism, imperialism, but also internationalism – the EuroAmerican academic household science movement infiltrated places as far apart culturally as Japan, New Zealand, and India. 'Legacies and meanings', the final chapter of the book, addresses the two pressing questions of why the movement fizzled out and what difference it actually made.

The coverage of the book is ambitious, because its subject is itself, if allowed to be, both vast and important. However, none of the chapters that follow should be read as comprehensive histories. In the interests of space and readability, I've had to be selective. Footnotes have been kept to a minimum, mostly to anchor direct quotations. Each chapter has a list of the other sources on which the text has drawn. An Appendix at the end gives the names and dates of the characters who feature most often.

'Just a housewife'

The Science of Housework comes half a century after my earlier attempt to endow housework with some academic status: *The Sociology of Housework* was published in 1974. It began life as a very academic PhD thesis, and reflected an emerging concern (my own and that of many others) with describing and analysing gender inequality. At the time, universities in Britain were still places that welcomed independent, innovative scholarship, and so, I thought naively, a sociology of domestic labour might be able to flourish there. Not so (the story of this book). To hedge my bets, but also to spread the message that housework is important, I published a companion volume which was called simply *Housewife* and carried the slogan 'High Value-Low Cost' on a red, blue and white cover borrowed from a well-known washing powder packet.

My original interest in interviewing women about housework had two sources: personal experience of the subject; and an intellectual crusade to make sociology less of a masculinist theory-based venture and more of a discipline that could record, and make sense of, people's everyday lives. Looking back, I can see that *The Sociology of Housework*, along with its predecessor *Sex, Gender and Society* (which started out as part of the housework PhD), established what would become the theme of my entire public working life: the bringing out into the limelight of subjects that have been concealed or forgotten and are hence missing from our cultural recollections. While *The Sociology of Housework* remains in print and has been reissued in new editions several times (and translated into several languages), it has largely acquired the status of an historical artefact. How interesting that someone thought to study housework 50 years ago, but the world has moved on: homes, women, gender, families and housework are all hugely different now, and in any case we have other ways of treating the topic. We have, for example, enormous databases of statistical information about labour and gender; and we have sophisticated post-modernist discourses that deconstruct the very terms of the subject itself.

It's true, and I've drawn on some of these in *The Science of Housework*. But let's revisit for a moment its ancestor, *The Sociology of Housework*. Chapter 1 of that book attacks sociology for its masculinist bias. This was quite an original thing to do at the time, and it was certainly relevant to my discovery that nothing much resembling a serious study of housework had been published before. British sociologist Hannah Gavron's *The Captive Wife* came out in 1966, but this (originally another London University PhD) was a study of conflicts and dilemmas in the lives of young mothers, not a project examining housework as work. Helen Lopata's American survey of *Occupation Housewife*, which frightened me as a potential competitor to my own by being published around the same time, focuses on social roles without making much of a distinction between housework and motherhood. This disappearance of housework into the mammoth hole of everything else women do is an obstacle to any who want to navigate their way to the beating heart of household labour.

Chapter 2 of *The Sociology of Housework* is called 'Images of housework' and it discusses the two contrasting views of housework that prevailed in the early 1970s in the United Kingdom and elsewhere: housework as oppressive, degrading, self-negating work, on the one hand, and housework as a form of creative aesthetics, on the other. The chapter asks where the attitudes of the 40 urban housewives I interviewed fitted into this dichotomy. I quote from page 37:

> Throughout the forty interviews a clear perception of housework as work emerges. The women in the sample experience and define housework as labour, akin to that demanded by any job situation. Their observations tie in closely with many findings of the sociology of work; the aspects of housework that are cited as satisfying or dissatisfying have their parallels in the factory or office world.

Asked what are the best things about being a housewife, the dominant response from the women was, 'you're your own boss'. Asked about the worst things, most of the answers cited either the housework itself, or its monotony, repetitiveness and boredom.[3] Many women also made critical references to the often-used and demeaning phrase 'just a housewife'.

The term 'housewife' that I and my interviewees used in the 1970s is more or less defunct in the 2020s. Few women today describe themselves as housewives. (The term has never been popular in the United States.) The 1971 UK Census defined a housewife as 'that member of the household, male or female, who is mainly responsible for household shopping'.[4] Because there was no actual question on this in the Census, a set of convoluted rules for selecting who in each household would count as a housewife were developed by a consortium of government departments, the Royal Statistical Society, the Market Research Society and the Institute of Practitioners in Advertising (the latter presumably keen to identify markets for promoting their products). Using another outdated term, 'head of household', the rules defined all women heading households as 'the housewife' and then went to some lengths to escape defining men as housewives by specifying that single men, or married men not living with their wives, would only count as housewives if there were no females over 20 in the household (whether not they were related to the man). The same rules applied in the 1981 Census, but by 1991 they had been replaced with the gender-neutral option 'looking after the home or family'.[5]

I use the term 'housewife' in this book because it was current in the period I'm writing about. But I do wonder whether we might be at the beginning of a new epidemic of idealised domesticity. 'Why would you want two jobs out of choice?' asks Alena Kate Pettitt, a British 'lifestyle blogger' and pursuer of 'nostalgia-inspired homemaking'. 'That's not empowerment, that's walking into bondage. ... Put as much energy and passion, if not more, into your role as a homemaker as your contemporaries who work outside the home do in their jobs. You'll walk away with so much more than just a payslip to show for it.'[6] In Richmond, Virginia, Estee Williams is a 'self-proclaimed traditional housewife' who spends between three and five hours a day cooking, and never allows her husband to lift a finger (apart from hanging heavy pictures) in their home. So traditional are their roles that he hunts with six guns and a bow and arrow at weekends and they have a freezer full of his meat to supply her recipes.[7]

The shift in my own gaze from the sociology to the science of housework was a gradual process. It was partly powered by research for my book *Women, Peace and Welfare* into the networks of women who in the late 19th and early 20th centuries pioneered social science research, welfare reform and the emancipation of women. 'Sanitary science' and 'municipal housekeeping' were planks in their argument that clean, well-ordered homes and cities are fundamental to any thriving society. These women, many of whom founded and lived in social settlements, developed a participatory social science.

Both in their work and the way they lived they did much to break down the barriers between public and private spheres that have so inhibited the systematic study of domestic spaces. I came to see that 'settlement sociology' and the household science movement were two great forces driving women's entrance into many areas of public life and to be heard as authoritative voices in policy making. It was through the research for *Women, Peace and Welfare* that I first encountered women like Ellen Richards, the uncompromising founder of household chemistry in the United States who never went anywhere without her water-testing equipment and whose work led to the first food adulteration legislation in the United States; the British economist Mabel Atkinson, who took Adam Smith to task for the misogynistic neglect of housework in his famous *Wealth of Nations*; American feminist economist Helen Campbell, who wrote a textbook on *Household Economics* in 1896 and called for a national commission to apply scientific methods to the home; and Alice Ravenhill, who taught household science to everyone she could in the United Kingdom, attended the extended disciplinary arguments at Lake Placid, and then emigrated to Canada and did it all over again. I was struck by the absolute certainty of these women that housework could, and should, be scientific, and only thus would public health improve. They didn't see housework as a private affair but as an activity of world-shattering importance in determining the health of nations. I was stirred by their stories of what they went through to convince people that this was true. Here is Alice Ravenhill talking about the evening lectures she gave to village women in Lincolnshire in 1894:

> Transport was difficult. It was a winter of deep snow and prolonged cold, the drive in an open gig along the wind swept dykes without even a wisp of straw to cover the feet is a test of endurance indeed. The welcomes were always warm but the beds were cold.[8]

It was Alice Ravenhill who led me to the King's College of Household and Social Science story, which is explored in Chapters 6 and 7. Discovering that the archives of this extraordinary institution had been preserved meant that I had no choice but to write this book.

The oppressive nature of household science

A disputatious relationship between the meaning of household science and the politics of feminism has helped to obscure the story told in this book. Feminist scholarship and feminist politics have (almost) to a woman ignored the history of household science as a sustained, professional effort to improve public and personal health. For example, in her *Wasting Girls' Time: The History and Politics of Home Economics*, the feminist historian Dena

Attar argues that home economics isn't only about 'sexist indoctrination' but has caused 'general educational harm'.[9] Teaching it to girls and women has made no positive contribution to their lives: furthermore, home economics is imbued with middle-class ideology, and it would be better not to have it all. This is very similar to the case put by Barbara Ehrenreich and Deirdre English in their pithy and panoramic *For Her Own Good: 150 Years of the Experts' Advice to Women*. However, *For Her Own Good* does admit there's something refreshing about the 'resolute unsentimentality' of the domestic science movement, its insistence that the home wasn't a retreat from society, 'it was just as important as the factory, in fact, it *was* a factory'.[10]

When the American feminist Robin Morgan stood before the American Home Economics Association (AHEA) in Denver, Colorado in 1973, she upset many of the home economists present by declaring that she was there 'addressing the enemy'. Observing that American homemakers work appallingly long hours for no pay in a job which society holds in contempt, Morgan argued that the AHEA was simply preparing women for that appalling fate. Their attitude was condemning multitudes of depressed suburban women who were consequently turning to drink – here Morgan echoed Betty Friedan's famous portrait in her *The Feminine Mystique* of 'the happy housewife heroine' who was anything but that. Later Robin Morgan admitted that, had she researched the history of home economics, she would instead have directed the AHEA to stop what they were doing and go back to their own roots.[11]

The dismissal of home economics, household science, or whatever you choose to call it, as a device for oppressing women means that the other goals of the household science movement discussed in *The Science of Housework*, of raising the status of work in the home, and creating new technical and educational opportunities for women, have also fallen by the wayside. In this, feminist scholars have aligned themselves with armies of other historians, economists, anthropologists, sociologists and policy makers who have similarly failed to give any thoughtful attention to housework. This explains many gaps and sidelinings. Here are two examples relating to cookery and public baths. As Yuriko Akiyama found in her study of nutrition and health in Britain before the First World War, the rise of cookery education had a substantial impact on nutrition in hospitals and in the army and the navy. Yet this development isn't highlighted in any of the relevant histories, because domestic science as a factor in national health improvement has been neglected.[12] Historian Sally Sheard, examining the development of public baths and wash-houses in the United Kingdom between 1847 and 1915, faced a very considerable research literature on large-scale sanitary infrastructure reforms, but very little on the smaller-scale and more intimate, but arguably equally important, matter of public baths and wash-houses.[13]

These played a key role in the reduction of many transmissible diseases including typhoid, which is spread by lice whose favourite homes are dirty bodies, clothes and bedding.

Matter out of place

Another cause of historical neglect with respect to housework as science can be traced to anthropology. The anthropologist Mary Douglas published her book *Purity and Danger: An Analysis of the Concepts of Pollution and Taboo* in 1966. This is famous for the aphorism that dirt is 'matter out of place'. For example, 'Shoes are not dirty in themselves, but it is dirty to place them on the dining table.' Douglas contended that we'll come to understand how 'often our justification of our own avoidances through hygiene is sheer fantasy' once we lay to one side the erroneous notion that there's something objective about dirt.[14]

An 'acknowledged modern masterpiece [sic]' of anthropology,[15] *Purity and Danger* has been an enormously influential book, not least because it elevated to academic respectability the study of the mundane and everyday life. But it has a lot to answer for when it comes to the science of housework. Douglas's argument is that ideas about dirt and cleanliness are ways of creating social order: dirt is essentially disorder, something that exists in the eye of the beholder. Therefore all our efforts to chase and eliminate dirt are about reordering our environment and making it conform to an *idea*. Douglas derived these observations from two main sources: intensive fieldwork with the Lele, a Bantu ethnic group living mainly in the Democratic Republic of the Congo; and her own experiences with the material environment of the West. While writing *Purity and Danger* she was housebound with mumps, looking after her two children, and probably engaging in a number of cleaning 'rituals' to keep the household safe.

Her work continues to prompt a cache of studies in which cleanliness, housework and the culture of consumption are defined principally as classificatory rituals: 'Through the magical rituals related to the subjective meanings of clean and dirty, the consumer tries to maintain a particular "reality", which can be defined as his/her geo-social position', claims one, for example.[16] I can almost hear Alice Ravenhill, Ellen Richards et al shouting in horror at the idea that dirt is defined by culture, not science. They spent their lives introducing people to germs and teaching them about the ill-effects of contaminated water, food and houses. It requires a considerable effort of the will to see this as a form of mass delusion. Nancy Tomes in her study of microbes, *The Gospel of Germs*, invites us to imagine another anthropologist looking back at the AIDS epidemic in a hundred years and labelling preventive measures such as condoms and bleach-disinfected needles as 'gestures of separation and classification'.[17]

The approach of *Purity and Danger* does, however, make it easier to dismiss the household science movement as a means of social control imposed on the working classes by matronising middle-class reformers, which is a case that has been powerfully argued by some. There was undoubtedly an element of that in the household science movement. Here is British sanitary reformer Margaret Pillow, a figure we'll meet later in this book, describing the target of domestic economy teaching in England in 1897: 'The deplorable ignorance of the women of the poorer classes upon the subject of cookery, the waste, and want of knowledge of practical household economy which often brought about unnecessary poverty' (what would *necessary* poverty be?).[18]

Finding household science today

Our current cultural amnesia about household science is evident from any casual internet search. Using the search terms '"science" and "housework"' proves quite unrevealing. An American website, 'Ask the Scientists', recommends housework as a way of dealing with stress:

> Next time you wash your dishes, try to focus on the sensations you are experiencing. What does the soap smell like? How hot is the water on your hands? Paying attention to these sensations will help ground you in the moment … this can help alleviate some of the stress in your life.[19]

A considerable number of sites sponsor housework as good physical exercise, as benefiting the brain, and as slowing ageing – all reasons, one might think, that would help to iron out the notorious gender divide. Changing the search terms to '"housework" and "public health"' is equally unproductive, although it does uncover a wealth of references to research carried out with 'elderly' people, for instance, a byzantine study of 36,240 elderly men and women in seven countries that found longer housework hours to be associated with better health – for men.[20]

Taking the quest to the academic journal literature results in further disappointment. Searching for 'housework' in the *International Journal of Food Microbiology* and the *Indoor Air Journal* produces nothing; 'household science', 'housework' and 'domestic labour' in the *British Journal for the History of Science* yield one reference, to a 17th-century female botanical artist called Margery Power. An interesting revelation is that the major concern of cleanliness today is with institutions, not homes. Hospitals, schools and other public spaces acknowledge the importance of housework to health by producing elaborate sets of guidelines. The National Health Service's *National Standards of Healthcare Cleanliness 2021*, for example, runs to 56 pages and includes detailed cleaning plans and scheduled frequencies and methods, all 'based on sound evidence'.[21] In contrast, the ideology of the home as a private space wraps a veil of mystery around the houseworker's own solitary confrontation with microbes: 'There are no enforcement officers checking whether the fridge is hygienic or whether there is cross-contamination from handling raw meat and then making a sandwich.'[22]

Conclusion

The lessons of household science remain with us today as 'the sanitary underpinnings of everyday life',[23] while their origins in the steadfast, impassioned and informed crusades of the first household scientists have gone somewhere else. In this they join the labours of other early women scientists, which the US historian Margaret Rossiter, in her book *Women Scientists in America*, demonstrates to have been eclipsed 'due to the camouflage intentionally placed' on their work.[24]

Writing a history is a way of reclaiming it, or of inserting alternative narratives in an accepted story. Or of changing the story altogether. *The Science of Housework* doesn't quite do that, but it brings together diverse segmented histories – of women's education and their penetration of erstwhile masculine professions; of how science and technology have impacted everyday lives; of the ways in which notions of womanhood, gender and domesticity have shifted, hardened and sometimes released radically reconfigured visions of what is public and what is private. But most of all the book is testament to the iron convictions and untiring work of the people who set out to clean up homes, make our food safe and nourishing, and improve national health.

2

Gender and germs: housework today

Géraldine and Bernard le Fecht, a French couple who took part in a research study of how men and women arbitrate the doing of domestic laundry, are firmly committed to the idea that everything in the home must be shared equally. They're so convinced of this that they decide to do their laundry separately. The problem for Géraldine and Bernard is that they don't each generate enough dirty clothes to fill the machine, so they reluctantly agree that they will have to fill it together. They continue to store their dirty laundry separately, though, and they arrange to meet in front of the machine to put it in, and again to take it out and bear it off to be dried. Naturally, the ironing is also done separately which means that none of the shared household linen ever gets ironed. Whether it was the pain caused by negotiating these delicate arrangements or some other incompatibility, by the second interview in the study Géraldine and Bernard had agreed to live apart.

Reading this account, and the others in Jean-Claude Kaufmann's *Dirty Linen: Couples as Seen Through Their Laundry*, delivers a strong sense of just how heartfelt and time-consuming these conversations about housework can be. This chapter considers some of the modern evidence relating to the theme of gender that is so firmly embedded in the history of housework. It introduces us to a second theme that is equally firmly embedded and much discussed in later chapters of this book but much less evident today: germs. A collision of these two themes occurred in the COVID-19 pandemic that began in China in December 2019. Early signs in the first British lockdown suggested that this virus might actually be accomplishing what numerous campaigns had failed to, namely reducing women's share of housework: 'An unexpected upside to lockdown', *The Guardian* newspaper called it: 'experts suggest that this could lead to a lasting change in gender norms'. Both *The Guardian* and the experts were wrong: it didn't, and six months later the newspaper had to admit that the novelty of doing more housework had already waned for men.[1]

Sing happy birthday while you wash your hands

As the first line of defence against the spread of the COVID-19 virus, governments around the world promoted hand hygiene – the vigorous, repetitive and meticulous washing of hands. We were bombarded with public health messages about the most effective way to handwash: with soap, hot water, scrubbing under nails, and doing it for long enough – hence the mnemonic of singing 'happy birthday' twice, an activity which would take the necessary 15–30 seconds. It's not clear who first thought of this. British Prime Minister Boris Johnson was only one of many politicians who recommended 'happy birthday', although some of his colleagues in the Conservative Party thought the first verse of 'God Save the Queen' should be chosen instead. In any case, when researchers at Lund University in Sweden got singers to perform 'happy birthday' into a funnel, so that they could assess the respiratory droplets coming out of it, they found that the words of this particular song contain an unhealthy number of big aerosol-spreaders in the form of the consonants B and P.[2]

That's why you need science. Today, as noted in Chapter 1, the science of housework hides in obscure places and is hard to find. In 2016 the *International Journal of Applied Microbiology*, for instance, published a study relevant to the COVID-19 experience: the study looked at four hand-drying methods: paper towels; a textile roller towel; a warm air dryer; and a jet air dryer. The latter two proved to be competent ways of *spreading* rather than containing microbes since the machines ejected them a metre or so through the air on a journey to land on other people. Paper towels were the winners.[3] The European Tissue Symposium, a trade association based in Belgium, funded this study, which could be regarded as making it slightly suspect. The promotion by commercial companies of many household technologies, something we now absolutely take for granted, was itself a child of the cleanliness project described in later chapters of this book.

On the other hand (an appropriate metaphor?), efficient handwashing *has* emerged as a helpful mechanism for reducing infection in domestic work activities. The same *International Journal of Applied Microbiology* published a study of household laundering practices in 2022, which used a 'quantitative microbial risk assessment' to demonstrate that hand hygiene at critical points in the domestic laundering process is the most effective way to prevent infection. Clothes-launderers should constantly wash their hands since household clothing and linen are heavy carriers of bodily fluids, dirt and food debris, all of which provide nutritious meals for pathogenic bacteria such as *Salmonella* and methicillin-resistant *Staphylococcus aureus* (MRSA).[4] These bacteria can survive on clothing for weeks. As well as the frequent handwashing, hot water and bleach are needed to get rid of them. Some common household items such as pillows and mattresses that can't (easily) be washed provide other good homes for bugs because they absorb bodily fluids and grow bacteria which are kept at an ideal temperature by the warm bodies lying on top of them. As one scientist has said, 'If you had to come up with a medium to cultivate bacteria, besides a Petri dish with agar, a pillow is pretty much as good as you can get.'[5]

Think of other things hands do that can spread germs: mobile phones, for example, the most commonly used electronic device in the world and found in most homes in pockets or handbags or on the kitchen table. In the wonderfully named journal *GERMS*, a 2017 study of 27 mobile phones belonging to Estonian teenagers located on these instruments a plethora of more than 20 types of viruses and bacteria, including *Escherichia coli, Staphylococcus aureus* and *Streptococcus*. This added up to ten times more bacteria than lurk on toilet seats.[6] Mobile phones share with kitchen sinks the counterintuitive distinction of being dirtier than either toilet seats or the soles of shoes. Also beware the germs on toothbrush holders and toothbrushes, which arrive there when the (relatively clean) toilet is flushed. Also counterintuitive is the finding that half of reusable shopping bags contain faecal bacteria: 'some people have more faecal bacteria in their grocery bag than in their underwear, because they at least wash that'.[7] And while we're on the subject, a salutary 81 per cent of the world's population do not wash their hands after contact with excreta. On the basis of 2012 data gathered from 42 studies, it has been calculated that handwashing with soap on such occasions has the potential to save some 296,872 lives annually.[8]

Kitchen dangers

Cleanliness research, dug out from these hidden fissures of the scholarly world, shows that much modern housework is a matter of rearranging invisible dirt. Researchers have been very ingenious in developing methods that prove this. In 2021, eight researchers published the results of a study of 'consumer practices' in 87 domestic kitchens located in six European countries. Their research was driven by the fact that some 40 per cent of all foodborne infections are acquired in the home. The researchers studied the extent to which the preparation of a chicken and vegetable meal involved encounters with three common pathogens causing foodborne disease: *Campylobacter, Salmonella* and norovirus. The researchers tracked the presence of the three pathogens on raw chicken, kitchen surfaces, clothes and sponges, and they went to unusual lengths to do so, following study participants to the shops, observing the transport home and unpacking of food items, and the whole meal preparation process, then making video and audio recordings, carrying out interviews and, of course, a great deal of microbial sampling. The main culprits – vehicles for cross-contamination – turned out to be cutting boards and sinks: using the same unwashed board and/or knife for preparing both the chicken and the vegetables, and the same unwashed sink or unchanged water for rinsing both. Practices in the different countries varied. For example, while 80 per cent of chickens hosted *Campylobacter* in France and Portugal, this figure was only 8 per cent in Norway. The UK households came top for the highest number of kitchen surfaces contaminated with

Campylobacter. In one of the 12 UK homes studied, the 'elderly' man who lived there prepared his meal in a visibly dirty kitchen without washing his hands and he used the same knife to get the chicken out of its wrapping and to cut up spring onions.[9] (Surveys by the Global Hygiene Council do show UK homes to be the dirtiest of those in all developed countries.)

One reason for dirty behaviour is that people's perceptions of risk and safety often differ from those of the experts. Since the kitchen is the heart of the home, it must, 'almost by definition', be safe.[10] Doing the research for this book, I became quite mesmerised by the roles items like dishcloths, brushes and sponges play in increasing or decreasing the chances of some pathogen-caused illness. 'Death as surely lurks among the dish-towels of many kitchens as it does in the rubbish piles of back-alley ways', wrote a Mrs E.H. Chase pre-scientifically in *The American Kitchen Magazine* in 1897.[11] These days scientists engage in some disgusting practices to investigate this problem. The journal *Environmental Health Review* reported in 2021 a study of the aerobic colony count on dishcloths. These were 'inoculated' in a beef slurry for 48 hours and then subjected to one-minute treatments with bleach, lemon juice, vinegar, tap water or microwaving. Which method did best? Sadly for those of us who might prefer 'natural' alternatives, the best approach was the microwave, followed by bleach and vinegar, with lemon juice and water coming last.[12]

Dishcloths aren't the best tools for kitchen cleaning and sponges are definitely the worst. The moist and porous surfaces of sponges (like pillows) provide cosy homes for hordes of bacteria, and one day's use of a new one will load it with over a billion bacteria.[13] Bacteria love wet conditions, so brushes are better because they dry out.

Figure 2.1 shows an unusual map of Europe based on the prevalence of these different washing-up aids. Brushes are traditional in some countries, including Norway and Denmark, but in the United Kingdom, France, Germany, Greece, Hungary, Portugal, Romania and Spain, infested sponges are preferred.[14]

The kitchen is the site of most serious domestic accidents, particularly those that affect children, women and old people. In the United Kingdom, some 6,000 people die every year because of domestic accidents, and the resulting annual cost to the National Health Service has been estimated as £43.63 billion.[15] Knives injure with depressing regularity, but so do wet floors, ovens, food blenders and laundry baskets. As the Royal Society for the Prevention of Accidents (RoSPA) in the United Kingdom observed in 2019, domestic hazards typically don't attract the same level of public scrutiny as accidents outside homes because they happen behind closed doors, and aren't seen to merit the same level of regulatory scrutiny. The RoSPA report lists many simple things that can be done to reduce these hazards: slip-tested flooring; fire guards for stoves; ovens at mid-height; lockable cupboards in bathrooms and kitchens (most houseworkers, myself included, store poisonous bleach in open

Figure 2.1: Cleaning utensils for dishwashing in ten European countries

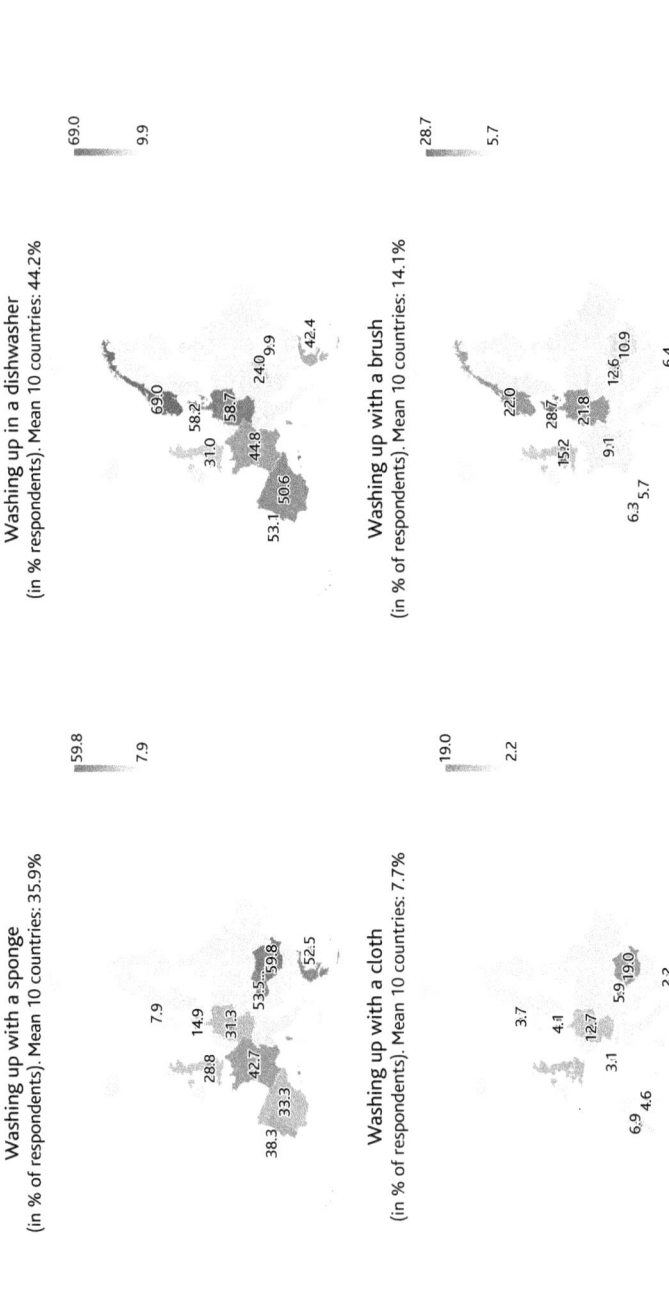

Source: Møretrø, T., Moen, B., Almli, V.L., Teixeira, P., Ferreira, V.B., Åsli, A.W., Nilsen, C. and Langsrud, S. (2021) 'Dishwashing sponges and brushes: consumer practices and bacterial growth and survival', *International Journal of Food Microbiology*, 337: 108928, p. 6.

cupboards under the kitchen sink). Architects and planners don't put domestic safety first; they rate aesthetics and economy as more important than the impact of home design on human health. This wasn't always the case (see Chapter 5).

The ecosystem of house dust

House dust is a prime character in many of the chapters that follow: its prevalence, meaning, prevention and, above all, removal. Like many other aspects of housework, its science is seriously understudied today. My enlightening excavations of the hidden scientific literature uncovered an uncomfortable study by a Dutch scientist of house dust biology. It was written for 'allergists, acarologists and mycologists' (acarology and mycology are the scientific study of mites and ticks, and of fungi, respectively) published in 1981, and it looks at house dust as an ecosystem of its own. Johanna van Bronswijk shows us how architects and housekeepers together create the conditions for an entire community of insects, mites and fungi to flourish. In a section called 'living with silverfish, dust lice and house mites', she says, '[t]hese dust feeders usually go unnoticed because of their hidden life and partly nocturnal habits. Occasionally they are seen in high numbers, causing damage to fabric, books or wallpaper. A nervous breakdown of the housekeeper who finds her beautiful, clean home crawling with vermin is also possible'.[16] Silverfish, for example, conduct nightly forays, emerging from the crevices of a room and moving about on the floor, cupboards and walls, making short runs with long pauses in between: Figure 2.2 depicts a colony on one such expedition.

The house dust inhabitants of most EuroAmerican homes are well-protected against cleaning procedures, which simply aren't thorough enough to threaten them or their food supply. Sweeping floors, for example, only displaces a fraction of the dust into cracks and crannies, thus creating better living space and food conditions for house dust-feeders. Vacuum cleaners are much more threatening. These should also be used on beds, because the protein content of bed dust is higher than anywhere else in the house due to the human skin cells which fall off bodies. Washing sheets and blankets can result in a severe shortage of food for the minute inhabitants of beds, but only for a few days. Mattresses with buttons should be avoided as bed mites congregate around the buttons. Bed-making causes dust, mites and microorganisms to become airborne, 'providing other dust layers in the home with new organisms to replace those lost by housekeeping procedures'.[17] And then a whole other world can be found under the bed, in those charming balls of dust that collect, especially on hard floors, and which have been found to contain multiple substances: cat hair, human and animal dander; limestone; iron oxide; quartz; cigarette ash and combustion products; fly ash; salt; sugar; starch; tea; rust; cotton, wool, silk and paper fibres; sulphur; chlorine; silicon;

Figure 2.2: Silverfish foraging in the nightly hours

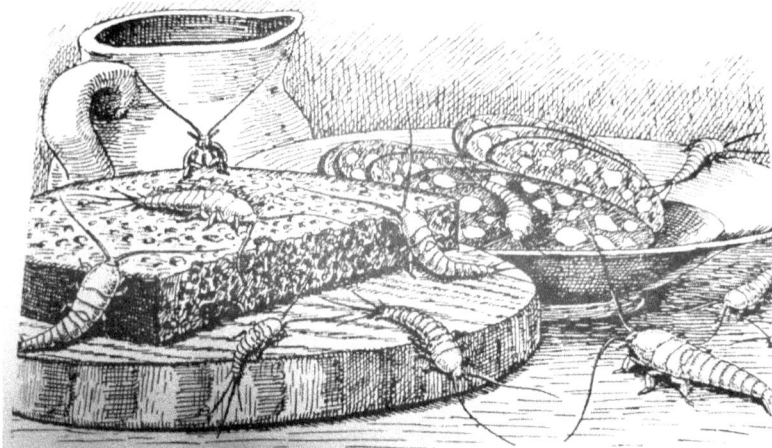

Source: Van Bronswijk, J.E.M.H. (1981) *House Dust Biology for Allergists, Acarologists and Mycologists*, p 54

iron; aluminum; potassium; calcium; and chromium. (It may be advisable not to look under the bed at all.)

Like almost everyone else who ventures out into this untapped landscape of housework, van Bronswijk comments on the lack of interest it appears to hold for most scientists, both medical and social. The rise of allergies, and of the shaky 'hygiene hypothesis' – that our homes are *too* clean – helped to spur the scientific study of dust in the 1960s, but otherwise who in their right mind would want to come face to face with something so common, so disagreeable and so utterly devoid of monetary value?

The chapters that follow describe the cleanliness project that washed EuroAmerican culture in the half-century or so that spanned 1900. The project was driven by various interconnected forces: the scientific discovery of germs; growing concern about the health-damaging effects of industrial capitalism; the changing role of women; the rise of a consumption culture. These conspired to highlight homes and the private behaviours they contain as potentially dangerous to human health. Homes were reinvented as places of danger, which was an image that struggled to engage with their traditional reputation as safe havens (for men and children, though not usually in the same way for women).

Women: the cleaner sex?

Unpaid care work is 'one of the most glaring manifestations of inequality between men and women around the world'.[18] The United Nations has called it 'an infringement of women's rights'.[19] Women's housework hours are more than three times those of men, and 606 million women of 'working age' globally do it full-time, compared to 41 million men. Girls aged from five to 14 spend 40 per cent more time than boys on household chores and collecting firewood and water in those countries where this is still a daily task. It is a gendered pattern that cuts across geographic regions, household income, religions and cultures.

Most of *The Science of Housework* is therefore about domesticity as a female project. Does cleanliness appeal to women because women are cleaner than men? Study after study of handwashing, body-washing and clothes-changing habits do indeed show that women are the cleaner sex. The gender difference is unlikely to be genetic: it's entirely plausible that women are cleaner because cleanliness has been held out to them as a desirable feminine trait. The superior cleanliness of women was noted by the Hungarian physician Ignaz Semmelweis in his landmark handwashing observations of 1847. Semmelweis showed that three times more women died from puerperal fever after childbirth when attended by male doctors, freshly laden with bacteria from the postmortem room, than when cared for by female midwives whose jobs spared them these infectious encounters. (Semmelweis met an unfortunate end because no one believed him, and colleagues had him committed to an insane asylum, where he died of an infection.) Today the same gender difference prospers in health-care institutions where improper handwashing is the main cause of infections acquired there.

The pest control firm Rentokil fixed sensors on toilet doors and on handwash dispensers in order to monitor the handwashing habits of 10,000 British office workers in 2015; it reported that 38 per cent of men but 60 per cent of women washed their hands after visiting the toilet. As a result, the firm was able to promote its 'ground-breaking new product', an alert-system called HygieneConnect.[20] In two US Midwestern city shopping malls in 2001, observers dressed as college students with clipboards and spreadsheets hidden in shopping bags watched people entering public restrooms. The disguised researchers 'entered a stall to record data'. After doing this 599 times, they arrived at the result: only 32 per cent of the observed toilet-users washed their hands adequately; 19 per cent didn't wash their hands at all; and 26 per cent just rinsed them with water. But the women were cleaner: 45 per cent washed their hands properly, while only 12 per cent failed to wash their hands at all and 17 per cent used only water. The men's figures were twice as bad as the women's: 18 per cent, 26 per cent and 36 per cent.[21]

In the study of Estonian teenagers' mobile phones referred to earlier, the median number of bacteria on girls' phones was nine, compared with 15.6 on boys' phones. Women's clothes are washed more often than men's (although not often enough to fill washing machines on their own, as Géraldine le

Fecht found). According to the Norwegian researcher Ingun Klepp, the largest gender difference is for underwear: 94 per cent of women but 59 per cent of men say they change it every day. The figures for socks are 71 per cent and 56 per cent.[22]

Divided labours

Men do engage in housework, and the division of tasks between the sexes/genders has a ritual aspect. Figure 2.3 is taken from a UK survey carried out by the public opinion and data company YouGov in 2019 of 1,314 British adults living with partners. Men specialise in putting the bins out and gardening, women in bathroom-cleaning, laundry, dusting, polishing, cleaning the oven, bed-making and mopping. For the endlessly taxing topic of laundry, the survey reported that 27 per cent of men have all their laundry done for them by their partners, whereas only 1 per cent of women enjoy this prerogative.[23]

A general notion pervades the atmosphere almost as universally as household dust – the idea that men do actually do *more* housework than they used to. This is certainly a valid observation when today's domestic division of labour is set against the patterns prevailing in the late 19th and early 20th centuries. But change is relative, and also very slow. An analysis of time-use diary data for British couples in 1975, 1987 and 1997 showed

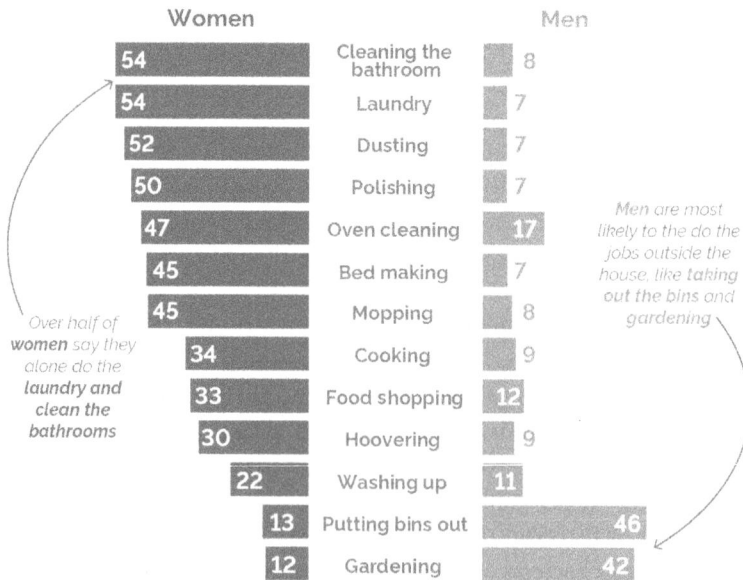

Figure 2.3: What housework do Britons say only they do at home?

Source: Ibbetson, C. (2020) 'Do men do their fair share of housework?', https://yougov.co.uk/society/articles/27710-do-british-men-do-their-fair-share-housework, courtesy of YouGov

that men's contribution to cooking and cleaning went up by less than 15 minutes a day in between the survey years. This averages out at less than one minute a year over a 22-year period.[24]

Also unequally shared is the *truth* about gendered housework. The pattern extracted from survey and interview data is that men generally say they do more housework than their female partners say they do. According to another YouGov survey of 1,520 British men and women carried out in May 2022, men were more likely than women to say that housework tasks were shared. The proportions of men saying they always did a task were uniformly higher than the proportion of women who said their partner always did that task: for example, 34 per cent of men said they always took care of the household finances, but only 10 per cent of women said their partners did this.[25] They can't both be right.

When Jean-Claude Kaufmann asked the couples in his study of household laundry the question, 'Do you consider laundry to be essentially a female domain?' most couples vehemently rejected the idea. Some, conscious of the huge discrepancy between their answer and the facts of their own case, went to great lengths to justify the contradiction, 'for which they had all sorts of excuses'. The men in this study who did participate actively in housework were keen to boast about it: 'Their voices swell with pride, they portray themselves, with some exaggeration, as modern heroes.' Women wanted to be the partners of such men, and so tried to present their own partners in this light 'by heaping praise on pathetic attempts at doing the vacuuming, or the Sunday barbecue'. Extraordinarily, women expressed more guilt than the men did about the lack of male domesticity.[26]

Constructing Mrs Consumer

The purveyors of household products have found the idea of male domestic incompetence extremely useful. As a dramatic device, it's a way of portraying women as the real authorities on housework, which naturally makes them the dedicated consumers of household products. It's the housewife who has the sense to argue for the replacement of the old kitchen with a new one, to persuade her family that industry-produced food is actually a superior, and perfectly safe, source of nourishment. An excellent demonstration of this commercialised female hyper-rationality is the popular 'housewife films' that were screened in Norwegian daytime cinemas during the 1950s, 1960s and early 1970s – an era when the notion of married women as housewives still carried a good deal of currency. Housewife films were made by a consortium of marketing consultants and home economics experts in an unusual hybrid format which mixed advertising, entertainment and education. The aim was to display all the latest household technologies in such a manner that women were persuaded to buy them. The entertainment breaks inserted in the films were hosted by a comic male figure whose exaggerated domestic stupidity was designed to create a feeling of confident solidarity among the watching women. Insidiously, too, the (accurate) representation of housework as real, laborious work in the films stood its cultural trivialisation on its head, for those brief, dreamy afternoon hours.[27]

Conclusion

Housework is an enormously important, contentious and socially structured aspect of the occupational world. Its neglect by academics reflects a cultural relegation of domestic labour to a box of mundane, taken-for-granted, ordinary, uninteresting activities. *The Science of Housework* explores a time before this cultural silencing, when conversations about bacteriology and the behaviour of dust mites and the correct temperatures for food storage and preparation were to be heard in all sorts of unlikely places, including the laboratories and lecture rooms of universities. Housework was important then. It still is. So what happened?

3

Teaching girls about housework

In the early 1900s a social investigator and welfare worker called Cécile Matheson undertook to explore for the British Board of Education how some European countries set about the business of training girls for the performance of home duties. She personally went to look at many different kinds of schools in Germany, Austria and Switzerland. In one she visited, in Cassel (now Kassel), Germany, domestic hygiene was taught in a ground-floor kitchen with a tiled floor, a light green dado and cream-coloured walls, around the top of which were painted a series of mottoes: 'The little kitchen builds the big house', 'Your home is your kingdom – stay there'. The 25 children who attended the class Matheson witnessed were 'bright and tidy', although some wore the patched clothes that told of poverty.

The lessons Matheson attended mostly took the form of question and answer. The children were asked such questions as: 'What are the constituents of the body and why do we need food?' 'What are the chief kinds of food and why are they mixed?' In the lesson she witnessed they were taught how to make a milk soup. Glasses of sour milk, strainers and plates were fetched from the attached larder and store room, and the class considered what milk is made of and what it can be made into. The children were already, noted Matheson, 'acquainted with the action of bacteria, the value of ice, boiling, covering, and, above all, of cleanliness in the preservation of milk'. 'Homely illustrations' were used to demonstrate the unappetising details of how milk is digested and acted on by the gastric juices. Once the soup was made, the class was shown the best way to extend hospitality, with a clean tablecloth and a vase of flowers. The meal that followed provided an 'opportunity for the practice of the politeness and good manners which are too often obscured in home when the pressure of poverty is great'. Science and good manners went hand in hand as markers of future womanhood.[1]

This chapter looks at the place of science in the history of teaching girls about housework. The history of instructing girls in domestic matters was there to draw on when the proselytisers of domestic science teaching in the late 19th- and early 20th-century seized on the new knowledge about germs and nutrition to design university courses in household science. They didn't have to campaign for the recognition of housework as a female activity: this already existed. But they did have to reframe it in language more suited to changed social conditions and the growing politics of women's rights. The chapter moves between countries, just as the household science movement did. It attempts to capture the essence of the different currents that prefaced the full-blown movement for household science, rather than to sketch a comprehensive history of developments in different countries.

The most famous housewife of them all

The American domestic writer Catharine Beecher published her world-famous *A Treatise on Domestic Economy for the Use of Young Ladies at Home and at School* in 1841. In Figure 3.1, the most-used image of her, she is 77 and evidently still busy writing. The general domestic advice literature, of which Beecher's text was the pioneering example, was an important tradition for the new proponents of housework teaching to call on. Beecher grew up in a large New England family with three Black servants, two of them 'bound' (indentured and unpaid), and she lived a contradictory life: an expert on domestic economy, she had no home of her own; she wrote on the moral education of children but had none; she urged women to become teachers but she didn't teach herself.

The science element in Beecher's approach gets little attention in many accounts of her life and work. In the Preface to the revised edition of her *Treatise*, Beecher explained her position:

> The author of this work was led to attempt it, by discovering, in her extensive travels, the deplorable sufferings of multitudes of young wives and mothers, from the combined influence of *poor health, poor domestics*, and a defective *domestic education*. The measure which, more than any other, would tend to remedy this evil, would be to place *domestic economy* on an equality with the other sciences in female schools. This should be done because it *can* be properly and systematically taught (not *practically*, but as a science), as much so as *political economy* or *moral science*, or any other branch or study; because it embraces knowledge, which will be needed by young women at all times and in all places; because this science can never be properly taught until it is made a branch of study; and because this method will secure a dignity and importance in the estimation of young girls, which can never be accorded while they perceive their teachers and parents practically attaching more value to every other department of science than this.[2]

According to Beecher, housewives needed to be jacks of all sciences: architecture, pneumatics, hydrostatics, calorification, floriculture, horticulture, animal husbandry, botany, hygiene, physiology, domestic chemistry and economics.

Figure 3.1: Catherine Beecher aged 77

Source: Public domain via https://commons.wikimedia.org/wiki/File:Beecherc.jpg

Her book treated every aspect of domestic life scientifically, from the building of a house to the setting of a table; she used crisp diagrams and put forward ingenious ideas for the invention of labour-saving devices, many far ahead of their time, for example, converting a barrel into an early type of refrigerator. Beecher was very much into evidence; she credited all the medical sources she used, and made the critical point that anybody who wished to could also access them.

Domestic science for girls (not boys) at home and abroad

By the time social investigator Cécile Matheson carried out her observations of domestic science lessons in Germany, Catharine Beecher's idea that all girls should be scientifically trained in housework at school had come to be widely accepted. Figure 3.2 is from Catherine Buckton's *Food and Home Cookery* (1879), described as 'a course of instruction in practical cookery and cleaning' for elementary school pupils, but it could be any number of images of any group of children anywhere. These ones look alarmingly compliant and composed.

Figure 3.2: Girls learning cookery at school in Leeds

Source: Buckton, C.M. (1879) *Food and Home Cookery*, London: Longmans, Green, facing p 36

There was considerable cultural variability in curricula for teaching girls household skills. A good housewife in Germany might not recognise all the habits of her counterparts in Austria, Belgium, Denmark, France, Norway, Sweden, Switzerland or the United States – all countries that were covered in the series of Special Reports published by the British Board of Education in 1905–1907. In Belgium, for example, the 1,116 schools in which domestic economy was taught to girls in 1899 included 'the study of nourishing and medicinal plants'.[3] Swedish rural teenagers were taught how to grow fruit and vegetables and how to make good use of the wild berries that proliferate in the Swedish countryside. In predominantly rural countries like Sweden and Finland, girls were taught in peripatetic classes. The teachers brought their own stoves and kitchen utensils along and taught courses lasting six weeks to young teenage girls. In France, the menus young girls were asked to cook were, as might be expected, quite ambitious: one summer menu recorded by the Board of Education researcher was *vermicelle au beurre*, followed by *restes de mouton en émincés ou braisés* and *pomme de terre en purée avec saucisses*, rounded off with *fromage à la crème*. 'Lunch ready, the little cooks sit down and relish with good appetites the work of their own hands.'[4]

In every country, needlework rather than cookery was the first domestic subject to enter the school curriculum. One reason was that it required very few resources – only a few chairs, needles, scissors and thread. In the United Kingdom needlework became an elementary school subject in 1840, and was made compulsory in 1862. The general subject of domestic science, conceptualised as 'domestic economy', joined needlework as a compulsory subject in elementary schools in 1878, to be followed by cookery in 1882, laundry in 1889 and housewifery in 1900. 'Housewifery' covered the warming, cleaning and ventilation of dwellings, and the general rules of health and sickroom management. By being made compulsory, these domestic subjects became useful grant-earners in state-run Board schools. This had a huge impact on the numbers of girls exposed to them: for example, the 844 girls taking domestic economy in 1874 had become 59,812 by 1882.[5] The same move to define domestic education as compulsory happened in the United States: by the second decade of the 20th century many schools/school districts there had made home economics mandatory for girls. In 1921, the US Bureau of Education reported that in two-thirds of all the larger school systems home economics was required of all girls in the 7th and 8th grades (12–14 years), and in many cities also in the 5th and 6th grades (10–12 years).[6]

One covert reason for training girls to do housework was getting some of the housework done. In Belgium, an explicit function of school needlework classes was making or mending the family clothes: 'I saw many and varied examples', wrote Helen Matheson, sister of Cécile (the Mathesons were a very public-spirited and investigative family) in her report for the British Board of Education. 'Putting new sleeves in a mother's bodice; patching a father's working trousers or coat; making a father's old trousers small for a little brother (the most usual).'[7] Another common practice was for girls to clean the buildings in which they were taught, wash its linen, and serve meals to other students, staff and education officials, and sometimes to (other) poor children in the locality. In France, pupils got their practical housework polishing tables and chairs, cleaning ranges and stoves and dusting shelves in the School Director's own house.[8]

An absolutely central point emphasised in the education regulations of different countries and much campaigning material was that cookery was a means of teaching the *general* importance of cleanliness in the home: 'the girls are taught to wash up the utensils, &c, to clean the knives, scrub the pastryboards and tables, polish the tins, clean the sink, and leave the kitchen cupboards, &c neat and clean', enthused the domestic economy teacher Margaret Pillow, Britain's first female sanitary inspector in 1897.[9] In Belgium, the ministerial directives issued in 1887 for the middle stage of primary school (8–10 year olds), began with 'Order and cleanliness', moved on to the exciting topic of brooms and brushes and the danger (unspecified) of using a feather brush; ventilation; and hygienic personal advice (don't sit in draughts, have wet feet, get too near the fire, wear woollen scarves and caps in rooms, eat unripe fruit or drink when perspiring).[10]

Like many features of gender-divided public and private life, the ordinance that girls and not boys should be taught about housework was mostly treated as unremarkable: women do the lion's share of the housework worldwide, so the logic of preparing them as girls for this duty must surely follow. This harsh gender divide was adhered to rather less strictly in Scandinavian countries than elsewhere in the late 19th and early 20th centuries: in Swedish primary schools the boys sewed, darned, and so on, alongside the girls for at least the first three years of their school lives.[11] But generally the gender difference attracted little comment. In a book about English high schools for girls published in 1907, Sara Burstall, headmistress of the academic Manchester High School for Girls from 1898 to 1924, was unusual in tangling with the topic of biological sex differences. Concluding that there *were* differences that had to be respected educationally – in bodily strength and needs, possibly mental differences in the direction of boys showing more originality – she added:

> It is when we come to consider the work of education in fitting young people for the life that the real difference comes. It is the natural duty of a man to defend his country in war, and he must be trained as a boy for this natural and inevitable duty; it is the natural duty of a woman to do housework, and she must learn it at school.

The effect on girls of learning domestic arts is that '[t]he girl wakes up, becomes more orderly and less troublesome, acquires a new self-respect'.[12]

The British reformer Alice Ravenhill, whom we met briefly in Chapter 1, took a more even-handed approach to the gender question. In her book *Household Foes: A Book for Boys and Girls*, published in 1910, she used the formula of conversations between two children, Robin and Ruth, and their Aunt Rachel, who is training for the very modern occupation of bacteriologist. Both children are exposed to pedagogically frightening information about domestic dirt, decay and disease, and the argument that as citizens they have the power to control all of this. Illustrations, as was usual in such texts, are lurid: horse manure, from which moulds are sprouting; the house-fly, with larva and pupa; a boy with ringworm, and so forth.

One profound effect of the focus on domestic education for girls was the narrowing of their educational opportunities. The 1871 British Code of educational regulations, for example, listed the optional academic subjects of animal physiology, mechanics and chemistry as available only to boys: girls were directed to domestic economy, cookery and laundry.[13] The impact of this on scholars' experiences was noted by the English writer Flora Thompson whose memorial novel, *Lark Rise to Candleford* (1945), records her attendance at a village school on the Oxfordshire/Northamptonshire border in the 1880s. While all pupils studied reading, writing and arithmetic, girls spent every afternoon doing needlework and the boys continued with the 3Rs. The Regulations for Secondary Schools made housewifery a compulsory female subject in 1905 and went on to add the further gendered injunction that, since girls all had to take domestic science, the time they spent on mathematics could be correspondingly reduced. In 1907 came a further dramatic decision when the Board approved a scheme of 'Practical Housewifery' entirely to replace science teaching for girls over 15 years old.

The domestic science education movement did, however, recognise that there were situations in which boys and men needed to study the practices of healthy living as specified by Alice Ravenhill and many like her. When boys and men worked in occupations which separated them from women they would have to cater for themselves. Soldiers and sailors fell in this category; both the army and the navy in Britain were pioneers in food reform. The navy discovered the importance of clean, nutritious food in the cramped and unhealthy conditions in which sailors often had to live: the quality of food could be literally a matter of life and death. Nautical Cookery Schools were opened in the 1890s and early 1900s. They offered tuition in how to cook in flooded, unstable galleys on long voyages with ancient provisions, no fresh water, and live animals which had to be cared for and then killed and reinvented as palatable meals. The Merchant Shipping Act of 1906 highlighted the role of poor food at sea as a factor in hugely accelerating rates of desertion: a scientific approach to naval food was thought to offer the additional benefit of encouraging young men to stick to the seafaring life. The Act specified that every vessel over 1,000 gross tons would henceforth have to carry a trained cook. Despite their critical life-preserving role, naval cooks came very low down in the status hierarchy of jobs on board; their occupation, tinged with the caste of femininity, defined them as very different creatures from the manly deck seamen.[14]

Learning how to cook

Cookery first entered the educational scene for British girls in workhouse schools as an explicit means of training them for domestic service, and it was the cookery and cleaning curricula of these schools that formed the basis for the rollout to public elementary schools.

A pivotal moment in the cultural history of cookery in Britain, the moment that established the methodology of formal classes as practical ways of changing culinary behaviour for women as well as girls, occurred when a Mr J.C. Buckmaster, of the Science and Art Department in the South Kensington Museum, was hired for an international exhibition in 1873 to give a series of public lectures on the application of scientific principles to cookery. A colourful, largely self-educated character, Buckmaster wrote books about physics, inorganic chemistry, magnetism and electricity and scientific agriculture. He knew nothing about cooking until he was asked to take on the task by the committee organising the exhibition which wanted to encourage public interest in the importation of different foodstuffs. He stood at a rostrum in the Exhibition Hall in Kensington lecturing twice a day from May to November, with the actual practical work of cooking managed by a French chef and carried out by four women, 'all four performing the same operations simultaneously at different parts of a counter stretched across a wide hall'.[15]

The Buckmaster lectures have been much quoted and were wildly popular, attracting streams of visitors, including members of the royal family. Queen Victoria went, and complained that she had to listen to a rather tiresome lecture before being exposed to the equally tiresome demonstration of how to cook an omelette. Buckmaster was clear that cookery was as much a scientific subject as chemistry, requiring 'caution, thought, intelligence, judgment'. 'The education of women for the proper work of women is about as bad as it can be', he complained, 'they go to boarding-schools and colleges and learn all about the transit of Venus and the Zanzibar contract, and often get married without knowing how to boil a potato'.[16] One of the books to which Buckmaster subsequently contributed was called *300 Ways of Preparing and Cooking Potatoes*.

Once Buckmaster had done his bit for the science of cookery, philanthropic and domestically minded campaigners took up the cause of cookery education. Schoolteachers who could provide this were badly needed. The result was the foundation in 1874 of the National Training School of Cookery in Kensington on premises lent by the Museum's Science and Art Department – the very same collection of corrugated iron buildings erected for Buckmaster's lectures. Here, under its leaky roof, cookery teachers were trained for jobs in elementary schools, hospitals and the armed services. In the early years many students were 'ladies of rank' who wanted to show their support for the idea that domestic tasks should be reconceptualised as skilled scientific subjects. They were encouraged to bring their cooks with them, but the ladies went off the idea of sophisticated French cookery later when they realised how much time it took (and their cooks weren't terribly enthusiastic either).[17]

Cookery curricula became increasingly scientised. A good example is a textbook on *Public School Domestic Science*, published by the Canadian home economics campaigner Adeline Hoodless in 1898. Out of its 140 pages, 132 are devoted to the composition and 'pecuniary economy' of food, its relation to the body, and how to prepare it. On the eight pages occupied by other housekeeping topics, dishwashing comes with a list of ten different stages or processes, ending with the time-consuming task of scalding and then boiling with a teaspoon of washing soda for half an hour anything that has been used to cook fish or onions. There are multiple injunctions about sanitation in the kitchen, which is characterised as an intensely hazardous place:

> All waste pipes, from that of the kitchen sink to that of the refrigerator, become foul with grease, lint, dust and other organic

matters which are the result of bacterial action. They are sources of contamination to the air of the entire house and to the food supply, thereby endangering health.[18]

It was due largely to Hoodless's efforts that the Canadian Ministry of Education decided to introduce domestic science in public schools in 1902.

One result of all this public interest in cookery education was that soon more and more girls were being schooled in the subject: in the United Kingdom, the 7,597 girls in 457 schools who qualified for the cookery grant (four shillings per head) in 1882–1883 had risen to 134,930 in 2,729 schools by 1885–1886.[19] The National Training School of Cookery issued the first teacher's diploma in cookery and also the first teachers for the new cookery schools set up between 1874 and 1877 in Edinburgh, Glasgow, Leeds, Leicester, Liverpool and Manchester. The courses weren't particularly stringent – three months with a three-hour examination paper on cookery theory and a demonstration lesson in household cookery.

The Liverpool Cookery School was started in 1875 by a woman whom the nursing pioneer Florence Nightingale (someone who was, as might be expected, much interested in scientific approaches to housework) called the 'saint of the laundry, cooking and health'.[20] Fanny Calder, the daughter of a Liverpool cotton merchant, became convinced through the kind of philanthropic work with the poor expected of middle-class young ladies at the time, that the real problem wasn't so much material poverty as 'absolute ignorance of the essential methods of "making a home"'.[21] For 50 years Calder, a tall, striking but reserved woman, fought assiduously for the universal instruction of girls in domestic skills.

Calder worked with colleagues in other cookery schools to set up the Northern Union of Training Schools of Cookery in 1876 and collaborate on standardising curricula and issuing teachers' diplomas. She followed this with the first national organisation in the United Kingdom, the Association of Teachers of Domestic Science, in 1897. After several changes of name, this organisation would survive to become the National Association of Teachers of Home Economics in 1991.

Slow and express trains

School domestic science teaching early acquired a reputation as a second-class education for girls who couldn't quite manage anything more demanding, a theme that would resurface later in the debate about university-level domestic science. The Manchester headmistress, Sara Burstall, broke ranks with other academically oriented headteachers when she introduced a 'Housewifery' course there in 1900. Her original intention was to come up with a scheme for encouraging girls to stay on at school, and for this purpose she also launched a secretarial course. Burstall called the girls who took these courses 'slow trains' compared to the 'express trains' of girls destined for university. The Housewifery course was for girls who would not attend university or follow a profession.[22]

What kinds of girls would or should take domestic science courses? A Miss D.E. Crick wrote in the *Journal of the Royal Sanitary Institute* in 1912 about her experience teaching the first year of a domestic science course for 15–16-year-old girls at a Ladies' College in Edinburgh. 'The course is intended for girls who mean to remain at home, for those who are going to take up domestic science', she explained, 'and for those who wish to follow other professions which do not involve residence at a University'.[23] But the Edinburgh course does, nonetheless, sound quite demanding. It lasted two years, with one-third of the girls' time being spent on general subjects and two-thirds on cookery, laundry work, needlework, housewifery, applied science, hygiene, economics and 'home problems'. There was a good deal of science: the study of air and water; the use of the microscope to examine the effects of heat, acids and ferments on food; the verification of facts by experiment. The students were also exposed to a quite radical economics curriculum which took in the position of women and the household throughout history; theories about production, consumption and exchange of wealth; family budgets and women's wages; sweated labour and housing problems. In defence of this panoptic approach, which would later be copied in higher education, Miss Crick quoted from a book on economics written by two household economists who are central figures in the story of King's College of Household and Social Science told in Chapters 6 and 7: Margaret McKillop and Mabel Atkinson.

School training for girls in domestic subjects was classed as a form of *technical* education. As such, it was treated as the counterpart of boys' training in manual trades. The two were often connected, not only ideologically but architecturally. In her visit to look at domestic science teaching in the United States, Alice Ravenhill was especially impressed by the example of the Wade Park School in Cleveland, Ohio, where the girls' kitchen and the boys' carpentry shop were placed next to each other in an annex to the main school buildings. In 'light, airy, suitably arranged apartments' with cloakrooms and sanitary conveniences attached (such details never escaped her), pupils were also schooled in gender-appropriate social interaction: while the girls entertained the boys with their cocoa and cake, the boys reciprocated by presenting the girls with small specimens of their skill.[24] The paralleling of these two enterprises, domestic science for girls and woodworking, metalwork and similar manual occupations for boys, is nicely represented in many of the 199 centres established in Chicago schools by 1915; the girls worked in cooking laboratories with adjoining dining-rooms that were filled with tables and chairs made by the boys in the manual training classes.[25]

The American sanitary chemist, Ellen Richards, confronted those educational critics who deemed housework could in no way be considered the equivalent of boys' manual training. 'Let the skeptic go into one of the school kitchens', she ordained in *Domestic Economy as a Factor in Public Education* (1889),

> and see the girls standing at their benches, with the measuring cup and scales, instead of a foot rule, with the moulding board and rolling pin instead of the plane, the dough for a loaf of bread instead of a piece of pine board, their hands the most effective tool of all.

Watching all this, and the girls' bright faces 'as the soup is tasted', would prove the value of such classes as 'a mental exercise in judgment, exactness and neatness'.[26]

An industry of textbooks

The household science movement demanded manuals of instruction for both teachers and students. These had to be written. Thus a tsunami of domestic education literature flooded the educational landscape in the 1880s and 1890s.

A few UK examples will illustrate the range and rhetoric of these. Fanny Calder in Liverpool co-wrote, with the headteacher at her cookery school, the first laundry work teaching manual in 1891. 'There is no department of science which can be of more benefit to the public generally than the chemistry of common life', she pronounced in the Introduction to *A Teachers' Manual of Elementary Laundry Work*, 'and that branch which is applied to the processes of laundry work can be made extremely interesting to school girls if taught intelligently'. Well-done laundry was most important because much disease was due to 'want of cleanliness'. Thus, Calder argued, to understand the laws of chemical action involved in proper cleaning would prevent many harmful mistakes, 'and will give that common sense acquaintance with the materials which conduces to thrift in purchase and in use'.[27]

Henrietta Barnett, a woman otherwise famous for her contribution to the settlement house Toynbee Hall, and the creation of an idealised community, Hampstead Garden Suburb, in London, wrote a textbook, *The Making of the Home*, in 1885. In it, she tangled, a little awkwardly, with the need for domestic science teachers to mention a number of unsavoury subjects: water-closets, drains, bad smells, dustbins and the failure of men and boys to wear sufficient under-clothing. She was frighteningly dictatorial on the subjects of sweeping and dusting, but her instructions do give a flavour of what housework in middle-class homes involved at the time. Sweeping and dusting should be done at least once a day, said Barnett. Before the sweeping came the pinning up of curtains, bed valances, and anything else that hung on the floor. Next all movable objects – ornaments, looking-glasses, small furniture – should be relocated to the middle of the room, and draped with dusting-sheets. Carpets and rugs had to be removed, shaken and beaten. Only then could the daily sweeping begin. 'We must go on our knees with the dustpan and short-handled broom, being careful to get into every corner, as well as under the beds and other furniture.' Not only the floors but the walls had to be swept because the dust that had been raised by sweeping would be found clinging there.[28]

Sanitary inspector Margaret Pillow, in her unmarried name of Scott, co-wrote with the Medical Officer of Health for Brighton, Arthur Newsholme, one of the first detailed textbooks on domestic economy for use in schools. The book, *Domestic Economy: Comprising the Laws of Health in their Application to Home Life and Work*, was published in 1893. The authors stressed the need for the 'scientific study of hygiene' to replace the rather haphazard lessons on cookery and housework to which many schoolgirls were exposed. 'We cannot expect to understand how to avoid errors in food or clothing, or personal habits, if not familiar with the scientific basis of facts on which a rational knowledge can be built', they decreed.[29] The book was full of scientific facts about almost everything concerning the material side of domestic life: how the human body works; food, its function, properties, preparation and conservation; principles and methods of ventilation, heating and lighting; water and the removal of waste; laundry-work; hygienic clothing and home decoration; home nursing; domestic service – the latter an occupation Scott and Newsholme thought mothers – working-class mothers – should encourage their daughters to go into 'in preference to entering upon indifferent callings which frequently entail late hours, injury to health, and exposure to temptation'. There was nothing especially tempting about housework, and it takes a sound constitution to get through Scott and Newsholme's text without feeling some repugnance for the whole subject. Sections on the digestion of food with details about mastication and insalivation precede highly magnified pictures of starch granules in the cells of potatoes; diagrams of misshapen feet warning girls off the wearing of high-heeled boots; and information about how the human body exudes the waste products of between 40 and 50 fluid ounces of urine and four ounces of faeces per 24 hours, the 'proneness to putrefaction' of these substances rendering the proper removal of both from houses of singular importance.[30]

How much of all this teachers actually *used* when talking to their captive pupils is of course unknown.

An international movement

Despite her opinions about slow and express trains, Manchester headmistress Sara Burstall was in many ways an enlightened headteacher for her time, and part of this enlightenment was her interest in finding out about educational developments in other countries. In 1893 she visited the United States in time for the great Chicago World Fair, and then she went back 15 years later to take another look. Her first trip was funded by a charity, the Gilchrist Trust, which responded to the public interest in the education of girls and women by funding five women teachers to go to the United States for two months. It was Burstall's exposure to American education, which much impressed her with its superior level of organisation and technical equipment, that led to her decision about the need for non-academic courses in girls' secondary schools.

This is one of many examples of transatlantic transfer in the theory and practice of domestic science. In the other direction, from the United States to both England and France, came the popular culinary instructor and celebrity cook Maria Parloa, who started cookery classes in 1876 in New London, Connecticut, and who travelled to Europe two years later to observe cookery classes at old London's National Training School for Cookery and in Board Schools. This experience inspired Parloa's *First Principles of Household Management and Cookery: A Text-Book for Schools and Families* (1879). Like Burstall, Parloa paid a return visit in 1894 for a further three-year stint of comparative research on the domestic education systems of France, England and Germany. (Sadly, she remains a mysterious figure with much of her work and life undocumented.)

European domestic science campaigners also often visited one another to find out about and use the newest developments. In Norway, the domestic science teacher Helga Helgesen took herself to Germany and then to Scotland in her efforts to find the right way of educating both boys and girls about hygiene and nutrition. She came back from Scotland with a certificate from the Glasgow Training School of Cookery and started a programme of domestic science teaching in 1891 at a school in Kampen, now a quaint tourist site in Oslo, but at the end of the 19th century a poverty-stricken area housing brickyard workers and their families. Helgesen and another Norwegian campaigner wrote the first Norwegian textbook for domestic science courses in primary schools in 1894; it was used in a number of revised editions until the 1970s.[31] In neighbouring Sweden, the first Cookery School in Stockholm was set up in 1889 after a Swedish reformer, Anna Hierta-Retzius, went to study the teaching of domestic economy in London Board Schools. As she described its purpose, the Stockholm School was intended to help the working classes 'get better wives and more useful daughters' by teaching girls aged 14 to 20 how to cook.[32] Further visits took place in 1891 to England, Scotland, Germany and Belgium, funded partly by the Queen of Sweden. (Royal patronage crops up everywhere in this story.) Hierta-Retzius went on to open the first domestic economy teacher training course in Sweden.

This was only one of her many achievements, which included founding the first women's rights organisation in Sweden, and establishing evening schools, a bank and a library for women. Many, but by no means all, of these trailblazing domestic scientists had strong connections to women's rights movements.

A different slant on the function of domestic instruction in American schools, compared to those in the United Kingdom, was the accumulation in congested cities of new immigrants from Europe who brought with them different cultural traditions. The famous Hull-House Settlement in Chicago added training in cooking, needlework, cleaning and childcare for working-class girls to its multifarious list of community services. 'The girls wore white aprons and caps for lessons in how to boil potatoes, sanitize the floor, and mend clothing.'[33] And there they are in Figure 3.3. Hull-House also opened a public kitchen, under the guidance of the Boston sanitary chemist Ellen Richards, where they offered nutritious soups and stews to an immigrant community that staunchly preferred its own recipes.

The indefatigable Alice Ravenhill

No history of domestic education in the period covered by this book can get very far without encountering Alice Ravenhill's strenuous attempts to promote the scientific study of hygiene as the foundation of both private

Figure 3.3: Girls in cooking class with instructor

Source: Wallace Kirkland, photographer. JAMC_0000_0117_0140, Hull-House Photographic digital image collection, Special Collections University Archives, University of Illinois at Chicago

and public health. 'A busy, alert, shrewd, straight-backed Victorian ... keenly aware of the contemporary world',[34] Ravenhill was born in 1859, the same year as Charles Darwin's *On the Origin of Species*. She was the daughter of a marine engineering and cloth-manufacturing family who overcame formidable opposition from her family and others to carve out a very influential career teaching and researching domestic science. Ravenhill wasn't allowed to be a nurse, or to enrol at a cookery school, but she did manage a newly created diploma course in hygiene offered by the National Health Society. This was at the time the only educational course available for women who wanted to go into public health. The Society later nominated Ravenhill to the Co-operative Societies as a lecturer on sanitary law, in which role she attempted to teach village women in Bedfordshire and Lincolnshire how to run their homes more scientifically: we read about the uncomfortable nature of this task in Chapter 1.

Alice Ravenhill's work crossed seas and continents. In 1900 she attended the Annual Congress of the Royal Sanitary Institute in Paris – a daring step for a single woman at the time. In her autobiography, *Memoirs of an Educational Pioneer* (published in 1951 when she was 92), she recalls that much prominence was given at the Congress to American methods of teaching what they called 'home economics'. Returning to England, Ravenhill took herself off to the Special Report Department of the Board of Education to request that more information be sought on this new subject by a suitably qualified investigator. They gave her £30 to take on the job – not enough money, so she raised some more. Ravenhill, like many of the women whose trails across the landscape of domestic science we follow in this book, was an arch-networker: she already knew the American sanitary chemist Ellen Richards, and it was Richards who arranged Ravenhill's three-month tour of the United States in 1901.

Ravenhill was an active participant in the transatlantic traffic of the household science movement. On her American tour she went to New York, Philadelphia, Washington, Indianapolis, Buffalo, Boston, Providence, Rhode Island, Salem, Worcester, Framingham, Cleveland, Columbus, Toledo, Urbana, Chicago, Ann Arbor and Detroit, travelling at night in order to fit it all in. She also managed a short trip to Canada to look at home economics in Toronto schools. Ravenhill found much to admire in American methods of teaching domestic science, describing them as:

[T]he first systematic educational efforts to introduce to girls some of the fundamental problems concerned with the home: for instance *why* heat applied to foodstuffs in various forms effected familiar but hitherto unexplained changes in their appearance or digestibility; *why* certain substances cleaned fabrics or wood or metal without injury and *why* others were destructive; why experience had dictated certain methods in the running of the home, and why, in the light of modern knowledge, many of these could be revised with advantage.[35]

The emphasis was on the method of scientific experiment, as it would be later in the United Kingdom. 'The causes and sources of household dirt, and the reasons why the different cleansing agents attain their object', wrote Ravenhill,

> are usually treated in detail; experiments are made with the cleaning of metals with different materials, and their effectiveness is compared; e.g., tarnished brass articles are rubbed respectively with rottenstone [a type of porous rock], with rottenstone and water, with rottenstone and oil, with vinegar or with lemon juice; the results are turned to account for the inculcation of underlying scientific principles.

This approach, which linked theory and practical application closely together, was no easy option. Learning about sanitary house construction, for example, meant that every girl had to write plans for a healthy dwelling:

> [H]ere she is required to have good reasons for all her details and to be as practical in her knowledge of plumbing possibilities and risks as she is in her scheme of colour decoration for the rooms. Calculation of cost must be carried out with care and the economics of family life studied.[36]

This concentrated attention to methodical scientific principles reappeared as a theme in Ravenhill's textbook for teachers. The way to teach girls how to clean a room, for instance, was to take a square metre of butter muslin and divide it into three. The first should be left dry, the second should be moistened with water and the third with a few drops of kerosene. A room should then be dusted with each method in turn and results examined.

Little housewives as the road to health

The Manchester Guardian, reviewing Alice Ravenhill's book on the domestic science scene in the United States in 1905, captured the contemporary concern about what was happening to women. 'Whether we like it or not, we are confronted with the undoubted fact that women of all classes are showing a marked distaste for what has been considered to be peculiarly their work', the reviewer noted.

> Even women who by any stretch of language cannot be justly called either idle or snobbish prefer to exercise their gifts and energies in any

work other than household work. ... The modern girl ... does not see any attractions in household work, which brings her no freedom, no salary, and no interest.³⁷

Although *The Manchester Guardian* reckoned it was too late to scold young women back into housewifely ways, the school training of girls in domesticity received a massive injection of enthusiasm in the late 1890s and early 1900s when public health campaigners settled on poorly run homes as a national disaster. The main culprit was maternal ignorance. This widespread accusation came particularly from doctors, who identified women's deficient knowledge of, and inclination for, scientifically informed motherhood as the principal cause of infant mortality.

Set against this ideological onslaught on mothers, however, was accumulating evidence of how bad housing and inadequate nutrition affected everyone's health. Social scientists were getting seriously into the documentation of social conditions. In the United Kingdom Charles Booth's mammoth survey of *Life and Labour of the People in London*, published in 17 volumes between 1889 and 1903, was the most cited, but there were many others. As philanthropy and social investigation revealed the appalling conditions of much working-class housing, especially in cities, so women and girls became the focus for renewed efforts to spread the sanitary housework message. It was hard to imagine just how awful conditions were, and difficult to see how educational instruction could solve the problem. Nonetheless, the campaigners campaigned. Margaret Pillow reminded readers of her texts about the parameters of urban working-class housing in Britain: 'No housing regulations existed to ensure decent living conditions; and houses with no adequate ventilation or sanitation were built back to back or in squalid courts, with a single common stand-pipe to supply twenty or thirty houses with water.'³⁸

Doctors and public health specialists went to town in blaming unhealthy homes for a litany of problems: the American Medical Association, for instance, in an 1899 editorial on the topic of 'Public school instruction in cooking', endorsed the need for domestic science education for girls on the grounds that it would lead to reductions in infant mortality, contagious diseases, 'intemperance' (in eating and drinking), divorce, insanity, pauperism and 'competition of labor between the sexes'.³⁹ Intemperance was a key target. 'Danger of alcoholic drinks', warned the hygiene syllabus for Belgian primary schools, 'alcohol does not nourish;- it is a poison; - it leads sometimes to crime and madness'.⁴⁰

Doctors in the United Kingdom were no less convinced that the health defects of the poor could be cured only by systematic school instruction of the female population in hygiene. In 1906, 15,000 of them petitioned the Board of Education for the obligatory teaching of hygiene and temperance in public elementary schools.[41] In her own textbook, Alice Ravenhill argued rhapsodically that it behoves teachers

> to drill their millions of recruits into obedience to the primary laws of practical hygiene, until a diminished rate of mortality, brighter skies, cleaner cities, purer water-supplies, healthier homes, and better proportioned figures and happier faces replace the gloom, dirt, dilapidations, deformities, and largely preventable sicknesses which now so injuriously affect life in town and country.

The scope of this realm, 'hygiene', was enormous, even at school level: entries in the index to Ravenhill's manual include both the expected (for example, 'antiseptics', 'chemistry of cleaning', 'drain pipes', 'mattresses, inspection of') and the less so ('chromatic aberrations', 'habits and environment', 'stuttering and stammering').[42]

The greatest boost to domestic subject teaching in England and Wales in the early 1900s was the famous Report of the British Interdepartmental Committee on Physical Deterioration in 1904. The Report, which has been much written about in medical and social histories, owed its origins to the recruitment of soldiers for the Boer War, which had revealed an alarming incidence of physical defects among would-be combatants. General questions were raised about the state of the nation's health, especially in the context of statistical information about high rates of infant mortality and declining birth rates.

Most of the evidence given to the Committee came from men, who had forceful opinions about the wanton domestic neglect of women. In the Index to the Report the entry 'neglect of home and domestic duties', inserted appropriately between 'needlework' and 'nervous disease', ran to two columns and included such items as 'carelessness accounted for more than poverty'; 'cooking appliances, lack of, among the poor'; 'sloppiness of mind'; 'laziness of working-class women' and 'increase in disinclination to attend to domestic duties'. This last entry referred to evidence submitted to the Committee by Charles Booth.[43] The Report put particular emphasis on the links between food and physical health. All in all, school training in home economics for girls was deemed a crucial, if not *the* crucial, remedy. Lessons in cookery and household management should be compulsory decreed the Report, especially towards the end of school life, when other subjects could be dropped to make enough room for them. So desperate were the authors of the Report to make this happen that one idea they seriously entertained was the curtailment of girls' non-domestic education altogether. Might not parents simply apply to keep their daughters at home when there were domestic tasks to be done?

The Physical Deterioration Report came at a watershed moment for the evolution of housewifery. Increasing industrialisation and urbanisation, the rise in women's employment outside the home, the shift of homes from producing to consuming marketed outputs, the growing availability of tinned and other pre-processed food: all these spoke of a change in the economic position of households which would permanently alter the practice of housework.

The focus on urban life as a breeding ground for social problems explains why most of the early formal housework teaching for girls happened in towns and cities. This wasn't, however, invariable: in Norway the first initiatives sprung up in the countryside as cures for the dirt and ignorance that were thought especially to scar rural life. The driving force here was a book called *On Cleanliness in Norway* published in 1869, the first in that country to give the subject any serious attention. It was written by a sociologist called Eilert Sundt, who was a skilled infiltrator of people's homes and confidences about all kinds of matters. (No English translation of this volume has ever appeared.) Sundt's book was the outcome of a competition born out of the Norwegian king's interest in the relationship between living conditions and disease. Competitors were asked to address leading questions about girls' education and household work; Sundt disliked the idea that women, not men, needed reforming, and was more interested in finding out about women's housework experiences and expertise. He didn't win the competition, but continued with his research anyway. Sundt features in an intriguing episode called 'the great porridge feud' in which the traditional household practices of women came into direct conflict with the advice of the domestic scientists (see Chapter 11).

Conclusion

The inclusion of cooking, sewing, cleaning, washing and other forms of domestic labour in the school curriculum for girls laid the groundwork for the move of these subjects into higher education. The schoolgirl's body was subject to moral and physical regulation as her character was being prepared for its adult mission of housekeeping. Around the world a huge variety of different kinds of institutions evolved or adapted themselves to teach domestic economy: state primary and secondary schools; private schools; evening schools; continuation schools and classes; special housekeeping, cookery or needlework schools; peripatetic teachers lugging their own stoves around the country to show rural housewives how to cook more efficiently. All this, for the girls themselves, was a lesson in the fabric of patriarchy: through their saucepans and scrubbing brushes teachers hammered home the notion of domestic life as a female responsibility.

There was resistance, of course. Time spent on training schoolgirls in housework wasn't always appreciated in the girls' homes, where many parents were sceptical of the whole endeavour to fill school time with what they saw as non-educational subjects. Mrs Hewitson, a pupil in the early 1890s at Rawlinson School in Barrow-in-Furness, recalled taking home 'dirty-looking' scones that none of her family would eat (and starched and ironed collars which her mother insisted on re-washing).[44] This literature is scattered with references to the manifold resistances of working-class women to the efforts of middle-class reformers. The proselytisers of school domestic science sometimes had to work hard to drive their message home. At times it was even necessary to frighten pupils into listening: the Belgian *écoles ménagères* (technical housekeeping schools for young teenage girls) deployed lurid poster art in which harassed housewives were pictured engaging in such hazardous activities as pouring oil on a slack fire and then, having been burnt to a cinder, lying in bed in terrible agony.[45] The initiative of the *écoles ménagères* was often not appreciated by the working classes, and especially not by mothers who could see no point in it. In the end it was decided to bribe the girls by offering money for the purchase and preparation of the Sunday dinner: 'When the father has had a good meal he is delighted, and becomes a warm partisan of the school.'[46]

The all-important and ever-recurring theme of science in domestic education was highlighted in an address on school training for women's home duties given to the British Association for the Advancement of Science in the summer of 1906 by a professor of chemistry, Arthur Smithells, a man whose role in the campaign that produced King's College of Household and Social Science will be highlighted in Chapter 6.

Smithells's lecture summarised succinctly the views of many in the household science movement. Much school-teaching was far too divorced from the everyday life of pupils; the world was full of

> schoolmistresses ... with high degrees in science who can give no intelligible account of the hot-water system of the ordinary house, cannot tell you what it is that yeast acts upon when it is mixed with dough, and have no opinion as to whether a hand-mirror is a satisfactory test for a damp bed. They do not know why washing soda goes white or brass grows green. ... They know nothing of gas meters, filters, or clinical thermometers, and are paralysed before a smoky chimney.

This 'vast undeveloped intellectual region connected with the domestic work of women' could, and should, easily be incorporated into the educational system so that 'the minds of the pupils are awakened to the fact that the household is ... a laboratory of applied science that may constantly engage the intelligence'.⁴⁷ The most important objective of science teaching in relation to housekeeping was not the information imparted but the inculcation in students of *the habit of scientific thinking*.

In the next chapter we look at how the domestic science campaigners managed to create a transnational social movement around this central idea.

4

Sweeping science into the home

A book called *Women, Plumbers, and Doctors* attracts our attention with its mysterious title, signifying something of interest in the association between three normally unconnected occupations. And indeed, Mrs Harriette M. Plunkett, who published the book in 1885, saw a very intimate connection between women, whom she declared should make plumbing their business, and preventive health, which she saw as curtailing the demand for doctors: a wise sanitary woman would keep the doctors away. The book's subtitle, *Household Sanitation*, stated its allegiance to the emerging movement for domestic science. It wasn't a proper movement yet, but there were signs all over the place: there were the cooking schools and the cooking classes; the tide of enthusiasm for girls' domestic education; the first textbooks were emerging; and European and North American reformers were busy meeting to exchange ideas.

This chapter engages with several important preludes to the academic household science movement. The emergence of germ theory, which happened just as Harriette Plunkett was preparing her text, revolutionised the scientific underpinnings of housework. As germs appeared on the landscape of conversations about housework, servants increasingly, but coincidentally, disappeared. The conjunction of these two historical moments created a stage on which women reformers' espousal of sanitary reform could more easily penetrate the private world of the home. At the close of the 19th century, this strengthened scientific rationale for housework formed the basis of a ground-breaking meeting of household science reformers at Lake Placid in the United States. The Lake Placid convention was a launch moment for all kinds of energetic currents and ideas that helped to propel household science into the world of higher education. Most importantly, the subject acquired an evidence-based theoretical approach which was a great aid to countering the dismissive derisions of those critics who saw housework as merely women's work and not worthy of any serious academic attention at all.

The trouble with drains

Harriette Plunkett was a woman with ideas. A respected New England matron, she wrote her book in the middle of a typhoid epidemic, and in it she grappled with that iconoclastic historic moment when the old miasma theory of disease was giving way to the new knowledge about germs. For a long time it was believed that disease was communicated atmospherically, although no satisfactory explanation of the process could be put forward. Then the new science of bacteriology emerged from the 1870s on with its startling evidence that microscopic living particles were the culprits. Either way, scientifically minded housewives were necessary, but the implications for housework were different in each case.

When disease was thought to enter human bodies through the air, bad air, caused by defective drains and plumbing and by the odours of rotting matter, was considered to be the direct cause of illness and premature death: the recurrent epidemics of cholera, typhoid, dysentery, tuberculosis, influenza, yellow fever and malaria, and the steady loss of infant life due to gastroenteritis. The primary target of miasma theory was sewer gas, the gas thought to arise from decaying faecal matter and emanate from leaky sewers and improperly vented drains, as well as from open sewers flowing through city streets. It could happen anywhere, and, indeed, it did, including in England where typhoid fever was recorded as the cause of Prince Albert's death in 1861, and ten years later was responsible for the near-death of the Prince of Wales. In the White House in Washington, DC, at least three presidents were brought to death's door by its serious plumbing inadequacies and location overlooking a marsh of stagnant sewage.[1]

Narratives such as Harriette Plunkett's directed at women and aimed at encouraging the proper care of drains had, by their nature, to be very detailed. There were long expositions of the air- and water-tight system of pipes, drains and traps needed to prevent sewage vapours fouling the interior air supply. Writing just as miasma theory was beginning to give way to germ theory in the public mind, Plunkett considered it important still to give much instruction about drains. Most of the 50 illustrations in her book feature drains: 'defective plumbing and draining, and no ventilation'; 'willow-root penetrating a drain laid without cemented joints', and so on. Figure 4.1, which is taken from Plunkett's scary manual, shows dreadful health-damaging sanitary design.

Sewer gas 'while escaping into a house, will ... cause feeble health, diarrhoea, dyspepsia, headaches, sore throats, and boils', stated the British National Health Society's leaflet on 'How to keep fever out of houses'.

> The pipes through which Typhoid Fever can enter are the discharge and waste pipes of each sink, water-closet, and bath; or the overflow pipes of the water cistern. ... To avoid this, allow no dark filth corners to exist inside, or immediately in connection with your dwelling. Burn the flue from the floors, rubbish, and all inflammable refuse.[2]

A favourite device for making sure these systems worked was the peppermint test. Peppermint oil was poured into the domestic waste pipes at their

Figure 4.1: 'The antique "pan-closet" – the sanitarian's horror'

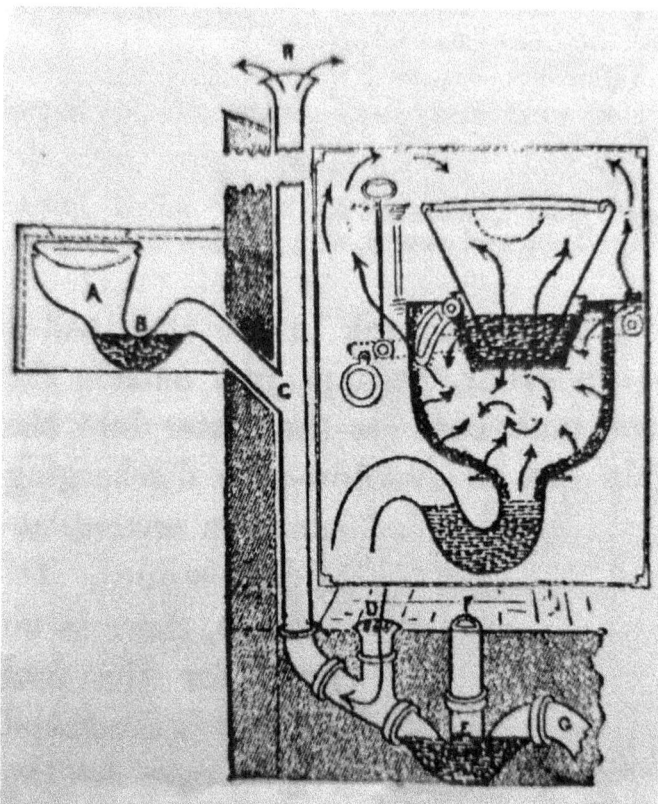

Source: Plunkett, H.M. (1885) *Women, Plumbers and Doctors; or, Household Sanitation*, New York: D. Appleton and Company, p 118

highest point and then the air in every room was sniffed to see if the smell of peppermint could be detected. Sanitary lecturer Margaret Pillow, writing in *Our Paper*, the monthly magazine of an organisation called the Women's Help Society, said the drains should be flushed daily and also disinfected with permanganate of potash.[3]

Like other sanitary science writers of the period, Harriette Plunkett took people painfully through all the structural elements of house-building needed for a fully sanitary life, and quoted all the international sanitary and scientific experts (Chadwick, Cohn, Farr, Koch, Pasteur, Virchow, and so on) on the way. She referred particularly to the authority of Dr R.B. Richardson, president of the British Medical Association, who decreed that the progress of the sanitary movement depended entirely on woman, 'the presiding genius of the home'.[4] Richardson could have been responding to the advice offered by Margaret Pillow, who deferentially but authoritatively noted in a paper given to the International Congress of Hygiene and Demography in 1891 that:

> Men, as they should be, are the pioneers of sanitary and hygienic reform; but they may sit in council, they may originate schemes, they may bring legislation to their aid, and they will find that most of their efforts are as a sounding brass and a tinkling cymbal, if they enlist not the sympathies and aid of women ... in women's hands the health of the nation lies.[5]

Harriette Plunkett's own understanding of current medical theory was aided by motherhood, as her son, who wanted to be a doctor, became totally blind, and she coached him successfully through five years of medical school.

These links between personal experience and professional work crop up frequently in the history of housework's reincarnation as a matter of science. In Canada, Adeline Hoodless founded both the domestic science movement there and the international Women's Institute Movement in 1897 after her youngest child died aged 14 months of the 'summer complaint' – an intestinal infection caused by drinking contaminated milk. In Hamilton, Ontario, where the Hoodless family lived, and in many such places, milk was delivered in open containers; cows were fed on kitchen refuse and were pastured in fields of raw sewage.[6] Milk was adulterated with chemicals like saltpetre, boracic acid and baking soda in order to make it seem fresher. As late as 1900 in both the United Kingdom and the United States, the milk supply was seriously contaminated with tuberculosis, typhoid, scarlet fever, diphtheria and streptococcal germs.

A woman's work is never done

'The air is full of sanitation', Plunkett wrote at the end of her *Women, Plumbers and Doctors*. Nearly every month saw a new book on the subject, 'so thoroughly illustrated that any quick, nimble-minded woman can take it in'.[7] Hers is actually quite heavy reading. But easier pieces in such organs as the *Popular Science Monthly* and *The New England Kitchen Magazine* also issued forth from her pen, and in two of these she drew attention to a very important aspect of the background to the domestic science movement: the staggeringly enormous amount of housework that had to be done in the days before the ready availability of running water, gas, electricity and industrially prepared food, clothes and domestic equipment. Cooking and heating was by means of open fires, which had to be kept going day and night. Cooking was a notoriously hazardous occupation, with a tendency for aprons to catch fire. In rural areas, wood in four-foot lengths was brought in and still had to be cut up without the treadmill sawing machine. Water had to be brought up

Figure 4.2: Housework in the old days

Source: Roghman, G., 'A Woman Doing Housework', Plate 5 from 'Five Feminine Occupations' (c. 1648–50) from the Elisha Whittelsey Collection, The Elisha Whittelsey Fund, 1956, The Metropolitan Museum of Art, https://www.metmuseum.org/art/collection/search/383483

and carried from wells, which was all very well on a summer's day but not with the mercury near freezing and a barn full of cattle to be watered.[8] In Figure 4.2 the 17th-century Dutch artist Geertruydt Roghman treats us to a more realistic view of Dutch domesticity than her contemporary Johannes Vermeer with his softly glistening domestic interiors. As Susan Strasser put it in her *Never Done: A History of American Housework*, 'tainted water supplies, rancid food, soot and skin burns from open fires, and full chamber pots' were the order of the day for the presiding geniuses of homes. Food arrived in the kitchen unprepared: live chickens had to be killed and plucked; green coffee, whole spices and cocoa had to be ground; loaf sugar to be cut; heavy flour full of impurities sifted. The dirty products of 19th-century heating and lighting settled everywhere, causing yet more cleaning, and there were also chimneys, wicks and oil lamps requiring attention. These tasks didn't begin to disappear until the beginning of the 20th century. Nor did the heavy manual work of washing, which could involve carrying loads of 40–50 lbs. Catharine Beecher in 1841 and the American economist Helen Campbell in 1881 both recommended the same time-honoured routine: soaking articles overnight; washing several times in hot suds (for which the water had to be hauled in and heated) using a washboard; wringing, starching, drying; and ironing with cumbersome flatirons.[9]

Much the same regime was followed in England; one woman, recalling her childhood in a Lancashire town in the 1920s, regaled everything that had to be done for the weekly wash: getting up early on Monday morning to start the kitchen fire; using a big tin cup to fill up the boiler in multiple trips with water from the one available cold tap; waiting for the water to boil and then putting in the clothes that had been soaked all night; transferring them after boiling to two big wooden tubs for rinsing; dragging them out and wringing them through a solid iron wringer with big wooden rollers. That wasn't the end of it, as the clothes next had to be put back in a tub of cold water with 'a dolly blue' (a powder containing a blue dye) to whiten them, and starch, before being put through the wringer again, and only then hung outside to dry.[10]

Unsurprisingly, washing was 19th-century housewives' most hated task. The first washing machines were available by the late 1890s, but these all had to be hand-cranked, and the water still had to be boiled, and the clothes soaped and rinsed by hand, so there was nothing very mechanical about it. Not often mentioned in histories of housework is the laundering burden of menstruation. Until well into the 20th century most women either just bled onto their clothes or used old cloths to absorb menstrual blood. These (called 'clouts' or 'rags') were hand-sewn out of cotton, gauze or flannel and were washed and reused. Imagine a household with a group of perhaps four menstruating women: some 40 stained cloths a month. The American efficiency expert Lillian Gilbreth (who features in Chapter 5) was hired by one sanitary product company in 1926 to assess the profitability of mass production: she came up with a figure of 4,576 cloths for each 'menstrual life', in other words a market well worth plundering.[11]

Another essential context for the immense amount of sanitary literature directed at housewives in the late 19th and early 20th centuries was the appallingly low standards of hygiene that often prevailed inside homes. At the International Health Exhibition held in London in 1884, public spaces were depicted as clean and pure, and domestic ones as riddled with poisons and dangers.[12] Housewives' ignorance was implicated in this, but so were the structural circumstances over which they had no control: leaky roofs, cracked, damp walls and privies; lack of fresh air; mounds of rubbish in halls, alleys and streets. Filth was the major health problem: filthy tenements, houses and farms, filthy streets, filthy water, inadequate or non-existent sewage systems, and filthy human bodies.

In her oral history of working-class women living in Lancashire between 1890 and 1940, Elizabeth Roberts notes that as late as the 1940s it wasn't unusual to board a bus in the area and 'be repelled by the overpowering smell of unwashed human bodies and/or dirty clothes'.[13] Soap was a rare commodity, time-consuming to make, and clean water was scarce. By the early 1840s some wealthy homes in the United Kingdom had toilets, but wastes from these were usually deposited in cellar cesspits and/or discharged directly onto the streets. In big cities like London, New York and Chicago, kitchen rubbish and the contents of chamber pots were routinely dumped outside on the streets. As late as the final years of the 19th century it was common to see streets two or three feet deep in household refuse and animal and human excrement. Rats, flies, cockroaches, ants, ticks and bedbugs were unavoidable.

Microbes and microbe-hunters

Beginning in the late 19th century, science brought new foundational characters called microbes into the drama of domestic science. As Harriette Plunkett put it most colourfully in the 18 pages of her book given over to the germ theory:

> [T]he conviction is spreading ... that reproductive parasitic life is at the root of epidemic disease; that living ferments, finding lodgment in the body, increase there and multiply, directly ruining the tissue on which they subsist, or they destroy life indirectly by the generation of poisonous compounds within the body.[14]

By this time science was firmly established as the new secular authority. It was a new discipline and a new profession, with the word 'scientist' only in common use from the 1830s, and university degrees in science possible only after 1870. Science meant systematised knowledge designed to understand the everyday world. It was practised by an intellectual elite, who had a huge impact on the public by affecting almost every aspect of life: food production, transport, communications, fashion, art, literature, politics, religion and national prestige. Both what science discovered and how science was done – the scientific methods of empirical observation, experiment, quantification and measurement – were central to this impact.

The German bacteriologist Robert Koch was the first to demonstrate in the early 1870s the relationship between a specific bacterium – that causing anthrax – and a specific disease. In 1882 Koch isolated the bacillus responsible for tuberculosis. Around the same time in France, Louis Pasteur, jointly regarded with Koch as 'the father of bacteriology', disproved the old idea that diseases could arise spontaneously, and gave his name to the process of pasteurisation, or sterilisation, which, when applied to milk, would have saved the life of Canadian home scientist Adeline Hoodless's son. Between 1880 and 1900 scientists discovered pathogenic organisms at the rate of about one every two years.[15]

The discovery of microbes reframed disease from an accident of fate to a process under human control, most notably the control of women. A new occupation for women, that of microbe-hunter, was invented. Women as microbe-hunters were in charge of the private side of public health and were earnestly taught through lectures and books 'the new lessons of the laboratory: that microscopic living particles were the agents of contagion, that sick bodies shed germs into the environment, and that disease spread by seemingly innocuous behaviors such as coughing, sneezing and spitting, sharing common drinking cups, or failing to wash hands before eating'.[16] Much fear came to surround ordinary household objects: 'contagion by telephone', 'infection and postage stamps' were topics of public alarm.[17]

Microbes were enemies with a powerful rhetorical image. Live and invisible, 'they lent themselves like nothing before to the demonization of dirt and dust'.[18] As products of real scientists working in real laboratories, microbes inspired parallel images of housewives as scientists working in the laboratory of the home. The British domestic writer Mrs Beeton, back in 1861, had called the kitchen 'the great laboratory of the household' in her *Book of Household Management*.[19] (Like almost everything in that book, the sentiment probably came from somewhere else: Isabella Beeton and her publisher husband Samuel were clever exploiters of other people's work. Nonetheless, the book, an exhausting read at 1,112 pages, was so popular that Isabella's death in childbirth four years after its publication was concealed so that people would believe she was still a living expert.[20])

The arrival of microbes enormously fertilised the metaphor of homes as laboratories. Sophronia Maria Elliott's *Household Bacteriology* was published in 1905 from the launch pad of Simmons College for women in Boston where Elliott taught household economics. It firmly instructed women to become laboratory technicians and apply the scientist's methods to an understanding of household dirt. 'The facts of bacteriology underlie so firmly all our daily living that there is no need to go far afield for illustrations', she counselled. 'But a thorough knowledge of the science can be gained only through laboratory methods and with a microscope. ... Many of the daily occurrences in the

Figure 4.3: Bacteria in the 'eyes' of potatoes

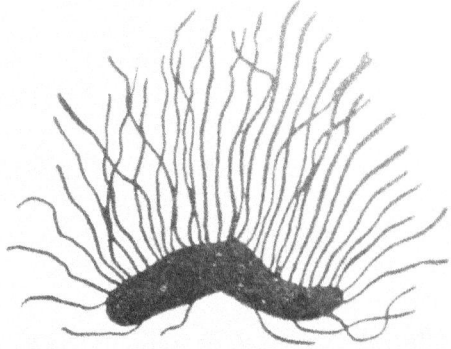

Source: Elliott, S.M. (1905) *Household Bacteriology*, Boston and Chicago: American School of Home Economics, p 45

home give rise to questions which may be readily answered if we will but turn our kitchens into laboratories and try some simple experiments.' Thus would women be able to attain 'a peep into this world of the unseen'.[21] Figure 4.3, which is from Elliott's book, quite put me off potatoes.

That, of course, was the crux of the matter. Microbes were invisible without the aid of science: in order to be believed, they had to be seen. Much was made in Elliott's book, and many others, of something called the 'dust-garden' methodology. Dust was cultivated in order to demonstrate exactly how many bacteria it could carry. Elliott's instructions for how to do this occupy eight pages, and they would have taken quite a lot of the housewife's time over a period of a week or more. The culture medium, made of minced boiled beef, water, bicarbonate of soda and gelatin, had to be prepared and then allocated to different bottles, which, treated in different ways, would show the propensity of bacteria to flourish differentially according to particular conditions. One of the pictures, Figure 4.4, Elliott included as an invitation to grow dust, showed an impressive yield. When exposed to air, specks of marvellously myriad hues would appear on the culture plates – pink, orange, yellow, green, blue, red. Less pleasantly, the smell would be 'sensible proof' of putrefaction. There were direct implications for housework. 'The next time you are tempted to leave a piece of meat exposed', remarked the sagacious Elliott, 'remember the dust-garden, and cover the meat with a cloth to keep out dust'.[22]

Dust was treated to sensational descriptions, becoming an enemy of gigantic proportions. Theophil Mitchell Prudden, the first professional pathologist and medically trained bacteriologist in the United States, took time off from his exciting work in Germany with Dr Koch to write a

Figure 4.4: A dust garden

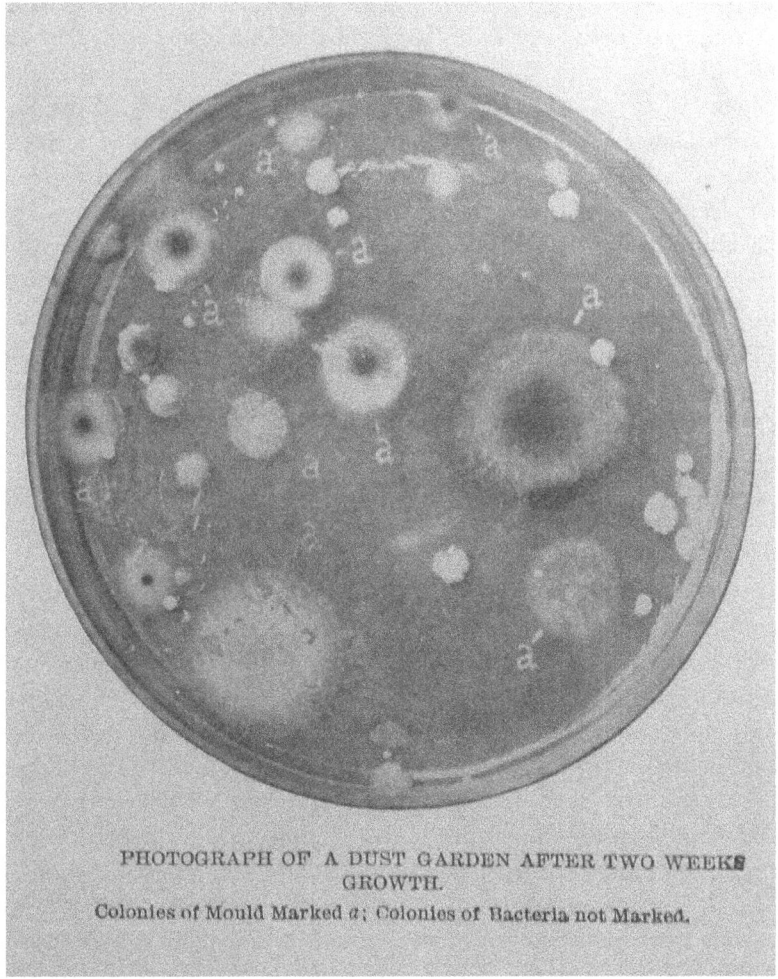

Source: Elliott, S.M. (1905) *Household Bacteriology*, Boston and Chicago: American School of Home Economics, p 12

disturbing book called *Dust and Its Dangers* in 1910. This was a foundational text for the domestic science movement. In it Prudden defined dust as 'fine, dry particles of earth or other matter so attenuated that it may be raised and wafted by the wind'. Dust was full of the most unsavoury items:

> small fragments of sand, broken fibres of plants, pollen, fine hairs, the pulverized excreta of various domestic animals, ashes, fibres of clothing and other fabrics, particles of lime or plaster or soot, parts of seeds of plants, masses and clusters of various kinds of micro-organisms, and other partially ground up materials of kinds too numerous to mention.

In the interests of science Prudden grew dust-gardens from material gathered in six New York settings on a dry, breezy day in April 1890, and he included photographs of the results in his book. In these six places – Central Park, Union Square, a library in a private house, a large dry goods store, a park railing in Broadway, and a street through which the carts of the Street Cleaning Department passed on their rounds – the number of germs that settled on the petri dishes went from 34 in the library to 5,810 where the street cleaning vehicles had been.[23]

The marriage between dirt and disease had profound implications for the hygiene of everyday household life. The preparation and preservation of food, for example, required an understanding of fermentation and decay; cooking and serving utensils had to be scalded in boiling water, dishtowels boiled. Domestic science reformers were convinced that women needed not only to keep their dishcloths clean but to understand *why* they had to be clean and the exact mechanisms of what would happen in the presence of unwashed dirt. Such an understanding, if it had really caught on, might have changed the dishcloth map of the world in the 2020s which we looked at in Chapter 2.

Increasingly in the early 1900s manufacturers and advertisers of domestic equipment, food and other products seized on germs as a way to raise their profits. Because food was a particularly dangerous source of germ-borne infection, the new teaching on germs settled on methods of acquiring, storing and cooking food as a core part of the new domestic science. There was no hesitation about using bacteria to advertise domestic technologies: a company in New Jersey, for example, selling a new model toilet in 1915, included in its promotional material a drawing of the typhoid microbe magnified a thousand times.[24] The word 'sanitary' was inserted in thousands of advertisements as an aid to their selling power, and new appliances were launched with ambitious claims about their disease-reducing potential: in 1909 the Bohn Refrigerator Company argued that its new appliance would greatly reduce infant mortality.[25]

The argument that housework needed to take advantage of technological innovation was paralleled by other habits of the scientific method: cooking recipes, for example, originally presented as rather laissez-faire narratives, had gradually been growing more precise in their lists of ingredients and the steps taken to turn them into a meal. Cookery books began to use standardised, quantified values, and to describe recipes based on actual laboratory experiments. Isabella Beeton broke down the menus that crowded into the 900 pages of her *Book of Household Management* into ingredients, mode, time, average cost, seasonableness and number of portions. The air of authority thus conveyed would have made cooking less of a hit-and-miss affair, while commending it as an activity that required a basic mathematical (scientific) education.

Women and sanitary reform

In 1893 the role of women as sanitary enforcers was formalised in Britain when they were allowed to join the ranks of male sanitary inspectors who, since the public health legislation of the late 1840s, had been responsible for patrolling the 'nuisances' of living: the emptying of cesspools; the removal of rubbish, animal dung, offensive businesses and infestations; the inspection of slaughterhouses, water closets and water supplies. However, drains, along with sewers and slaughterhouses, were in the early years considered beyond the female sanitary inspectors' remit as unfeminine. Why? Margaret Pillow, the first woman to pass the sanitary inspector's examination, recalled her own steep unfeminine learning curve:

> I went practically to work by going into workshops and I learnt as much of plumbers' work as possible, to make joints, &c. I have spent hours over the practical laying of drains, water mains, and connections. I examined cisterns, learned to draw plans of houses, vertical section drainage of houses, &c. ... I thoroughly studied the Acts of Parliament and ... bye-laws framed by the Local Government Board. ... Among the places I visited were three dairies, one slaughter-house, two bake offices, sanitary arrangements of schools, several hospitals, disinfecting rooms and workshops, and one dust destructor.[26]

Women's entry into the male precincts of local government is a story about how domestic housekeeping became municipal housekeeping. 'What is the city but the larger house in which we dwell?' asked one American reformer in 1894. 'Good city government is good housekeeping and that is the sum of the matter.'[27] This extended self-appointed remit for housekeeping reform was a critical backdrop to the accelerating movement for the reframing and dissemination of housework as science.

Large numbers of sanitary women's organisations took up the new microbe-focused approach to the physical improvement of homes. The National Health Society, an outfit founded in 1871 by a group who met in the home of Elizabeth Blackwell, the first woman doctor in Britain, published a major series of leaflets in the 1890s with titles such as *Domestic Sanitary Works*, *Short Rules for Disinfection* and *A Short Leaflet on Dust*. The Society did much lecturing and also sponsored inventions: one lady member devised 'an exceedingly elegant drawing room ventilator – on improved scientific principles'; and in 1883 a fever-proof costume appeared in the Society's London offices. This was an early version, fashioned out of glazed mackintosh, of the Personal Protective Equipment we heard so much about during the COVID-19 epidemic of 2020–2022.[28]

The domestic science movement reframed women as intelligent, capable human beings who had been held back by the forces of (male) tradition and custom from assuming their full role in society. Science would help to release them from these constraints. If there's one image that lingers from a journey through all these sanitary texts it is of the woman keeping house as a *scientist*. Equipped with scientific knowledge, with a scientist's view of the world as a rational, physical, measurable, understandable universe, she was handed the power to have a demonstrable impact on the workings of this universe. By attending scrupulously to the cleanliness and healthfulness of everything concerning the home, she was elevated to its scientific guardian, akin in rhetorical importance to that of the doctor or the public health expert, but not of course equal to them in prestige or financial remuneration.

And the men

Most of the educative domestic science work that happened in the late 19th and early 20th centuries was carried out by women on a voluntary basis, but the men were there as well. They wrote books and they lectured on domestic sanitary subjects. A popular early tract in the United States was *The Handbook of Household Science* by the science writer Edward Youmans. His book was crammed with technical detail, for example, that the shine achieved on furniture by polishing is a consequence, not of the polish itself, but of the increased density of the outer surface produced by polishing, a revelation of perhaps dubious usefulness. Youmans' reputation owed much to the services of his sister Eliza who read chemistry books to him and carried out experiments, all of which was necessary since he had poor eyesight. Eliza herself contributed to a handbook for the New York National Training School for Cookery in 1879, and wrote many texts on botany and early childhood education. In the 1880s the male-run Sanitary Institute in London began a series of 'lectures for ladies'. In 1888 lectures on child culture, butter and cheese, were given; the following year Professor Lewes of the Naval College in Greenwich offered a lecture on 'The Chemistry of Cleaning', 'a subject which is too little understood … being one which cannot be adequately dealt with except upon a scientific basis'. Bread, and the domestic use of petroleum were also covered.[29]

Whose kitchen was it?

In telling the domestic science story, we cannot escape mentioning the fabulous Count Rumford and his New England Kitchen. These appear in many narratives as a convulsive episode in the scientisation of housework.

The 'Rumford' or 'New England' Kitchen was a model exhibit at the Chicago World Fair in 1893; it was devised to prove that nutritious meals could be prepared for a ridiculously small sum of money. Ten thousand visitors to the Fair were served scientifically prepared meals for 32 cents each; in a very modern gesture, there were menu cards at each table listing the exact weight of each dish, its precise ingredients, calories and nutritional value. Count Rumford, born as Benjamin Thompson in Massachusetts in 1753, was a maverick self-taught physicist and a chemist who applied his study of heat to everyday problems. He became a Count of the Holy Roman Empire for his work in Bavaria, where he reorganised the army, popularised the potato, and set up workhouses and soup kitchens: 'Rumford' was the place in the United States where he married the first of several wives. Count Rumford had a remarkable career in science and diplomacy in several European countries, which included trying to persuade George III to set up a public forum for the 'Application of science to the common purposes of life'. The result was the Royal Institution.[30]

The Rumford Kitchen was an offshoot of scientific research in Germany on food and nutrition. American chemist Wilbur Atwater applied German research techniques to American food and concluded that it was nutritionally deficient – too many sweets, not enough protein for the poor. He came up with the idea of a public kitchen providing affordable nutritious food for working-class families, and he discussed this with sanitary chemist Ellen Richards and another household scientist, Mary Hinman Abel, who was familiar with the latest German research through her husband, a professor of pharmacology who had also worked in Germany. The household science movement was strongly transnational: people travelled, met and worked with one another, exchanged ideas and initiated projects; few of these were solitary accomplishments.

In fact the Rumford New England Kitchen didn't belong to Count Rumford at all. The experiment of establishing a public kitchen grew out of this network of scientists, and began as an experiment funded by the Boston philanthropist Pauline Agassiz Shaw, and conducted by the chemist Ellen Richards. Shaw gave Richards US$1,000 to equip and staff a model kitchen which opened in 1890 in downtown Boston offering cookery demonstrations, instructions in housekeeping and cheap meals. The name 'Rumford' was chosen by Ellen Richards who wanted to see his scientific work on domestic processes more widely appreciated. This was the background to the Rumford Kitchen's appearance at the Chicago World Fair. The Boston poor didn't actually much take to the idea, and the Kitchen closed down several years later, but its subsequent removal to the Chicago World Fair ensured its eponymous place in the history of domestic science.[31]

The servant problem

Another critical context for the evolution of domestic science was the structural change in women's employment which saw far more women working in factories, shops and offices instead of in homes as servants. The decline in the availability of servants was statistically notable: in England and Wales indoor servants made up 6.1 per cent of the population in 1861 but less than half that, 2.7 per cent, in 1921.[32] The servant problem was widely discussed, and the scientific education of housewives was widely advocated (on little evidence) as producing better servants. Some of the early schools of cookery and housekeeping were intended for the training of servants rather than women managers of homes, but these had nothing like the success of educational initiatives aimed directly at housewives, partly because servants disliked attending them.

Middle-class complaints about the lack of servants focused the energies of domestic scientists on providing recipes for servantless homes instead of chapters on how to manage servants scientifically. A New Jersey enthusiast for household science, Mary Pattison, recorded in her *The Business of Home Management* (1915) her personal decision to give up three servants – 'a laundress and cook, a waitress and chambermaid, and a nurse and seamstress'. Organising the servants took her a lot of time, and they were expensive, so she decided to do all the work herself. For this she had to study 'like a student preparing for an examination', analysing 'the various departments of the work', and experimenting with different methods for each; she had to search for the best devices with which to achieve the desired results. Mary Pattison found this exercise intellectually stimulating. At the end of it she was pleased to boast that she could clean the seven rugs in the front hall efficiently 'while gloved and dressed for a reception'.[33]

We should not be surprised that domestic service as an occupation has been just as ignored by historians as all other aspects of domestic life. Household service was predominantly a female occupation; thus the status of domestic servants was closely tied to ideologies about the value of women. Not until 1891 did the English Census differentiate between hospital nurses and household servants, both of whom were dedicated to keeping bodies and the environment clean. Actually, in the United Kingdom before 1777, male domestic servants were relatively common, but a stiff tax, which was rigidly enforced, was imposed on their employment in that year – and not repealed until 1937. Female servants were taxed for a few years (1785–1792) at a lower rate. The object of the servant tax was to raise money for the war with the American colonists, and later the Napoleonic wars: male servants, paid at much higher rates than female ones, were taxed more heavily and were thus a richer source of income. By the time we get to 1911, 91.7 per cent of 'indoor servants' in England and Wales were female. In Ireland, without the tax, there was more gender equality.[34]

Nor should it come as news that it's mainly women researchers and historians who have taken this topic seriously, by studying the actual, everyday conditions of domestic labour in the decades around the early 20th century, or by fixing the long historical gaze on domestic service as an aspect of class and/or of racialised cultures. Lucy Salmon, an American historian who founded the history department at Vassar College in the United States and who believed in social, rather than narrowly political, history, published a book on *Domestic Service* in 1897. This covered the history and sociology of domestic service. Salmon dispatched 5,000 questionnaires to domestic servants and their employers, and these harvested the kind of detail she found fascinating but which political historians regarded as uninteresting. Her favourite historical document was the laundry list, from which one was able to learn a great deal about the inner life of households. Salmon's male colleagues criticised *Domestic Service* as unoriginal and unworthy of a historian because of its focus on the menial work of the home.[35]

In the rhetoric of the domestic science movement, the disappearance of servants contributed a new rationale for sweeping science into the home: the management of homes without servants could (theoretically) become a more fulfilling occupation. For women who treated housework as a servantless job, every little domestic task would, thus, according to American efficiency expert Christine Frederick, be transformed into 'a new and interesting problem'. 'Far from being dull drudgery, homemaking in all its details is fascinating and stimulating if a woman applies to it her best intelligence and culture.'[36] Moreover, efficient housewives would have more time for everything else: for their husbands and children, for self-education, for philanthropy. The possibility of serious professional work was less often mentioned.

What's in a name?

In 1899 11 people met at the Lake Placid Country Club in the wilderness of the Adirondack Mountains in upstate New York for a conference on something they initially called 'home science or household economics'. What to call it in fact occupied a good part of the discussion at that first conference and the succeeding nine. The Lake Placid conferences have eponymous status as the organised beginning of the international domestic science movement. The discussions that took place there effectively solidified a consensus among the scientific reformers of the home in the early 20th century that the only real route for securing the expansion and upgrading of home economics was to get it into the universities. The Lake Placid conferences are thus a key context for the case-studies about domestic science degrees in higher education which occupy Chapters 6–8 of *The Science of Housework*.

The conference format was quite intensive: organised meetings for up to a week each time, supplemented with evening sessions and recreational drives to abolitionist John Brown's grave and other nearby lakes and a steamer trip on Lake Placid itself; these excursions would have furnished enormous further networking opportunities. Topics for discussion in 1899 included: the definition, naming and classification of household economics; the results of experience teaching domestic economy in schools in the United States and Europe; the preparation of papers/brochures in domestic science for publication; the founding of state schools and chairs of household economics in state universities and the training of domestic science teachers; how domestic science can help 'the woman who does her own work'; simplified methods of housekeeping; and standards of living as affected by sanitary science.[37]

Among the participants at the first Lake Placid conference were Anna Barrows, the editor of *The American Kitchen Magazine* (a monthly journal of recipes and advice published from 1895 to 1903); Maria Parloa from New York, whom we met in Chapter 3; and Alice Peloubet Norton from Massachusetts, a home economics teacher who is part of the story in Chapter 8 about academic household science in Chicago. The original Lake Placid group had swollen to 700 five years later. Most were from the United States and Canada, with a small contingent from the United Kingdom. Alice Ravenhill went in 1901 to talk about 'women as sanitary inspectors' and 'practical hygienic teaching in England', this second slot affording her the opportunity to share the details of her own 30-lesson course for teachers in Yorkshire.[38] The Lake Placid conferences were dominated by women, but there were some male attendees. The chemist Wilbur Atwater attended some meetings, as did Charles Langworthy, Chief of Nutrition Investigations at the US Department of Agriculture, and Henry Sherman, a chemistry professor from Columbia University and a leading nutrition researcher.

The debate about names was heightened by the presence at the Lake Placid meetings of an eccentric individual with a passion for efficiency and time-saving called Melvil Dewey, who co-owned the Lake Placid Club with his wife Annie: both Deweys were librarians, and much given both to networking in the cause of the domestic science movement, and to methodical habits in every aspect of life. Annie was an arch-organiser of philanthropic causes, and she was the one who first dreamt up the idea of creating a community club which would advance 'the science of right living'. She found the Lake Placid site in 1890. From modest beginnings, the enterprise eventually expanded to 390 buildings, 43 farms, a general store, sports facilities and a library of 10,000 books, Melvil's particular interest. He was the originator of a method called the Dewey Classification System (or Dewey Decimal System) for classifying library books, which is still used today. One of the conference arguments was about where Melvil had placed home economics in his classificatory system. He put it as 'Domestic Economy' in category 640 under the subheading 'Useful Arts' at the same level as other applied technologies. But some of the Lake Placid participants thought it should be moved to a more prestigious position in 339 between Political Economy and Law and with Sociology.[39]

So what was it: domestic economy, domestic science, household economics, home economics, household arts – anything, presumably, would be better than the bland label 'housework'. After 'full discussion' the Lake Placid attendees settled on the name 'home economics'. This was what the whole general subject should be called. Most importantly, they decided it should form 'a distinct section of the general subject of economics' in order for it to 'find a logical place in the college and university course and not be confused with the mere "household arts"'. This was because 'household arts' would never form part of a university curriculum. The terms 'domestic economy' for younger pupils, and 'domestic science' for high schools were also suggested.[40]

A far more important person, for the future of whatever-it-was, than Melvil Dewey at the Lake Placid meetings was the world-leading sanitary chemist Ellen Swallow Richards. In most of what she did Ellen Richards was the first woman to do it: the first American woman to get a chemistry degree; the first woman student at the Massachusetts Institute of Technology (MIT) and the first female member of staff there; the first woman chemist to work for a State Board of Health; the first woman member of the American Institute of Mining and Mineralogical Engineers; the first woman, and indeed, the first person, to run a consumer products-testing laboratory and to set up a chemistry laboratory for women. Richards' Women's Laboratory opened in 1876 and was the first institution of its kind in the world teaching science to women. Her great professional concern was the quality of air, water and food as 'the three essentials for healthful human life'.[41] She carried out the first great scientific study of pollution, personally analysing 40,000 samples of local water, creating the world's first Water Purity Tables and something called the Normal Chlorine Map, which predicts inland water pollution and is still used in water studies today. The first water-quality standards and the first modern sewage plant in the United States were established as a direct result of her work. Richards' studies on the adulteration of food produced the first Pure Food and Drug Act. She was married to an engineering professor at MIT, who proposed to her in the chemistry laboratory, and whose salary helped to fund her early work. Their home was childless, but full of labour-saving sanitary ideas: vines and flowering plants instead of curtains; carpetless floors; air-purifying fans; meters to monitor fuel usage: 'a living laboratory', in other words.[42]

Figure 4.5: Ellen Swallow Richards, portrait with cat, 1860–1867

Source: Courtesy of MIT Museum

In most of Ellen Richards' available photographs, she looks straight at you, unsmiling and rather forbidding. In Figure 4.5 she permits herself a half-smile, perhaps in recognition of the (not so clean?) cat perched on her shoulder.

Richards was a woman with extraordinary ambitions for her subject. She propagandised for it, ran demonstration projects, conducted huge numbers of experiments, raised money, wrote many books, organised activities and professional associations, and trained and inspired many others. Her life was dominated by three themes: a passion for science; the furthering of women's education; and the home as a source for social change. These came together in her goal of raising sanitary science to the same academic status as Greek or mathematics. What she really wanted to call home economics was 'oekology', or 'the science of right living', but she gave up on this term when biology appropriated the term as 'ecology'. At the sixth Lake Placid conference in 1904 she tried euthenics, 'the science of controllable environment'. 'Euthenics' was an intentional play on the word 'eugenics'. As Richards explained in the book she published in 1910, *Euthenics: The Science of Controllable Environment*, euthenics means, '[t]he betterment of living conditions, through conscious endeavor, for the purpose of securing efficient human beings'. Human vitality, she said, depends on two things – heredity and hygiene: eugenics deals with 'race improvement through heredity' and euthenics with 'race improvement through hygiene'.[43]

The language of heredity and race reflected the biases of the time, and the dominance of the household science movement by White middle-class culture. While more than 30 million immigrants, mostly from Southern and Eastern Europe, Asia and Central America, settled in the United States between 1870 and 1914, there is little sign of this massive cultural diversity in the structures, pronouncements and products of the campaign to take science into the home (for more on this, see Chapter 10). Nonetheless, the distinction Ellen Richards made between what people could, and could not, control was an important one.

Her interest in domestic science was much broader than that of many of its other proselytisers. She saw it not only as a means of elevating women's capabilities but of ridding the world of all preventable disease and thus of creating a wonderful new one: 'When wise attention is paid to municipal sanitation, to school hygiene and household bacteriology, we may expect a social development hitherto Utopian.'[44] Richards was fond of the writings of H.G. Wells, himself a great believer in science as the tool of social progress. In Richards' utopian view, science would aid human beings to develop what she called the art of right living, and would curb the harm they were doing to the environment: she has been called the founder of environmental science.[45] At the heart of her perspective on domestic labour was the very modern reconceptualisation of housework as health-care work. Her many books, speeches and courses of instruction were designed to train citizens in critical thinking skills and to demystify science.

Conclusion

Bacteriological and other scientific discoveries in the late 19th century gave a new impetus to the household reform movement. New knowledge about the hidden dangers of domestic life could be cited in support of the thesis that housework is essential health-care work. Women as housewives were recast as savvy and informed first-line defenders of homes and bodies against the scourges of dirt and disease. While one might conclude that nothing would ever be the same again after this shift in perspective, it didn't prove to be quite as simple as that, as we will learn in later chapters.

The domestic science movement can be seen either as an attempt to raise women's status or as a strategy for the further oppression of women; either as an outlet for female philanthropy or as a critical element in the improvement of public and personal health. In reality it was all of these things, and it is in all these guises that we need to locate it as part of the social and economic transformation that produced our modern world.

5

This man-made world

The passion for injecting science into housework which gripped Europe, America and many other countries in the period between 1880 and 1940 didn't confine itself to recipes for cabbage soup, the persecution of dust and other microbial enemies of human health, and how to cook cheaply for the poor. Housework happens in people's homes and these – the way they're designed, manufactured and furnished – shape the extent to which housework can be converted into a scientific discipline. Thus, the *making* of homes needs to be as much a subject of discussion as the *doing* of housework.

The American writer Charlotte Perkins Gilman published a book called *The Man-made World* in 1911. Gilman is most famous for her terrifying fable, 'The yellow wallpaper', which is about the creation and treatment of depression in women. She is less well-known for what she was, the leading feminist intellectual of her day, and a prominent social theorist in the emerging discipline of sociology. In her autobiography Gilman described herself as 'a philosophic steam-engine', and she certainly propelled herself with enormous zest through most of the debates that raged in her lifetime about women, households, gender and social policy. She was the great-niece of Catharine Beecher whose 1841 text on domestic economy took the first sustained scientific interest in housework. Although this may have helped to fuel Gilman's own interest in the home as a place of labour for women, she didn't see the relationship between women and housework in at all the same way as her great-aunt. Indeed, Gilman devoted much energy to undoing Catharine Beecher's ideology of the home as women's natural domain. Between 1898 and 1911 she wrote books about the home, women and economics, human work, children, and *The Man-made World*, whose subject is the effect on human life of 'the unbridled dominance of one sex'. In this 'androcentric' culture, as she termed it, men have made homes essentially places for women and children, but without considering their needs.[1]

This chapter ties together various themes about house design, efficiency and economics in a story about how the domestic science movement developed in the period from around 1910 to the 1930s. A more housewife-centred approach to house planning; the transfer to household work of efficiency principles originally developed in industry; an economic analysis with productive housework at its centre; Gilman's reimagining of housework as a collective enterprise: all these form the backdrop to the university career of domestic science which we look at in Chapters 6–8.

Labour-making and labour-saving homes

Because men don't generally have to keep house, nor are they usually performers of housework, the details may easily escape them of how houses should be designed. So decided the British writer and journal-editor Constance Peel in her best-selling *The Labour-saving House*, published in 1917.[2] In an astonishingly varied career, Peel, who was married to an electrical engineer, wrote many books and articles about household management, and four novels, including one called *The Hat Shop* based on an establishment she ran with a friend where they provided hats for the actor Ellen Terry. During the First World War, Peel worked for the Ministry of Food, travelling round England to promote economical diets, and she was a member of the group that set up Women's Pioneer Housing in 1920, a co-operative association that converted buildings into cheap rented flats for single women and which continues its much-needed mission still today. Many such co-operative housing initiatives in the early decades of the 20th century could reasonably be seen as outcomes of the domestic science movement.

Peel's *The Labour-saving House* begins with the middle-class problem of not enough servants, goes on to discuss what a labour-saving house would look like, compares it to a labour-making one, and then discourses on the wonders of gas and electricity which would consign to the past the labour- and pollution-making work of heating and cooking with coal and wood. Scattered throughout her text are many pictures of electric and gas devices, with their manufacturers named for ease of purchase: by the 1920s household technology had become big business.

Another popular British book was Leonora Eyles's *The Woman in the Little House*, published a few years after Peel's, in 1922. Like Peel, Eyles attributed 'the supreme inconvenience' of many homes to their design by male architects: 'men don't live and move and have their being in their houses. They are more or less paying guests'.[3] Eyles spoke from experience, having being jettisoned from a middle-class marriage into lone poverty-stricken motherhood in a working-class neighbourhood of badly designed terraced houses after her husband abandoned her and their young children. So there was this young mother living in a small inconvenient dwelling in Peckham, South London, where the only place for the pram was in the kitchen, which was full of coal dust because the coal cellar opened off it, there was no hot water, and the sink emptied onto the floor. Eyles lived with her three little children in this house, and she worked in a garment factory to make money. Her book describes in dismal detail the life of the anonymised 'Mrs Annie Britain' who inhabits one of these nasty, cramped, insanitary homes and is reduced to constant misery by it and poverty and the endless routines of housework and family care.

In the United States, *The American Kitchen Magazine* provided a regular outlet for similar critiques of masculine-designed homes. The interior designer, geographer, feminist and later highly newsworthy survivor of the *Titanic* shipping disaster, Helen Churchill Candee, wrote this in 1900 about the shortcomings of men as house designers:

> He may be familiar with the temples of Greece and the chateaux of the Loire, and yet fail to provide a place for the flour barrel and the brooms. ... For a man to plan a house is almost as incongruous as for a woman to plan a manufacturing plant.

According to Candee, the space around the pantry sink was 'the architect's pet economy. He has never washed dishes, so how could he know that the piles of unwashed glass and china, and the piles set to drain, take up more room than those actually within the water?'[4]

The masculinity of the architectural profession and the house-building industry was an obstacle to the building of labour-saving homes. Architecture wasn't a profession for women. Actually, this isn't quite true, and the history of architecture shares with many other disciplinary histories a trail of buried women who were there doing it anonymously, forgettably and/or being mistaken for the men who were assumed to have done it instead. I do realise this is a deviation from the story of scientific housework – we'll get back to that in a minute – but I absolutely must mention Elizabeth Wilbraham, who was born in the same year (1632) as Christopher Wren, and who designed some 400 buildings, taught Wren architecture, and designed 18 of 'his' 52 London churches.[5]

Victorian homes were heavily patriarchal architecturally as well as ideologically. In middle-class British homes, the largest area of space and the most convenient position, accessible from the front of the house, belonged to the male heads of households. In homes of all classes, women's spaces were tucked away at the back, or in the basement. These spaces had no architectural embellishments: heavy housework was done in cramped areas next to privies and coal cellars. Little architectural thought was given to the need for light and air, for appropriate storage and furniture, and for the principles of hygiene and cleanliness that would aid women in their household labours and promote the health-giving, rather than the status-giving, properties of homes.

Among the British theoreticians of the domestic science movement was Clementina Black, an industrious novelist, social investigator, trade unionist, feminist agitator and founder of two internationally important organisations for the story of women and labour, the Women's Industrial Council in 1894 and the British Consumers' League in 1887. In 1918, Black published an article in *The Contemporary Review* called 'Domestic idiocies'. Here she railed against many of the common defects in house design that were due to men 'irreflectively but unanimously' making women's housework harder. For example, most doors open the wrong way, and they 'are almost invariably ill designed. Their panels are enclosed by sharply cornered and finely grooved mouldings, and their frames, adorned with similar mouldings, project from the wall'. And windows: 'The frames of windows, like those of doors, should cease to project from the walls. ... And is it not really an idiocy to build windows in such a way that they cannot be cleaned except by the employment of an extraneous man with a ladder?'[6]

Black's article was a foretaste of her book, *A New Way of Housekeeping* ('New' or 'Easy/Easier' were popular adjectives attached to 'housekeeping' in book titles in these years). The book contained a chapter on 'Labour-making houses' that expanded on the domestic idiocy theme, from the dirt-attracting simulated cockle-shells adorning many lavatories and the 'extravagant, inconvenient, and laborious kitchen range', to the intricate balusters of staircases for which no effective cleaning apparatus has ever been invented. This is why my mother in the 1950s hired a builder to fit unaesthetic but cleanable sides to them (see Prologue). Black's solutions to all this demanded a more sensible approach to house design, but she also, like Gilman, recommended the socialisation of housework itself. 'Consider the fifty women who all peel and boil potatoes – most of them badly – twice a day at the same hours', she counselled,

> and are all at work by-and-by washing up crockery in small lots, whereas all the potatoes might be prepared and well cooked, and all the crockery cleaned in less time, by five persons with proper appliances such as are used in a well-appointed hotel or restaurant. ... Let any man of business contemplate this spectacle steadily for half an hour and declare what he thinks of it as a method of carrying on one of the nation's largest and most essential industries.[7]

If women made houses

As noted earlier, most stories about the history of housework focus on the United States or Britain, whereas the domestic science movement was a distinct presence in other countries too. Women campaigners in many places attacked the masculinity of domestic architectural design. In France, the journalist and philosophy graduate Paulette Bernège gave the household science movement a respectable philosophical pedigree, as well as launching a severe attack on the thoughtlessness of male architects. One of her books, *De la méthode ménagère*, recalled the 17th-century French philosopher René Descartes' own *Discours de la méthode* (1637). Bernège argued that Cartesian principles – the deductive logic of science, the elevation of consciousness, the separateness of mind and body – are none other than the principles of 'philosophie ménagère' itself.[8] Descartes' injunction to separate every difficulty into its component parts in order to analyse and resolve it applies, for example, to cooking, which must be subdivided into mode, method, appliances, time, effect on taste, price and amount of work. The 19th-century experimental physiologist Claude Bernard is also a figure in Bernège's erudite landscape – for bequeathing to domestic science its core methodological principle of experimentation.

In 1928 Paulette Bernège published a book called *Si les femmes faisaient les maisons* [*If Women Made Houses*]. She wrote this in response to government plans that had just been issued to update France's housing stock. The government claims to have consulted all experts, Bernège protested, but where are the real experts, French housewives? In Bernège's popular *Si les femmes faisaient les maisons*, readers are invited to compare the performance of household tasks as they would normally do them, and then using the time-and-motion approach, with a stopwatch and a pedometer pinned to their bodices. The book's tone is playful but also confrontational. Among the many examples of waste Bernège invites architects to consider is that walking the 'vampiric' distance between her kitchen and dining room over 40 years would take her from Paris to Lake Baikal in Siberia. She proposes practical architectural reforms that include the usual minimising of dust-gathering staircases and corridors, networking homes to all utilities and using washable smooth building materials – getting rid of Clementina Black's 'domestic idiocies', in other words.[9] Figure 5.1 shows Bernège working in her rationally organised kitchen (the piles of books perhaps not so rational in this setting). The last French edition of *Si les femmes faisaient les maisons* appeared in 1969 and Bernège's own career as a celebrant of scientific efficiency continued well into the 1950s. The book was never, however, translated into English, like the other classic text *On Cleanliness in Norway* that we encountered in Chapter 3. Perhaps someone might be interested in making English versions of these important texts available now?

Bernège set up an outfit called the Ligue de l'organisation ménagère [Household Organisation] in 1923, and another the following year, the Syndicat des appareils ménagers et de l'organisation ménagère [Union of Household Appliances and Home Management]. Both these provided a network of female experts in house design and technology for architects and policy makers to draw on, if they so wished (which for the most part they didn't).

Cleanability and how to achieve it

The general message about house design that populated domestic science texts in this period concentrated on remodelling the interiors of homes so

Figure 5.1: Paulette Bernège in her rationally organised kitchen in 1930

Source: Courtesy of Schlesinger Library, Harvard Radcliffe Institute

as to pay much more attention to *cleanability*: 'The floor is of lignolith laid down in one sheet and carried up as wainscoting so that no crevice exists for entrance of insects or dust', explained Ellen Richards in her *The Cost of Shelter* of the kitchens scientific housewives should demand. For redesigning the bedroom, she quoted directly from H.G. Wells's *A Modern Utopia*: a fireplace-less room with six switches on the wall controlling the temperature of the floor, the mattress and the walls. The windows don't open: air is pumped in and out mechanically. In the recessed bathroom the water is heated by an electric spiral of tubing, soap is delivered by a machine at the turn of a handle, and that and the soiled towels are dispatched in a shaft (no detail is given as to where or with whom this ends up).[10]

In such texts, technology is offered as one answer to the deficits of the home as a place of labour. A move away from coal- or wood-fired heating and cooking meant gas or electricity, solutions of such gigantic importance that they have a chapter of their own later on in this book. Advice as to good household equipment appeared in many domestic science texts; one bestseller in the United States was a book of that name, *Household Equipment*, written in 1934 by Louise Peet, who was head of the Household Equipment Department at Iowa State College, and Lenore Sater, Chief of the Housing and Household Equipment Division at the US Department of Agriculture's Bureau of Home Economics. (The mere existence of such an organisation makes one tremble with admiration for the role scientific housework played then in US public policy.)

Like other household science texts, what was most notable about the Peet and Sater household equipment book was that students/readers were expected to understand, not only what appliances could do what, but the 'fundamental scientific laws' governing their manufacture and operation. Thus, '[w]here male agricultural engineering students took apart and inspected tractors, female equipment majors disassembled and evaluated ranges; while men in mechanical engineering learned the thermodynamics behind diesel engines, women systematically familiarised themselves with the physics of refrigeration'.[11] The level of detail in Peet and Sater's text might have overwhelmed many readers – for instance, aluminum is described as a metal found in clay that constitutes approximately 8 per cent of the earth's crust. Significantly, the housekeeper or homemaker (both terms are used in the book) needed to be able to repair her own household equipment, just as earlier texts in the 1880s and 1890s had made women responsible for detecting faults in the plumbing and sanitation of their homes. Housework, in this view, is about the intelligent understanding of *structures* as well as the scientific provision of *services*. Hence housewives must understand the internal workings of the gas meter (Figure 5.2), as they also must be sure to use the correct knife for each kitchen task (Figure 5.3).

Scientific management as applied to the home

Scientific housework received a significant injection of energy in the early 20th century from the movement for scientific management in industry. 'Taylorism', the name given to a method of scientific management developed by the American mechanical engineer Frederick Taylor, aimed to increase productivity by dividing shop-floor work into its component processes and studying the quickest way to get these done. Taylor gave his seal of approval to the women who wanted to extend his ideas to the home, although he

Figure 5.2: 'Inside the gas meter'

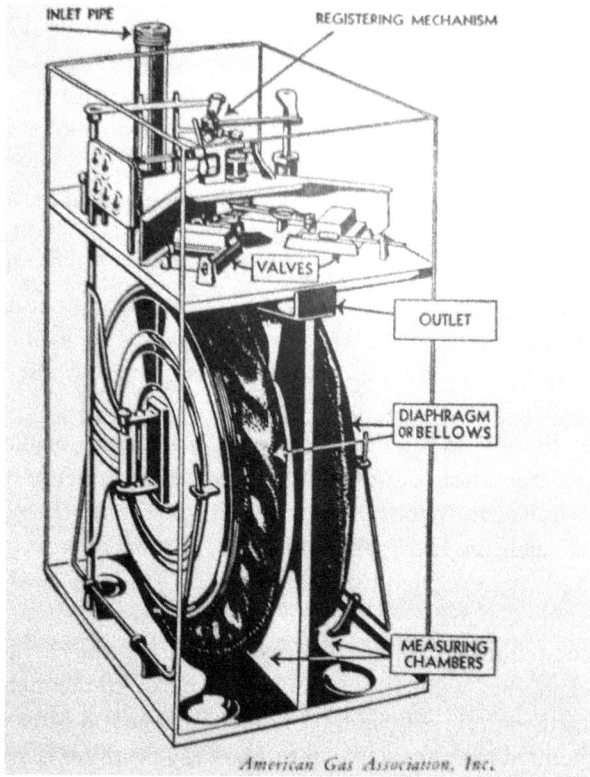

Source: Peet, L.J. and Sater, L.E. (1940, 2nd edn) *Household Equipment*, New York: John Wiley & Sons, Inc., p 103

perhaps went a little overboard in his Foreword to Mary Pattison's *The Business of Household Management* when he put her work in the same category as 'that of Leonardo da Vinci in his "Il Codice Atlantica," Newton in his "Principia," and Darwin in his "Origin of Species"'.[12]

Taylor's intensely mechanical approach entered the arena of domestic science mainly through the work of two tremendously energetic American women, Christine Frederick and Lillian Gilbreth, who led almost contemporaneous lives (1883–1970 and 1878–1972, respectively). However, a rich vein of ideas about efficiency and time-and-motion studies is present in earlier texts. All the good ideas (as well as the bad ones) come and go. This is from the American social scientist Helen Campbell's *The Easiest Way in Housekeeping*, which was first published in 1881:

> Let sink, pantries, stove or range, and working-space for all operations in cooking, be close at hand. The difference between a pantry at the

Figure 5.3: 'Select knives carefully to meet a definite need'

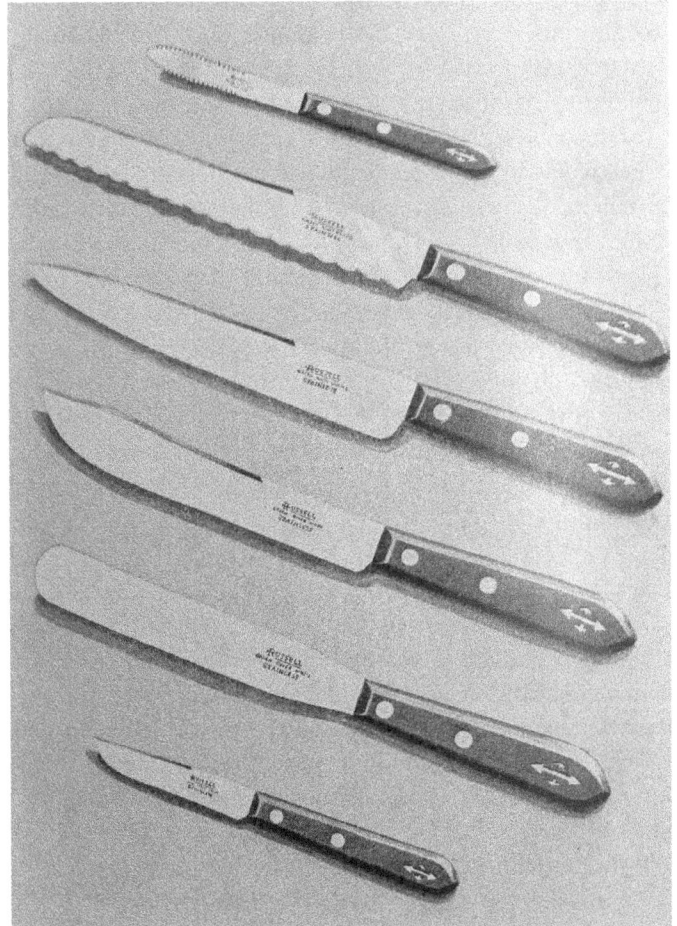

Source: Peet, L.J. and Sater, L.E. (1940, 2nd edn) *Household Equipment*, New York: John Wiley & Sons, Inc., p. 190

opposite end of the room, and one opening close to the sink, for instance, may seem a small matter; but when it comes to walking across the room with every dish that is washed, the steps soon count up as miles. ... Let, then, stove, fuel, water, work-table, and pantries be at the same end of the kitchen, and within a few steps of one another.[13]

Campbell would have much appreciated Paulette Bernège's calculation of the 'vampiric' distances she had to walk in her own apartment.

Gilbreth and Frederick were both introduced to ideas about scientific efficiency through their business executive husbands who were familiar with this regime as applied to industry. Both women leapt at the idea of using it to transform women's work in the home. They deviated, however, in their views about the place of housework in women's lives. Frederick's version of domestic efficiency tied women more closely to the home, particularly in their capacity as 'Mrs Consumer', while Gilbreth favoured the rationalisation of housework as a path to creating more female freedom. Despite (or because of?) their parallel statuses as domestic efficiency experts, the two women weren't close. Christine Frederick had been a biology teacher but she hadn't done any of the new training in household science. She came to the subject raw out of personal experience. In her *Efficient Housekeeping or Household Engineering: Scientific Management in the Home* (1915), she talks about how she first got interested in the subject. As the mother of two young children living in a small flat in the Bronx she struggled to do justice both to the housework and the children and was often too tired at the end of the day to listen to her husband talking about *his* day. When he told her about something called 'scientific management', she immediately saw its relevance to the problems she was facing. For example:

> There was the point of height – didn't I with hundreds of women stoop unnecessarily over kitchen tables and sinks and ironing boards? … Couldn't we perhaps standardize dishwashing by raising the height of the sink and changing other conditions? Did we not waste time and needless walking in poorly-arranged kitchens—taking twenty steps to get the egg-beater when it could have been hung over my table, just as efficiency insisted the workman's tools must be grouped?[14]

Applying to housework the principles of scientific management in industry, Frederick found she could save a third of the time it had previously taken and the work became a good deal more interesting once it had been recast as an intellectual task. Making housework more *interesting* was a common justification put by domestic science campaigners, implicitly recognising, of course, that housework is an essentially *uninteresting* activity.

Christine Frederick claimed that her methods could save the nation a million dollars a day.[15] In order to save time, a preset, scientifically determined schedule was needed for every task. She included a number of such schedules in her book. Table 5.1 shows one of them, for a woman with an (unbelievably compliant) small baby. This is not dissimilar from the one reproduced in the Prologue from my own life as a new mother in 1967. Both are notable for recording no social interaction with other adults.

In 1912 the Fredericks moved from the Bronx to a spacious rural home in Long Island called Applecroft. In what she termed her 'Applecroft Experiment Station' Frederick conducted numerous household science experiments. For instance, she demonstrated that merely by arranging

Table 5.1: Daily schedule for family of three

(One small baby on three-hour feeding period; small house or flat)

6:30–7:00 Rise and dress; give baby morning feeding

7:00–7:30 Breakfast. (Uncooked cereal, or cereal cooked in fireless [sic]. Table set night before)

7:30–8:00 Clear table; stack dishes; plan meals for the day; put on water for baby's bath

8:00–9:00 Bathe baby, feed and put to sleep; pick up after bath; straighten bedroom

9:00–10:00 Prepare baby's gruel, sterilized milk, etc.; wash baby napkins while watching food

(Baby naps 9:00–11:00)

10:00–11:00 Clean living-rooms, hall, etc., and dress ready to take baby for morning airing while marketing

11:00–12:00 Outdoors with baby while marketing

12:00–1:00 Return for lunch and baby feeding

1:00–2:30 Wash combined breakfast and lunch dishes; prepare vegetables, dessert and meat, if possible, for evening meal; brush up kitchen; empty garbage; sweep porch (Baby awake and playing outdoors, if possible, from 1–3; at 3 o'clock feeding and sleep until 4)

2:30–3:00 Iron baby clothing

3:00–4:00 Rest period; preferably nap with baby while it is asleep

4:00–5:00 Afternoon airing

5:00–5:30 Start supper

5:30–6:00 Put baby to sleep with night feeding

6:00–7:30 Own supper; supper dishes washed; table set for breakfast following morning (Baby's last feeding 10 P.M.)

Source: Frederick, C. (1923) *Household Engineering: Scientific Management in the Home*, Chicago: American School of Home Economics, pp 76–7

kitchen tools more scientifically, the time spent in peeling potatoes could be reduced from five to two minutes and the number of steps taken from 19 to eight; the washing of 50 dishes could be cut from 41 to 23 minutes.[16] She herself employed servants to get her own housework done in order to save enough time for scientific management. This pointed to a major flaw in the whole domestic efficiency idea – it added time and complexity to housework rather than shortening and simplifying it.

In her Applecroft Experiment Station, Frederick was an untiring tester of the new household appliances that were flooding the market. For example, in 1916 she wrote 'informative' articles about a new electric toaster, percolator and chafing dish. Exactly how unbiased the information was isn't clear, since she worked closely with manufacturers, who paid her for her labours, and she even maintained that the interests of manufacturers and consumers are identical, something which other household scientists vehemently denied.[17]

Lillian Gilbreth had a background in industrial psychology and a PhD on efficient teaching methods, but she had been unable to penetrate the male engineering community and so turned her attention to the home. Much of *her* own housework was done by her children. She and her husband Frank decided they would have 12, six boys and six girls, and this, most incredibly and efficiently, is, indeed, what happened. Together with Frank until he died in 1924, and thereafter on her own, Lillian ran a business and engineering consulting firm called Gilbreth Incorporated which disseminated the Gilbreth System of time-and-motion studies and which used the term 'therblig' (an anagram of 'Gilbreth') to describe the elemental motions required for individual tasks. The Gilbreths were excellent self-promoters. They measured time and motion to 1/2000 of a second and led an inexorably efficient domestic life which was well documented by two of their children, Frank Jr. and Ernestine, in two books, *Cheaper by the Dozen* and *Belles on Their Toes*, both of which were made into films (in 1950 and 1952, the former subsequently remade in 2003 starring Steve Martin). Using a 35mm hand crank camera, the Gilbreths themselves pioneered the use of short films as research techniques to expose inefficient working methods in both home and factory; this was a real innovation in research methodology.[18]

Gilbreth family life was run on strict Gilbreth System principles: the children were all allocated household tasks. Work charts were installed in the bathrooms, and every child old enough to write had to initial the chart in the morning after bathing, brushing her/his teeth and hair and making her/his bed. At night each child had to weigh her/himself and plot the figure on a graph. There was a gendering appropriate to the time: the boys cut the grass and raked the leaves; the girls swept, dusted and did the supper dishes; everyone except Frank made her/his own bed and kept bedrooms neat; the smaller girls dusted the legs and lower shelves of furniture, while the older girls attended to the table tops and upper shelves. Little resentment of these requirements is expressed in these memoirs of an extraordinarily regulated childhood.

Too much efficiency?

The Gilbreth memoirs could almost be fiction, and the whole notion of scientific household management did in fact lend itself very well to fiction. A raft of entertaining novels published between 1917 and 1927 made fun of the whole business.

The most famous of these satiric anti-scientific management novels was penned by the American writer Edith Wharton in 1927. Wharton was quite an architectural expert herself: she had designed her own house in Western Massachusetts, a Georgian revival with formal Italian gardens overlooking a lake that was modelled on the 17th-century Belton House in Lincolnshire, England. The title of Wharton's anti-efficiency novel, *Twilight Sleep*, makes a telling allegation about the effect on women of too much efficiency.[19] Wharton's take on scientific management was that it caused a drugged condition in women such that they lost touch with the way housework and family life made them *feel*. Too much science in the home destroyed the normal emotional chaos of life as it is lived. The 'Twilight sleep' of the title refers to a German method of using the drugs morphine and scopolamine to induce a state of amnesia in labouring mothers, such that they have no memory of pain. In the novel, Pauline Manford, a perfect elite home-maker, manages a perfectly run house with the aid of a 'pale resigned' English butler and a perfect cook who enables her to serve perfect dinners. Pauline has a passionate interest in dust, plumbing, electric wiring and every new household appliance and has her life of osteopathy, gymnastics, rest-cures and speeches for good causes organised for her by a perfectly efficient secretary. None of this makes her happy. Pauline's lawyer husband Dexter can't stand any of it and has at least two affairs; she herself enters into a liaison with her therapist. In a dramatic denouement Dexter mistakenly kills their daughter instead of his wife. The Efficiency Movement might not have been responsible for all this dysfunctional interaction, but it was clearly something about which people did feel very strongly.

The craze for efficiency infected the domestic science movement in many countries, although differently in each: Austria, Belgium, Czechoslovakia, Denmark (and other Nordic countries), England, Germany, Holland, Italy, Poland, Spain and Switzerland all subjected housewives to their own versions of scientific efficiency, with varying results according to culture and economic context. Christine Frederick visited Bernège in France and approved her work. Bernège herself was widely travelled (Belgium, Czechoslovakia, Italy, the Netherlands, Scandinavia, Scotland and the United States are all mentioned in accounts of her life). Frederick's *The New Housekeeping* was translated into German in 1921, with 'rational' substituting for 'new' in the title, *Die Rationelle Haushaltsführung*; the book enjoyed a successful career in Germany as a manifesto for young industrial designers. The German home economist Erna Meyer, a professional housewife like Frederick, took up the theme and published her own *Das Neue Haushalt* (*The New Household*) in 1926 which passed through 29 editions in its first two years.

Grete Lihotzky and the Frankfurt Kitchen

Scientific management in the home had lost much of its appeal by the late 1920s, as women increasingly sank under the burden of its administrative demands. But in the 1920s it gave birth to something of lasting importance today: the modern streamlined Western kitchen. It did this through

Figure 5.4: Margarete Schütte-Lihotzky (centre) at the age of 100 in 1997

Source: Public domain via https://commons.wikimedia.org/wiki/File:Werner_Faymann_und_Brauner_1997_(2721380957).jpg

the labours of a young German architect called Grete Lihotzky and the democratic socialist ideals of the Weimar Republic.

Margarete Schütte-Lihotzky, known as Grete Lihotzky, was a feminist and a communist, and an admirer of Taylorism and Christine Frederick's writings. She died in 2000 at the age of almost 103, having taken what became known as her Frankfurt Kitchen to the new cities of the Soviet Union and to Austria and Cuba. In Figure 5.4, a picture taken when she was 100 years old, Lihotsky looks happy at her achievement of, as she put it, having invented a kitchen that had saved millions of women many hours of unnecessary and exhausting labour.[20] Unlike the Rumford Kitchen, which appeared in Chapter 4, this one was aptly named, as it really did belong to Frankfurt. Grete Lihotzky worked for the architect and city planner Ernst May on an ambitious social housing project in Frankfurt aimed at working-class families (although two of their prototype homes catered for families with one or two servants, so these were at least the upper echelons of the working class). Lihotzky's kitchen design built on work she'd earlier done in Vienna in 1920–1922 for co-operative settlement housing and which delivered such ingenious devices as a 'natural refrigerator' – a container for eggs connected to the cold air outside. This exemplary kitchen, called a 'cooking-niche', was modelled on the restaurant car on trains. It was a small space-saving unit, 1.9 metres by 3.4 metres, designed on the galley principle and using the results of workflow research. It was fitted with units painted blue, because researchers had found that flies

Figure 5.5: A Frankfurt Kitchen in Frankfurt, 1927–1928

Source: Courtesy of Sammlung Werkbunderarchiv, Museum der Dinge, Berlin

weren't fond of blue, and beech surfaces, because beech resists staining, acids and scratching. It was crammed with ingenious devices, such as built-in food containers and a hinged draining board that could be angled to flow down into the sink or alternatively stowed away against the wall. Figure 5.5 is a picture of a Frankfurt Kitchen built on a Frankfurt housing estate in 1927–1928. Functional is the word: the kitchen had finally become a 'laboratory for housework'.[21]

The Frankfurt Kitchen met the twin Taylorist/Frederickist/Gilbrethian objectives of using limited space efficiently and reducing the distance the housewife had to walk in the course of her work. But it had a wider symbolic significance: 'In its gleaming metal surfaces, its high imageability, the specificity of its interlocking parts, its modular totality, and its largesse of technical fittings', it epitomised the modernist transformation of everyday life.[22] The kitchen had effectively become a machine, with the housewife as its operator, in a space no longer called a 'room' but a 'niche', tucked away from the eyes of the household. Grete Lihotzky went on to use the same approach in revising domestic education. She designed instructional facilities for Frankfurt public schools whose kitchenettes were miniature versions of her Frankfurt Kitchen. Girls were thus introduced early to the notion of the kitchen as a kind of mechanical space capsule. This was very different from the image of kitchens as sociable places, 'the heart of the home'.

Women houseworkers don't seem to have been consulted in the design of the Frankfurt Kitchen. Many of its recipients apparently tried to cram their chairs and family dining tables into its unforgiving spaces. As Karen

Hagemann found when she interviewed women in Hamburg in the early 1980s about their memories of the domestic rationalisation movement, an attitude of scepticism prevailed: these ideas were all very well, but working-class housewives had to manage their households carefully, rationally and economically anyway, modern technology could not be afforded, and the old Victorian furnishings were comforting, which Frankfurt Kitchens definitely were not.[23]

Some 10,000 Frankfurt Kitchens, which were prefabricated and lifted into buildings with a crane, were installed in housing developments in Frankfurt in the late 1920s and early 1930s. Although Lihotzky herself wished to reduce women's housework and free them for more imaginative pursuits, the motive behind the domestic rationalisation movement in Germany wasn't women's liberation but the benefits to men, children and the national economy of a more rational approach to housework. Domestic efficiency was an integral part of a wider rationalisation movement which infected most aspects of post-war life in the Weimar Republic, the regime that occupied the interregnum between the end of the First World War and the rise of Hitler. The sinister element in this movement, so far as women were concerned, was something called 'female redomestication'. Women's domain of the home was stripped of its sentimentality and converted into a place governed by reason and objectivity, so that it resembled men's place in the public world. Rationalisation, embraced by engineers, architects, educators, academics and politicians alike, became a slogan for productivity, science and modernism. Home economics had a secure place in state policy: it formed a department of the Reichskuratorium für Wirtschaftlichkeit or National Advisory Board for Productivity. This department carried out quantities of experimental work in the 1920s and 1930s on such familiar activities as potato-peeling and floor-cleaning – the latter a two-year project comparing the mop-and-pail method with the mop-and-oil one and leading to the conclusion that the quicker mop-and-oil strategy saved 43 hours 20 minutes per year but also cost three times as much.[24] This project, like a good deal of the time-and-motion work generated by the craze for scientific efficiency, was of dubious help to the ordinary housewife.

While the Frankfurt Kitchen, and the forgotten female architects of the Weimar and other republics, are now remembered in some architectural historiography, the history connecting these scientific advances to the domestic science movement is less well-known. The pedigree of the Frankfurt Kitchen can be traced back to Catharine Beecher. She, and her sister Harriet Beecher Stowe, wrote about it in their *The American Woman's Home* in 1869. Their ideal kitchen was a contrast to the sprawling sociable spaces of rural American domesticity. It was small, nine feet by nine. Glazed sliding doors separated its heat and smells from other living spaces. Its sides were lined with shelves.

On these shelves, and in the closet and boxes, can be placed every material used for cooking, all the table and cooking utensils, and all the articles used in housework. ... The cook's galley in a steamship has every article and utensil used in cooking for two hundred persons, in a space not larger than this stove-room, and so arranged that with one or two steps the cook can reach all he [*sic*] uses.[25]

Kitchenless homes

Kitchens had always played a key role in the schemes of domestic science reformers, but never more so than in reformers' most radical ideas about the need for co-operative housekeeping. Charlotte Perkins Gilman was clear about one thing – well, this assertive, uncompromising woman was clear about many things, but her central theme was that the private family kitchen had to go. It was wasteful, irrational, unscientific and depressing, and a main cause of women's oppression. She called 'preparing food by means of one cook and one kitchen to each family' an 'inherently and hopelessly wasteful method'. In a creative calculation, she proposed that kitchens in private houses, each of which had to be supplied with stoves, tubs, boilers, sinks, dishes, and so on, plus water, light, and fuel and amounts for breakage and depreciation, incurred a waste of 90 per cent. The rationalisation of housework calls for its abolition as a private household industry. Experts should take it over, thus transforming 'a general feminine function' into 'a particular social industry'.[26]

There can be no more thoroughly scientific approach to housework than devising methods to dispose of it altogether. Gilman's ideas about how to live co-operatively without private kitchens were most fully developed in her novels. In her first, *What Diantha Did* (1912), we see one young woman, bored with her constrained New England life, making the most of the great business opportunity – one of the greatest the world has ever known, according to Gilman – presented by the marvellous goal of deprivatising housework. In the fictional Californian community of Orchardina, Diantha Bell sets up a profit-making restaurant, a cooked food delivery service, a maids' hostel and placement service (yes, some utopias apparently do allow servants), an apartment hotel and a housecleaning service.[27]

Gilman's visionary ideas, both fictional and factual, appear in a work by the American historian Dolores Hayden, *The Grand Domestic Revolution* (1981), which charts the efforts of other American feminists to analyse, redesign and socialise domestic work. There was, for example, architect and city planner Alice Austin, who in 1915–1917 designed a city of kitchenless houses in California, with tunnels transporting laundry, meals, supplies and goods, and homes built specifically with the aim of cutting housework. There was psychologist Ethel Puffer Howes, who directed the wonderfully named

Institute for the Coordination of Women's Interests at Smith College in Massachusetts in the late 1920s. Howes's Institute, virtually unknown today, was unusual in targeting both housework and professional work at the same time. Set up in 1926, with a grant from a Rockefeller Foundation charity, it combined housework research and practical initiatives to socialise it, on the one hand, with efforts to expand women's entry into the professions, on the other. Thus it tackled three central problems of women's situation at the same time: the burden of housework, its social isolation, and the hostility to women of male professions.[28]

Co-operative or community housekeeping doesn't seem to have caught British attention in the same way. But in her *A New Way of Housekeeping*, Clementina Black did come up with a plan for housing federations organised around centrally managed domestic services. Every group of 50 houses would have a 'domestic centre'. The centre would be fitted with scientifically designed store rooms, kitchens, dining rooms, offices and lodging for servants (who would be supplied to individual houses as and when needed). A 'scientifically trained manageress' and a secretary (to keep accounts, check stores, and so forth) would run the centre. People would eat their meals either there or in their own houses, where the food would be brought 'in some sort of heat-retaining box, probably on little wheeled trucks' along with all requisite crockery and cutlery which would be collected afterwards for washing. Black credits the heated box and wheeled trucks ideas to Charlotte Perkins Gilman's novel *What Diantha Did*.[29] Fictional and factual narratives about the scientisation of housework sit side by side in both European and American literature. It's as if the same quality of imagination is needed for both: to envisage a world where housework is seen as a serious subject for study, and to dream of one in which what has been learnt becomes reality.

Economic man and the home

Our final theme in this chapter is the reworking of economic theory that was a necessary corollary of the household science movement. The reframing of housework as scientific work of huge national importance brought it into conflict with the way in which economists treated it – as a private function, unproductive, unquantifiable and without any calculable financial value. Being hidden from public view inside homes has always been one of housework's most toxic characteristics, and it has given (male) economists an easy excuse to ignore it.

Housework didn't/doesn't fit into traditional masculine models of how goods and services are produced and exchanged. The housewife's function is to *buy* things. In the American-Norwegian Thorsten Veblen's famous *Theory of the Leisure Class* (1899), the American woman is the physical embodiment of his newly coined term 'conspicuous consumption'. *Selling Mrs Consumer*

(1929) was Christine Frederick's own extremely popular contribution to the conceptualisation of the housewife as the shrewd or susceptible buyer of the capitalist marketplace rather than the producer of household health and welfare.

Female economists had to retheorise housework as productive labour. A background to their travails was the excision of housework from national accounting systems, itself a direct product of masculine economic thinking. At the beginning of the 19th century, women who worked for their families inside or around the home were defined as productive workers. Even in mid-century when female occupations were enumerated for the first time in British Censuses, women could be assigned to non-market household work as well as to paid domestic and non-domestic occupations. In the late 19th century, upper-class men – the political economists, the statisticians – reached a cosy, mostly covert, consensus about the unproductive nature of housework.[30] The moral elevation of the home as a refuge (for men) from the public world went hand-in-hand with the economic devaluation of housework (and women). A strong influence here was the Cambridge University economist Alfred Marshall, who took a distinctly patronising view of women – he fought the admission of women to the university, opposed the employment of married women, and, for those who had to work, he proposed lower wages as an incentive to persuade them back into the home.[31] As a result of his work, British Census classifications were changed at the end of the 19th century to cast all married women as 'dependents', along with children, the sick and the elderly. This was a vocabulary that derived from the masculine idealisation of the home as a refuge. It also, at the other end of the social hierarchy, had a good deal to do with the preoccupations of skilled male workers who were worried that women taking paid jobs outside the home would threaten their jobs. The male breadwinner model of family life, the notion of a 'family wage', was an expression of sectional economic interest, not a reflection of life as it was lived. It was this model that accounted for the exclusion of unpaid domestic labour from national accounting systems in the mid-20th century.

The year that Gilman published *The Man-made World*, two women who were closely associated with the household science developments at King's College in London described in Chapters 6 and 7 of *The Science of Housework* released their own *Economics: Descriptive and Theoretical*. Margaret McKillop, a domestic science lecturer, and Mabel Atkinson, a philosopher, economist and active socialist, startled the world of masculine economics by beginning with the everyday life of the household: how do houses get their water, gas, electricity, milk, mail; how is their rubbish removed; how are streets lit and policed; of what do household budgets consist? Beginning with the domestic space and using this to generate questions about how the economic system works was not the method generally used in economics textbooks. Economists' popular concerns – theories about wealth and exchange values and financial markets – ignored unpaid housework. This, said McKillop and Atkinson, is what directly produced the economic fiction of 'unoccupied' women – those human beings who perform the 'toilsome and important work' that sustains us all.[32]

In a chapter for domestic scientist Alice Ravenhill's edited volume on *Household Administration*, Mabel Atkinson was especially rude about Adam Smith, the 'father of economics': 'The founder of political economy showed so little insight into the real nature of the work carried on there as to class those whom he described as menial servants with unproductive labourers.' She went on to observe that '[t]he wife who cooks her husband dinner, or caters, organises, and keeps accounts for him, is really engaged in work which in any rational interpretation of the word has far more right to be called productive than is much of the labour employed in manufacture or business'.[33]

The absence of economic woman from the economists' landscape was seen as in these critiques as especially disastrous from two points of view. First, the *productive* labour that goes on in the home (producing goods and services, health and family care, men as workers, and children as the next generation of workers) is misclassified as *consumption*. Second, we really know very little about *how* and *how much* housework actually contributes to national economies. Gross domestic product (GDP) is a monetary measure of the market value of goods and services produced in a country. It's often considered to be the 'world's most powerful statistical indicator of national development and progress', even though it omits not only unpaid domestic and care labour but other non-trivial issues such as the impact of economic activity on the environment and on human health and well-being. Many people have tried to estimate what would happen to GDP were housework to be included. Their results vary from increases of 15–20 per cent using 'conservative estimates' to 70 per cent and more.[34]

Other female economists extended and elaborated on the arguments put forward by women like Mabel Atkinson, Margaret McKillop and Charlotte Perkins Gilman. Hazel Kyrk was Associate Professor of Home Economics at the University of Chicago from 1925 to 1941, and is part of the Chicago story related in Chapter 8. In her *Economic Problems of the Family* (1929), Kyrk remarked scathingly and correctly that:

> The wife who is inefficient as a household worker and manager may find herself elevated to a state of affluence through the earning power of her husband and the efficient household manager may find herself in a state of poverty through the financial incapacity or misfortune of her husband. In other words, here are workers for whom all economic laws based on the assumption of free competition fail.[35]

The doctrine of free competition so beloved of capitalist economists falls at the first fence when it comes to housework (it actually doesn't do very well for the rest of the economy either).

The new tradition of economic thinking Kyrk helped to sponsor sees the wealth of nations as reposing in the hands of 'unoccupied women', and it became an integral part of domestic science teaching and research in higher education in the 1920s and 1930s. This approach ought to have become part of mainstream economics, but didn't, because the women who proposed it were refused jobs in academic economics departments in case they contaminated its teaching with their unsettling ideas.[36] Thus economic theory was not enriched by their rational reworking of economic models. Economics joined other professions such as science, architecture and medicine, which used the back door of home economics as a route for accommodating women, as quietly and unnoticeably as possible, in the public world. Kyrk's own specialty became the economics of consumption: the empirical study and theorisation of household spending patterns. Empirical data, in which mainstream economists have never been terribly interested, showed that social influences work much better as a determinant of household spending than the standard doctrine of selfish, profit-seeking economic man that dominates conventional economic thought.[37]

It was one of Kyrk's PhD students, Margaret Reid, who made household production central to economic analysis. Her book, *Economics of Household Production*, published in 1934, observes that household production differs from industrial production in several key ways. In industry, large-scale production increases output per unit of labour and capital employed, thus increasing worker efficiency; labour-saving machines and a division of labour also raise productivity; the performance and the management of labour are separate activities. None of this applies in the home. Housewives as workers are unspecialised (they have to do lots of different things, often at the same time); they have no obvious incentive to make housework more efficient or to become expert at any particular task; they must criticise their own performances and do so – another difference from industry – in isolation from other workers: the only competition between housewives is on the social level. Careful economic analysis of household labour therefore reveals the fallacious logic behind the application of industrial management techniques to the home. Nonetheless, and as many female critics pointed out, if people only took the trouble to study how women housekeepers, especially in poor working-class homes, actually behaved, they would realise what efficient workers they have to be in order to make income and outgoings come within shouting distance of one another.[38] All housewives, as Mabel Atkinson had pointed out, have to make decisions about what to spend money on; they must constantly weigh alternatives, and make crucial and sometimes life-and-death economic decisions.

The budgeting needed to sustain families in poverty, the acute sense of economics/economies in everyday living, had totally eluded the attention of professional male economists.

Margaret Reid's work on what she termed 'consumption economics' inspired many male colleagues, including Theodore Schultz, Milton Friedman, Franco Modigliani and Gary Becker, all of whom got Nobel prizes, while her work was largely unacknowledged.[39]

Conclusion

As the domestic science reformers and educators continued their mission to elevate the status of housework, they met both help and resistance. Embracing ideas about scientific efficiency derived from workplaces outside the home appeared to offer an appealing injection of science. The redesigning of homes to reduce housework hours was a gesture in the direction of appreciating how little control over material conditions most houseworking women had. Imagined scenarios of kitchenless homes, and co-operative, professional housekeeping were rational and alluring but, despite many local initiatives, and for complex reasons, they didn't catch on sufficiently to liberate women from the tyrannies of solitary housework. Revised economic theories which took account of the enormous global importance of household labour informed the teaching of household science but had little impact on mainstream economics teaching.

This is the endlessly fascinating character of housework: that it *isn't* just like other labour, although it is also *the same* as other labour. Its split identity challenges attempts to make it fit with ideas that come from somewhere else. In the next three chapters we see how this logic operates when the university world tries to accommodate domestic science as a fully-fledged subject.

6

Lectures for ladies

King's College of Household and Social Science (KCHSS) in London, England, offered university degrees in household and social science for over 30 years, beginning in 1920. The King's College initiative is unique in the history of housework, not because it was the only institution to provide domestic science degrees – by 1920 there were many places doing that – but because of its independence as an institution from other university connections, its longevity, the sustained academic and political struggle that gave rise to it, the outstandingly comprehensive curriculum of research, teaching and policy work that went on there, and its legacy today in programmes of food and nutrition science that are known and respected around the globe. KCHSS has received little attention from historians of housework.[1] This is a pity, as tracing its rise, development and influence has much to tell us about the domestic science movement, and about its tight interconnections with the movement for women's higher education. The scientisation of housework and the education of women are like conjoined twins: recognising, and at the same time disputing, the closeness of their relationship. By following the development of household science at KCHSS we can see how the argument for scientific education in housework meshed with, and at times contradicted, the drive to get women accepted as equal citizens in the professional academic world.

This chapter and the next are based on many weeks spent in the marvellous archives of KCHSS which are now held in the library of King's College, London. Carefully preserved by assiduous (and very helpful) archivists, some of these records throw up clouds of dust that would horrify the protagonists of the domestic science movement. Thus these two chapters are different in tone and purpose from the others in *The Science of Housework* because their concern is with the meticulous details of ideas and arrangements, negotiations and social networks that gave rise in one particular place to a university degree in household science. Our journey through this story will cause us to re-encounter many names we have already met in previous chapters: the resourceful British sanitary scientist, Alice Ravenhill, for example; domestic science lecturer Margaret McKillop and her co-author, economist Mabel Atkinson; Arthur Smithells, professor of chemistry and supporter of a thoroughly scientific education for women; Clementina Black, who railed against the domestic idiocies of much home design and had her own brilliant remedial ideas.

The beginnings in Kensington

In the 19th century few women in the United Kingdom or the United States had any access to higher education. The only way in was through the partly opened door of private and community initiatives that offered protected spaces for women – away from male students, often with chaperones – where anxious parents could send their daughters for a few hours each week. One such initiative was a series of 'Lectures for Ladies' that were offered in Richmond, West London, in 1871. Reverend Canon Alfred Barry, who was the Principal of the all-male King's College in the Strand, was in favour of more education for women and he thought King's College should be part of it. With his encouragement, King's College staff who lived in Richmond and Twickenham, and who agreed with him about this, began an 'experimental' course of 'Lectures for Ladies'. A Ladies' Committee of 'respectable matrons' was set up, with a member guaranteed to be present at every lecture in order to allay parental anxiety.

Reverend Barry gave an inaugural lecture in May 1871. He talked about women's right to higher education, and argued, in tune with the tenor of the time, that 'the inconveniences of access through the bustle of the Strand would prejudice any attempt to open its teaching to ladies'.[2] The ladies must be catered for separately. A home was found in the Vestry Hall in Kensington High Street (now a bank) opposite the Metropolitan Railway Station (important as a means of access for further-away ladies) and a syllabus drawn up. In Figure 6.1 we see this historic building as it was in 2023, a smart, self-assured place.

Not much is known about the early years of the ladies' lectures until in 1877 George Warr, Professor of Classics at King's, and a supporter of many progressive causes, learnt that Maria Grey of the Women's Education Union was looking for an institution to organise lectures in West London. Grey was an educational reformer as well as a writer of novels and serious outspoken books about women – her *Old Maids* (1875) was a timely attack on the idea of unmarried women as unfulfilled and useless. Warr suggested to Grey that she might turn her attention to what by then had become known as the King's College Ladies' Department in anticipation of the future, 'as a warship is regarded as a floating portion of the British Empire'.[3]

In order to advance this empire, Reverend Barry called a conference in November 1877 on the subject of turning the ladies' lectures into a proper women's college. He was joined by Warr and Grey; the vicar of St Mary's Abbotts Church, Kensington; 'sundry prominent ladies'; and Cornelia Schmitz – the daughter of a noted German scholar who would steer the early work of this budding institution. The aims of the venture were described as:

> The promotion of the Higher Education of Women, first – by giving instruction in separate departments of Literature and Science; next by

Figure 6.1: 'Vestry Hall' in Kensington, 2023, where Lectures for Ladies began

Source: Author's photo

forming courses of Systematic Education ... and lastly – by preparing the way for the foundation of a College for the Education of Women in all those branches of Learning which enter into and together make up a University Education.[4]

The first official King's College classes for ladies in Kensington took place in February 1878. The minimum age of attendees was 17, and there were five groups of classes: holy scripture and church history (taken by the Reverend Barry); modern and ancient history; languages and literature: English, French and German, also Latin and Greek; arithmetic, algebra, geometry and astronomy; and the rather strangely grouped physics ('sound in relation to music'), geology and physical geography, botany and harmony. All the classes were for an hour each week, apart from holy scripture and church history and arithmetic and algebra, which merited two. The first of these was the cheapest, at 10s 6d per term and the second, along with modern history, the most expensive at £2 2s 0d. Fees were reduced by one third for ladies engaged in teaching, or where three or more from the same family were attending. Examinations were held at the end of term in each subject for those who were keen to possess something called a 'Certificate of Proficiency'.[5]

Because attendance in the first year exceeded all expectations at around 500, space rapidly became strained in the Vestry Hall. In 1879 a lease was taken on a nearby house, 5 Observatory Avenue, Campden Hill (now 9 Hornton Street). Cornelia Schmitz became the 'Lady Superintendent', carrying out her duties with enormous dedication for 15 years, before being forced to leave her post because of the bar on the professional employment of married women when she married the new Principal of King's College, the Reverend Barry's successor, Henry Mace.

By 1881 the 500 ladies who had attended in 1878 had swollen to 1,500. In that year King's College in the Strand celebrated its 50th anniversary and responded to the wave of interest in higher education for women by launching an appeal for money to expand the Ladies' Department into a larger and more comprehensive programme of work. The long list of financial contributors to this cause included the Principal and Staff of King's College, who gave £1,250; the Prime Minister, W.E. Gladstone, £100; the Dean of Westminster, a more miserly £5; and four city companies which together contributed £800. Aided by further creative fund-raising activities, the next landmark in the history of KCHSS was achieved in 1885 when King's College formally recognised the Ladies' Department as an official arm of its work.

The success of Lectures for Ladies can be gauged from the statistics of enrolment, but we know little about the backgrounds or experiences of the early students. Most of them came from Kensington or elsewhere in West London. The registration books in the archives preserve some of the names and subjects: in 1894–1895, a Mrs Atkinson of Bayswater took a class in wood carving; a Miss Armitage in Redcliffe Square, Kensington, attended lectures on the work of Robert Browning; and three Curtis sisters from Lennox Gardens, Knightsbridge, did singing, church history, architecture and Robert Browning (who seems to have been very popular).[6] Edith Morley, a literary scholar who became the first female professor in Britain in 1908, described in her autobiography her own Ladies' Department experience. Brought up with her four brothers in a house in Bayswater, Morley led the protected life usual for upper-middle-class girls at the time – she wasn't allowed out on her own even across the road to post a letter. She wanted to go to Bedford College, but her parents deemed the journey much too taxing. The pleasant walk of about 20 minutes, mostly across Kensington Gardens, that King's College Ladies' Department would entail, was much more suitable.

Edith Morley's admission to King's College Ladies' Department was a very ladylike affair. Her mother took her to Observatory Avenue one afternoon in October 1892: 'How well I remember that interview with Miss Schmitz – an elegant middle-aged lady who wore a cap and had a canary bird singing above her desk in the pleasant room, looking out on a garden where she received her visitors.' Morley described her fellow students as a mix of all ages and all levels of attainment, 'alike only in their sense of thwarted intellectual development and their longing for enlightenment'.[7] She would go on to become one of the first two King's College Ladies' Department students to achieve an Oxford degree (in 1899) and she was back there as a member of staff in 1902 teaching English language and literature.

There were other notable early students. One was Marguerite Radclyffe Hall, author of the novel *The Well of Loneliness* which was the subject of a famous obscenity trial when it was published in 1928; Radclyffe Hall is said to have attended the Ladies' Department around the turn of the century.[8] So also did the Stephen sisters, later the writer Virginia Woolf and the artist Vanessa Bell. Virginia's biographers describe her as self-educated, but they failed to notice that she went to the Ladies' Department in Kensington in 1897 at the age of 15 and studied a range of subjects there for five years. She took Greek, German, history and Latin, reaching degree level in some of these subjects. Latin was taken with her sister, who was registered as attending between 1898 and 1900.[9] Their father, Leslie Stephen, was an anxious parent. He wrote to his friend George Warr to say that Virginia was in a very nervous state, and he was allowing her to attend Warr's Greek class because he thought it would do her some good to have the occupation, but please could Warr remember this and not burden her with too much work?[10] Virginia Woolf's exposure to Greek culture at King's Ladies' Department became a lifelong interest, and various King's College staff are said to have contributed their characters to her fiction. Today she is remembered architecturally in the Virginia Woolf Building for Arts and Humanities, part of King's College, London, an undistinguished glass and concrete affair which also happens to house the wonderful mountain of archives I explored for this book.

By the time the Stephen sisters went to their lectures, educational provision in Observatory Avenue had expanded hugely. New subjects included physics, chemistry, economics, physiology, first aid, home nursing and hygiene, and law. John Cutler, Professor of Law at King's, offered a free introductory lecture on what might have been for some a rather inflammatory subject: 'the position of Married Women with regard to their Separate Property and their Contracts'.[11] The ladies' lectures had now been arranged so as to align with preparation for BA and BSc London University degrees, as well as Oxford Higher Examinations. The first hint of the household science enterprise to come was the appointment to the staff in 1898 of Margaret McKillop, who arrived to teach elementary science and chemistry and to prepare students' minds for the move towards a focus on household science in a lecture on

'The extent to which Natural Science now influences our lives. How far we require scientific training as an equipment'.[12]

Another change was that lecturers were no longer restricted to King's College staff. For example, Professor Hewins came from the London School of Economics (LSE) to enlighten the ladies as to 'the main features of the structure and organisation of modern industry and commerce, and the leading principles of economic science'.[13] There were social developments as well: a common room and 'a simple luncheon' were provided, and a number of student societies had been launched. An all-important (for the time) bicycling club was added in 1896. Weekly rides of 10–20 miles were held on Tuesday afternoons to places such as Pinner, Bushey, Hampton Court and Stanmore, the latter now urbanised and subject to considerable aircraft noise, but then 'a sweet little country village, unspoilt as yet by the railway, and possessing a very interesting Church'.[14] The bicycle was such a radical departure for women that, before allowing her to mount the saddle, Edith Morley's own worried father consulted some of his medical friends about the possibility that she might thereby permanently injure herself.

A further sign of expansion was the opening in 1900 of a hall of residence for students in 32 De Vere Gardens. This was managed by Eveline Faithfull, one of six daughters of an intellectual family in Hertfordshire and the sister of Lilian Faithfull, who would power the whole Ladies' Department enterprise into the field of academic household science. An article in the *Girls' Realm Annual* for 1899 describes the welcome given to girls wishing to reside in the new hostel. It confirms the impression of the gentle, ladylike atmosphere that pervaded that part of Kensington:

> Miss Eveline Faithfull receives her visitors in the drawing-room, a large, pretty room, facing the Square. Her taste has made the whole house harmonious and restful. The quiet colouring, the sober old English furniture, make for a simplicity and daintiness admirably in keeping with the olden character of the building.

The bed-sitting rooms in the hostel had tiny dressing-rooms, 'originally powder-rooms, sacred to the great Georgian ladies who used to drive in their chariots … or drink a syllabub under the trees'.[15]

Stirrings of household science

Lilian Faithfull's arrival in 1894 to take over from the now-married Miss Schmitz marked a turning point in the evolution of Lectures for Ladies into a fully functioning University College of household and social science. Lilian had read for a degree in English at Somerville College, Oxford, and she arrived in Kensington to take up the post (now renamed 'Vice-Principal') aged 29, full of energy and commitment to making it a place of serious academic study. She faced enormous problems, however. The first was that most of the clientele were not, as she put it, 'of the pioneer type':

> Women and girls of all ages from seventeen to seventy came to the lectures, some only to one course, once a week, and some to several. Old ladies followed a favourite professor and came year after year. … Married women arrived gasping for a 10 o'clock lecture, having snatched an hour with difficulty from their household duties at that time in the morning.[16]

But Faithfull's keen eyes did land on two intellectually ambitious students: one was Edith Morley, and the second was Caroline Spurgeon, a literary scholar who would become the first female professor at the University of London in 1913. Both, under Faithfull's tutelage, became the first King's College Ladies' Department students to achieve (first-class) Oxford degrees in 1899 (although women at Oxford were not actually able to claim their degrees for another 21 years).

The second problem Lilian Faithfull faced was a chronic absence of money, endowments and scholarships, and a sizeable debt on the buildings: 'I had to think twice before I could order a new hall doormat.'[17] Judicious financial management, successful fund-raising and careful nurturing of the appropriate staff enabled her to double student numbers and make the department financially independent of the main college during her 13 years as vice-principal. In 1902 she converted it from the 'Ladies'' to the 'Women's' Department (as the King's Professor of Medieval History, F.J.C. Hearnshaw, phrased it, 'women' take examinations, whereas 'ladies' do not).[18]

There are various versions of how the domestic science degree at King's was first conceived and planned. One of them is that it was Lilian Faithfull's idea – a way of expanding the educational agenda and attracting financial sponsorship. Faithfull did, indeed, in her first few years, mount a sustained assault on the virtual absence of science from the curriculum. In 1903, she established physics, chemistry and botany laboratories, moving out of her own rooms in the building in order to make this possible. Faithfull herself says that the plan for a domestic science course 'was conceived by one or two members of the Council'.[19] Nancy Blakestad, who wrote a PhD on KCHSS, identifies the indomitable household scientist Alice Ravenhill as the originator, and certainly Ravenhill's name crops up very often in the archival documents – in the minutes of meetings, in prospectuses and curricula, and as a name attached to the writing or signing of reports. Faithfull recalls the early discussions about a domestic science degree as incorporating the familiar argument that, just as men could be educated in agriculture or engineering, so women had the right to understand more about the occupation of housekeeping. The move to rationalise housework was part of that argument, as was the need for relevant research to be carried out in chemistry, bacteriology and other sciences. The research component in the case for academic household science was absolutely crucial, and, as in other sciences, teaching and research were regarded as essential to one another.

The keenest female protagonists for the household science venture on the King's College Women's Department Committee of Management were Margaret McKillop, Adèle Meyer and Thereza Rücker. The first of these we have already met. Adèle Meyer was a wealthy society hostess and social reformer, especially in the area of infant welfare, and she co-authored with social investigator Clementina Black in 1909 a landmark investigation into women's work in the dressmaking trades: Adèle Meyer was usefully married to Carl Meyer, a financier, director of the National Bank of Egypt and a considerable presence in the City. Thereza Rücker had helped her mineralogist father with his research and gone on to marry Arthur Rücker, an expert in terrestrial magnetism and the first Principal of the University of London in 1892, which also came in handy for some of the Kensington negotiations needed to create KCHSS. Thereza believed in higher education for women but thought they should be able to choose a form of it that would help them in their lives as wives and mothers. She was president of the Association of Teachers in Domestic Science, active in many social organisations, and a great believer in never wasting time, although she much distrusted the new household technology, habitually leaving plugs in all the electric sockets in her home to stop electricity escaping onto the carpets. In Figure 6.2 these helpfully wealthy matrons appear alongside one another and together with Lilian Faithfull and Alice Ravenhill. The extravagance of Meyer's picture, a portrait by the celebrated painter John Singer Sargent, is a good demonstration of the affluent connections that nourished the cause of household science at King's.

It was a multi-purpose vision: university-level teaching in order to equip domestic science teachers, but also the 'elevation of the dignity of the subject to its proper level' and 'for research into many problems affecting the health and economic welfare of the community'.[20] Instruction in household science was said to be something the ladies of Kensington (and elsewhere) were politely demanding. In March 1897, Faithfull told the Committee of Management that she had received several requests 'for a course of lectures on household management'.[21] She'd made enquiries concerning lecturers on the subject, and someone called Miss Margaret Lonsdale (probably Lucy Margaret Lonsdale, a nurse who had done part of her training at King's College Hospital in the 1870s) had been suggested as a competent authority. The first domestic science course, called 'Household management and thrift', appeared on the curriculum in 1900. The content was very reminiscent of many courses at other institutions in England and elsewhere: 'the soil,

Figure 6.2: Conspirators for academic household science at King's College: (a) Lilian Faithfull; (b) Adèle Meyer; (c) Alice Ravenhill; (d) Thereza Rücker

Sources: (a) Public domain; (b) Sargent, J.S., 'Mrs Carl Meyer and her Children' (1896), Tate, reference number T12988; (c) https://en.wikipedia.org/wiki/Alice_Ravenhill; and (d) public domain

aspect and position of a house in town, in the country'; the water supply; air; 'infection of house and person'; food; servants; and income. There were echoes of Harriette Plunkett's interest in plumbing: 'What it is necessary for householders to know about plumber's work.' The section on servants reads as though Miss Lonsdale was responding to local concerns: 'Details of housemaiding, parlour and scullery work, not usually attended to by the modern servant.'[22] Mysteriously, the course disappeared from the curriculum the following year.

But things would soon take off in a bigger way. In 1906 a small group centred on Lilian Faithfull, Lady Rücker and Dr Frank Heath, a civil servant at the Board of Education with an interest in scientific education, turned themselves into an Organising Sub-committee for Special Courses in Home Science and Economics, 'to consider the advisability of attempting to raise the teaching of this subject to the level of other University courses'.[23] The Committee engaged Hubert Llewellyn Smith, an economist who worked at the Board of Trade, to spend a year on scientific research into home problems; it also appointed Alice Ravenhill to lecture on hygiene and sanitary science and Mabel Atkinson as lecturer in economics 'at a salary which should enable her to give a great deal of time to working out the problems, before then untouched, in connection with the economics of a household'.[24] Adèle Meyer guaranteed the lecturers' salaries for the first 18 months.

Much impassioned debating followed as to what the syllabus should consist of, who should be allowed to take it, who should teach it, and how it could be accommodated and turned into a sustainable long-term enterprise. Recalling this period in her memoirs, Alice Ravenhill said that it was an uphill struggle to convince the professors of biology, physics, chemistry and, not least, economics, that their subjects were fundamental to the advanced study of household science. She and Rücker put together a report which was presented to the Faculty of King's College. Drawing heavily on the American household science literature, they argued that many recent scientific discoveries in human nutrition, for example the role of vitamins, were unknown to the public and that further research on all aspects of domestic life was needed as a foundation for social reform. The head of the Biology Department, Arthur Dendy, a zoologist and 'a most able but rather dour personality', was particularly resistant to their case and it 'taxed all our resources to win him over to a point of view which offered him no attraction'. But he was won over, eventually. The relatively new LSE, which might have been an obvious ally, offered little support on the relation of economics to household organisation. As Ravenhill phrased it, '[t]he mere suggestion was also startling, that provision must be made in the course for practical tests on foods and cleansing agents; on household furnishings; or on clothing materials. The group of men to be convinced had never given a thought to these details of daily life'.[25]

In 1907, special lectures on subjects related to women's life and work – hygiene, business affairs, physiology, sick nursing, anatomy and first aid – were given as an 'experiment'. The physiology/nursing courses were listed in the prospectus as being provided by a King's College Hospital surgeon, Peyton Beale, and those in business affairs by someone called Cecil Gradwell who had an unusual biography. Born Cecilia Gradwell in 1855, s/he was known as Cecil, was recorded in the 1911 Census as male, and lived as a man with a woman, Octavia Richardson, with whom s/he set up the Westminster School of Business Training for Women in 1893. There some 30 young women a year were inducted into secretarial/financial/clerical work.[26]

Naturally Alice Ravenhill taught the 1907 course on hygiene: ten lectures 'illustrated by practical demonstrations and experiments'. Hers was the most expensive of these preliminary courses, £2 2s 0d for the term. The lectures were comprehensive, going from 'The physical nature of man' through 'The relation of nutrition to health' and 'The preparation, preservation and protection of food', and lectures on the environment and health, physical exercise and school hygiene, to 'some public health problems' including infant mortality, housing and the growth of public health legislation.[27] As part of the experiment, members of the Women's Industrial Council contributed material on the relationship of the state to women's work. Among their lecturers was a sprinkling of well-known names: the social researcher Bessie Hutchins, who lectured on legislation affecting employed women; Mary MacArthur, the trade unionist, who talked about political organisation for women; the Labour Party politician Margaret Bondfield, who discussed women shop assistants; and the researcher and writer Clementina Black, who spoke on one of her favourite subjects, women in domestic service. The King's College Women's Department–Women's Industrial Council connection shows how thoroughly the household science initiative was embedded in the female reform and social science networks of the time. Domestic science wasn't an outpost of the main trajectory but a central part of it.

And then, just at this moment, when it looked as though household science as a university subject might be on the cards, Lilian Faithfull, who had done much as vice-principal to steer the campaign in the right direction, left to take up a post in the more settled waters of another Ladies' College, Cheltenham Ladies' College, a girls' school. Faithfull's replacement at King's College Women's Department was another Somerville graduate, Hilda Oakeley, a philosopher, whose contacts with the American domestic science movement gave her a highly developed interest in expanding this side of the work. Oakeley had spent time in the United States studying psychology at the University of Chicago and learning about women's education in that country. She would probably have discussed the household science agenda with some of her US contacts, especially Alice Freeman Palmer, the president of Wellesley College, with whom she stayed on her visit, and who had put a course in practical housekeeping on the college curriculum there. But of all the American examples she encountered, Oakeley considered the University of Chicago course in Household Administration closest to the spirit of the King's College Women's Department venture. In this she wasn't wrong, as we will see in Chapter 8.

'Teaching of a university standard'

The 1907–1908 prospectus for the King's College Women's Department carried a red sticker on the front reading, 'Home Science and Economics. Lectures and practical classes are being arranged for a complete three years' course in Household Knowledge and Economics'. The course was promoted as 'of use to many classes of women; to those whose position will give them control over estates and large households, to those intending to teach in secondary schools or in the many training schools of domestic economy, and no less to those going to live in the Colonies'. However, it was also anticipated that 'many who cannot devote so much time to the subject may nevertheless take such parts of the course as may be a useful preparation for home life'.[28] King's College Women's Department was maintaining its tradition, rooted in the very first Lectures for Ladies, of combining the provision of thorough academic study with more superficial tastings of academic and scientific culture for those whose backgrounds and/or interests gave them a more dilettante attitude towards learning.

In December 1907 the Organising Sub-committee of Home Science and Economics at King's College Women's Department recommended to the Committee of Management that a College Board of Studies in Home Science and Economics be established. This happened. The Board consisted of the Principal of King's College; the heads of King's College science departments (botany, zoology, bacteriology, chemistry, hygiene and physics); Mr Mackinder from LSE; and two lecturers in the Women's Department, McKillop and Ravenhill, plus Hilda Oakeley and representatives of the Headmistresses' Association and the Committee of Management itself. The membership changed as the drive to introduce fully-fledged university courses accelerated: by 1910, among the 11 female members of the Board were Mabel Atkinson; Florence Baddeley from the Gloucester Domestic Science Training School; Lilian Faithfull in her new post in Cheltenham; Maud Taylor, Chairman of the Association of Teachers of Domestic Subjects; Lady Rücker; and Mrs Woodhouse, headmistress of Clapham High School for Girls which lent its kitchens to the early household science ventures of the Women's Department.

The minutes of the Board's meetings give a flavour of the earnest and detailed discussions about the household science courses that took place over many months. In early February 1908, Alice Ravenhill was appointed as the Board's salaried secretary, conditions of student admission were debated, staff were asked to work on potential timetables, and a series of subject sub-committees were set up for chemistry, bacteriology and microscopy, sanitary science and hygiene, and economics and psychology. Professor Jackson, a chemist whose wide-ranging interests included investigating the action of soaps and solvents in laundry work, argued that a course on general physical science, which would include chemistry and physics, should be compulsory. This proposal generated further questions that were on the agenda for the next meetings: should the chemistry component be called applied chemistry? (Yes); How much science should students be expected to have done before they arrived? (Some); Should psychology include child psychology? (Yes); Which courses should be compulsory? (Chemistry, economics and sanitary science and hygiene). The discussions weren't without tension. For example, some overlap was apparent between the biology courses planned by Professors Dendy, Hewlett and Jackson and Miss Ravenhill's course: could she please adapt hers?[29]

Two courses were planned: the first was a one-year diploma and the second, more ambitious one, was a three-year course that would ultimately be recognised by the University of London as degree-worthy. The relationship of both courses to the related area of household arts occupied much of the Board's time in these months, requiring yet another sub-committee. Basically, household arts was practical housekeeping without the theory. The Women's Department did have a Household Arts Department. It was run by a woman called 'Miss E. Minot', who is a shadowy figure in this history despite obviously being deeply committed to teaching students how to look after stoves, remove stains from clothing, and so forth. Her proposed curriculum for the second year of the three-year household science course occupied 60 hours over two terms. It was devoted to the familiar subjects of dust and its removal; stains; the cleaning of metal, wood, all household articles of furniture and fabrics; and bleaching and disinfection of clothes and rooms. Students also had to commit to 90 hours in the kitchen laboratory doing practical experimental work. But the planners of the Board of Studies in Home Science and Economics, while recognising the importance of practical work, weren't willing to lose sight of their ultimate objective, which was to raise household science to the same level as other university science subjects. When the details of the full three-year household science course were finalised, only a quarter of the curriculum was taken up by household arts, leaving three-quarters of the curriculum for the fully-fledged science element.

Publicity for the planned household science courses made the most of the fact that 'there is at present no other University College where women can obtain in this subject a complete training of so high a standard'. It was noted as an aside that students might include men in need of 'administrative knowledge', but this theme was never developed. The publicity made it plain that the household science courses weren't simply about housework in private households. Their scope was much broader: 'The social economics included in the course will be of great value to those who wish to understand the problems with which they are confronted when serving as Guardians, District Councillors, or County Councillors, or on the Boards likely to be formed in connection with Poor Law Reform.' The training provided would be relevant to students intending to be factory inspectors or 'Managers of Institutions'. It was also hoped that, if King's College household science graduates took up teaching posts in schools and colleges, this would help to elevate the subject of domestic economy 'to the same level as other subjects taught to girls in schools by women with a University training, and that in this way more will be done to overcome the prevalent ignorance, in all classes, of the best methods of economic home management and child-rearing'.[30]

Educated charwomen wanted

In the landmark year of 1908 the Women's Department of King's College was inaugurated as an independent college within the University of London, and its name was changed to 'University of London King's College for Women'. The serious philosopher, Hilda Oakeley, as head of this establishment, had to face a whole new set of challenges consequent on the institutional coming of age. Apart from its symbolic importance – effectively making King's College itself co-educational, albeit on split sites – the creation of King's College for Women was enormously significant for the financial future of home science. It was now possible for the new College to get grants directly from the Board of Education, the London County Council and other bodies. This immediately opened up new vistas of financial support and extended intellectual and scientific expertise.

Courses in home science and economics started formally in October 1908. The aim of these courses was described as being 'to provide a thoroughly scientific education in the principles underlying the whole organisation of Home Life, the conduct of Institutions, and other spheres of civic and social work in which these principles are applicable'. In that year, two students arrived to take the three-year course; eight postgraduate students registered for the one-year course; and a further 30 students took the non-examination courses. The one-year course was intended for 'students of graduate standing', and the three-year one for 'students whose general education has reached the standard requisite for entry on University courses of the usual undergraduate type'.[31] Students could also choose a two-year course of training for social and public health workers arranged in conjunction with the Ratan Tata Department of Social Science and Administration at LSE. (Working with LSE wasn't easy, and this arrangement was to unravel later.)

Who were the first students? An 'N. Cowper' is listed in the Record Book as attending in 1908–1909. Her address is given as Maida Vale, and she took the three-year course. Forty years later she recalled in the pages of the KCHSS Magazine what it had been like studying in those 'tall, gloomy houses' in Kensington Square. She was constantly reminded that she was 'a shop-window advertisement' for the new household science course.

Arts students, meeting me on the stairs carrying a very black zinc pail, were horrified when I explained that I was experimenting with the cleaning of metals. One day the Cookery Lecturer and I were both down on our knees while I was solemnly instructed in the art of scrubbing, when the door opened – there was our gentle Warden [alias the Principal, Hilda Oakeley], engaged in showing a visitor over the college and blushing furiously at this embarrassing domestic scene.

For books, N. Cowper had to go to the British Museum or reference libraries as the library at King's College for Women was inadequate. For cookery, laundrywork and housewifery, she and other students travelled to the Domestic Economy centre at Clapham Girls' School. There were several external visits as part of the course: Cowper particularly remembered going to the Primrose Soap Factory, where an elderly French chemist sprinkled the students' hankies with a pungent violet scent. Ten days' attendance at the Army and Navy Stores Catering Department was vastly entertaining; they prepared food for balls in Covent Garden and roasted 400 quails for a regimental dinner. Less entertaining was a visit to Royal Holloway College, where, seated next to its Principal at dinner, she was told that the whole notion of studying household science was nonsense – any woman with intelligence could do it. With her new qualification Cowper got a job as matron-housekeeper at a London County Council training college where she catered for 250 people; later, during the First World War, she moved to a hospital where she catered for four times as many.[32]

Arthur Smithells, whose ambitions for domestic science education ended Chapter 4 of *The Science of Housework*, delivered the inaugural address for the King's College Home Science and Household Economics courses in October 1908. He saw the arrival of household science as part of a generic attempt to knit university studies more closely to the 'common occupations of life' and to break down the customary barriers between thought and action. The new courses were about emancipating people 'from the rule of thumb ... the spurious traditions and the mischievous credulity, that have gained such an extraordinary sway in the domestic world'; they would therefore bring about an 'economy of life, labour, time, and money'. He made a particular point of distancing the courses from those run in Domestic Economy Schools, which were, in his view, short on theory and science. He laid special emphasis on the need for household science education to be located in institutions where it could benefit from other allied studies and would lead 'to the prosecution of vivifying research'.[33] Smithells's own province of work was chemistry, and King's College for Women strategically made him an education adviser for their new courses.

The arrival of household science on the university curriculum was met with a huge and mixed storm of sarcasm, approval and disapproval. Press by-lines included, 'The dignity of housework: Educated charwomen wanted'; 'Management of the house: the chemistry of the wash-tub'; 'Doctors of Housewifery'; and 'Model Wives'.[34] The author of the latter piece in *The Leeds Mercury* could hardly restrain himself: 'In the detailed syllabus one notes development of the frog's egg', he observed acerbically,

> but the cooking of the hen's egg is not specified. … The initials S.D.A., representing Spinster of Domestic Arts, might be a valuable asset in the matrimonial market, but the M.D.A., or Matron's Degree, should only be available for wives who have been married five years, and are in possession of a husband's recommendation.

The Manchester Guardian observed that the three-year course might turn into a degree, but there was still a strong feeling among academics that kitchens weren't a suitable academic topic. It voted the experimental cookery promised at King's College for Women better than the sort usually done at home because the results of the academic one were normally thrown away.[35]

Plum puddings and houseflies

The financial future of household science at King's was not secure, however. Since the initial fund-raising efforts had covered costs only for the first three years, there needed to be a vigorous and sustained programme of further fund-raising and publicity. To achieve this, a new Ladies' Committee had been formed in 1907 by Ravenhill, Rücker and Maud Taylor. These three women knew the right people to convince about the desirability of investing time and money in academic household science. There were letters to the press and other inventive episodes such as a 'model market' held in a house in Queen Anne's Gate inhabited by a Mrs Loe Strachey in December, 1910, at which the articles for sale included 'cakes (large and small)', 'cream (thick and Devonshire)', 'game (rabbits, hares &c)' and plum pudding. A total of £165 was raised.[36] Lady Rücker arranged a series of 'drawing room meetings' in the homes of well-connected people. One in May 1909, at Grosvenor House, collected quite a lot of money from the Goldsmiths' Company, the Mercers' Company and the Merchant Taylor's Company, and four scholarships for the course were promised by the Surrey Educational Council. These results contrasted with the scanty contributions that were accruing at the time in answer to appeals for the support of religious education. As the King's historian Professor Hearnshaw put it, sanitation was clearly winning over salvation in the minds of the public.[37]

In 1910, the Women's Congress, part of the Japan-British exhibition held in London to promote trade between the two countries, sponsored a discussion on 'A University Standard in Home Science'. Thereza Rücker was a prominent speaker, declaring in her usual bold manner that '[i]nefficiency in women is as great a danger to the State as quackery in medicine'. President Theodore Roosevelt sent a personal message to the Congress giving his 'warmest approval and sympathy to the movement' at King's College.[38] This kind of publicity endeared domestic science to segments of the public who wouldn't otherwise be supportive of higher education for women. Patronage by the British royal family was another factor. This had been a constant theme right from the beginning, when Princess Louise, Queen Victoria's fourth daughter, had attended the inauguration in the Vestry Hall of the Ladies' Department in 1878. Queen Alexandra, then the Princess of Wales, first appears in the brochures as patroness in 1894. Three of Queen Victoria's numerous granddaughters studied in the Ladies' Department, one (at least) taking household science under the watchful eye of Margaret McKillop. A little later in this story, Queen Mary lent her name to the new hostel which was built in Campden Hill as part of the grand KCHSS scheme, and, even later, KCHSS ceded its name to Queen Elizabeth, becoming Queen Elizabeth College in 1953.[39]

Arthur Smithells was right about the edge in terms of theory and science the new King's College courses had over the educational provision of the domestic economy training schools. Students of household science at King's College had a heavy workload. Those taking the one-year course were confronted with 180 hours of practical work in applied chemistry; 60 lectures and 60 hours of practical work in sanitary science and hygiene; 60 lectures in economics; and 180 hours in practical domestic arts, of which 90 were taken in the Kitchen Laboratory. In addition they could take bacteriology and microscopy; psychology with ethics; or psychology with practical or experimental work. The applied chemistry component of the courses covered the constituents of the atmosphere; water analysis; foods, adulterants and preservatives; and the chemistry of cooking and of laundry work and other cleansing processes. The associated practical work included the 'qualitative and quantitative examination of water, milk, foods, etc., and of materials and chemicals in common use in the house, kitchen, laundry, &c' and 'the use of the microscope in analytical work'. In the sanitary science and hygiene course, students heard about the usual 'application of general biological principles to human hygiene', and the history and scope of sanitary legislation, and were also required to undertake 'a statistical study of the reports on the physical welfare of children and adults published by Municipal and other authorities'. There were 'practical demonstrations and laboratory investigations' on building construction, lighting, warming, ventilating, cleansing, and decoration of dwellings, schools, workshops, markets, and so on, and 'direct observations on children in schools and elsewhere'.[40]

Students who chose bacteriology embarked on a demanding journey through '[t]he general morphology, biology, structure, and classification of

Bacteria, Yeasts, and Moulds, their cultivation and isolation. Fermentation, and its application in bread making, alcohol and vinegar prod, &c' and went on to cover 'sewage pollution, sterilisation and pasteurisation applied to the preservation of foods, milk &c. Bacteria in water milk and foods. Mould and its relation to infant mortality. ... Micro-organisms in the atmosphere, dust, clothing, bedding, &c'. General biology began with the structure and life history of animals and plants 'so far as is necessary to illustrate the general principles of Biology': 'Amoeba, Paramoecium, Opalina and Nictotherus'.[41] This was followed with more possibly superfluous and somewhat disgusting information about malarial parasites, earthworms, liver flukes, tape worms, crayfish, blowflies and houseflies, and instruction on the anatomy of whiting, pigeon and rabbit. Cecil Gradwell (listed here as 'Miss') taught the management of business affairs. This was a blatantly middle-class agenda that covered how to index and file, how to write business letters, correspond with solicitors, make wills, manage bank accounts, deal with stockbrokers, make investments and reclaim income tax.

Mabel Atkinson, teaching economics, covered a tremendous amount of ground, as would be expected from someone who believed that the science component of household science should cover a new sort of economic science with household life at its centre. She started with how and why the whole topic of household economics had been neglected, went on to give a sketch of how English households had developed from the Manorial System through to, and beyond, the Industrial Revolution, and then focused on the statistics of those engaged in housekeeping, and the nature of their work from the point of view of economic theory. She covered housing problems; town planning; domestic service; and experiments in co-operative housing, before moving on to the economics of consumption, 'a neglected branch of the science'. Atkinson's powerful economic analysis of women's position meant that students would also have to take account of women's work beyond the household: issues of pay, unionisation, factory legislation, philanthropic work, and so forth.

The Record Book of students taking the household science courses in 1910–1913 contains 44 names, together with details of fathers' occupations (for 32 of the names) and some information about students' own backgrounds. They are a mixed lot, socially much more mixed than the clientele who had crammed themselves into Kensington's Vestry Hall to attend lectures for ladies. Seventeen of the 44 were taking the one-year postgraduate diploma. Of the 11 whose fathers' occupations were given, three fathers were teachers, two were described as a clergyman/clerk in holy orders, two as a printer & stationer/printer & publisher, and one each as a builder, a commercial traveller, a GP and a 'stock and share broker'. Among the 21 out of the 27 students doing the three-year course whose fathers' occupations were listed, there were also one clerk in holy orders, one stock and share broker, one editor, and one 'literary man'. Three fathers were builders and four were described as merchants of minerals, seeds, timber and marble respectively; there was one grocer, one cotton agent, one manufacturers' agent, one secretary, one bank manager, one HM civil servant, one barrister and one father of independent means. The last two students had fathers who worked as an acetylene gas engineer and a science demonstrator, so presumably these daughters had the edge over the other students in terms of scientific knowledge.[42]

The domestic science training colleges were ambivalent about the exciting new courses at King's College for Women. On the one hand, any progress in elevating the status of housewifery was to be welcomed; on the other, many colleges felt they had been doing for years what King's College was hailing as an original development. Hilda Oakeley had to be diplomatic in the speech she was asked to give to the Gloucester School of Domestic Science in the winter of 1911. So she began by referring to the 'bonds of no light nature' that connected the two institutions, and by telling her audience that the Gloucester Principal, Miss (Florence) Baddeley, had been very helpful in developing the King's College programme. Both institutions were benefiting from – indeed, had helped to create – the extraordinary public interest now being shown in domestic science: 'At one time hardly admitted to an intellectual equality with the three Rs, it may now be said almost to take its place amongst the Muses.' She recalled the history of this transformation:

> Social reform did not at first appear to have anything to do with the home – that seemed to be a private matter. Certainly it had to do with housing, with the hygiene of life, with feeding the hungry, providing for the homeless, educating the ignorant. But the notion that there is a kind of education in the making of home life, which is a part of social reform, was very slow to be grasped. The reason for this seems to have been the way in which we – rightly – oppose the home to every kind of public life. It must not be invaded by the forces we call to our aid in the battle of life beyond. It must be moulded by other influences than those which make us successful in the professional and industrial world. Does it therefore follow that we are to eject knowledge from a place in the moulding of home conditions?[43]

Of course not.

Conclusion

By 1911, when Oakeley gave her diplomatic speech, household science at King's College was well on its way to owning a proper university career.

Figure 6.3: King's College for Women, June 1911

Source: Courtesy of Archive Centre, London Borough of Sutton

These very proper university ladies and some of their students are shown in Figure 6.3.

A panoply of motives – raising the status of housework, improving public health, educating women or confining them to the home – had come together as a kind of unholy alliance that eventually guaranteed the moment in 1928 when both Lectures for Ladies and King's College for Women would vanish and be replaced by a completely independent King's College of Household and Social Science. The resistances of academia crumbled – or were forcibly dissolved by the relentless campaigning of household science proselytisers – allowing housework a transitory moment of academic glory. The campaigning vision expanded to encompass the creation of a whole new set of architect-designed buildings in Campden Hill to replace the much-loved but shabby, dark and cramped premises in Kensington Square. Fully equipped laboratories for hygiene and bacteriology, physics and physiology, and biology and chemistry, a grandly proportioned teaching kitchen, a comprehensive library – all these would rise from the ashes of Lectures for Ladies to produce both 'the perfect housekeeper' and 'the thoroughly trained and scientific woman'.[44]

7

Alice through the cooking class

The King's College for Women (KCW) magazine, *King's Minstrel*, drew parallels with Lewis Carroll's *Alice in Wonderland* when in March 1929 it celebrated the college's formal transformation into King's College of Household and Social Science. The London University Senate had resolved that the Household and Social Science Department of KCW should now be recognised as a wholly independent school of the university. Thereafter it would conduct its own business, and all links with King's College in the Strand were severed. But had the Senate been in its right mind when it took this decision, asked the magazine's editorial? The question was followed with a short piece called 'Alice through the cooking class': 'For some minutes, Alice stood without speaking, looking in all directions over the kitchen – and a most curious kitchen it was.' Alice stands in this curious kitchen looking at a 'luxurious parsley tree' through one window and a kitchen garden with rows of shining pans and gooseberry bushes hung with sieves, strainers, whisks and spoons through another. White Pawns and Knights leap over tables laden with food, while the White Queen issues cooking instructions. She addresses the White Pawns, all lined up in front of her, each with a slate and a piece of chalk (just like the KCW housework students themselves): ' "The time has come", the White Queen said,/ "To talk of many things;/ Of stews – and chips – and cooking caps -/ Of cabbages – and King's -/And why the fat is boiling hot -/ And whether pigs have wings".'[1]

Lectures for Ladies had come a long way from its tentative, chaperoned beginnings in Kensington's Vestry Hall. There were three constants, however. First, it was still an institution located in West London, some distance from the other University of London colleges. This geographical separation helped to foster a distinct curricular identity. Second, the commitment of its staff, supporters and students to creating a university education that met women's needs had in no way faded: on the contrary, the years since the first household science course had appeared in the prospectus had been full of hard-won achievements, intellectual innovations and imaginative expansion, all amidst unpredicted but consequential academic manoeuvrings which we will hear about in this chapter. Third, the original vision, of making housework a truly scientific subject, truly a part of a liberal education, still illuminated the floor on which Alice stood, marvelling at the culinary other-world in which she found herself.

At the point of its independence in 1928, King's College of Household and Social Science (KCHSS) was a thriving institution with its own architect-designed set of buildings in Campden Hill, Kensington. Student numbers had gone up to 212. Many students now came from academically ambitious secondary schools and/or prominent families. Colonel Hugh Bonham Carter, of the well-conected Bonham Carter family, sent his daughter Hilary there in 1919, and then spent some time complaining about the services the college offered. On one occasion he told them that Hilary had reported herrings at lunch so high that 'a procession was formed and a dish of them was buried with much solemnity in the garden'. (The herrings were investigated and determined to be perfectly good, the problem was that the students didn't like them.)[2] Another distinguished student was Ishbel MacDonald, the daughter of the politician Ramsay MacDonald, who arrived in 1923 to take the three-year household science course. Her attendance was terminated abruptly when Ramsay became Labour's first prime minister in 1924. Since his wife had died some years before, Ishbel withdrew from her household science education in order to become the youngest-ever hostess of 10 Downing Street.

A party at the castle

So the question arises: how did the modest enterprise that struggled to find its feet in the genteel air of Kensington transform itself into the much more extensive arrangement of 1928? Such transitions are rarely simple stories of ambition and achievement. Serendipity and social networks play key roles.

In 1911 a chance meeting at a motte-and-bailey castle built by William the Conqueror generated a much grander ground plan for household science than its original enthusiasts had conceived. At a weekend party in Warwick Castle, a young doctor called John Atkins got into conversation with Adèle Meyer, the reformer and socialite who had taken over managing the Ladies Committee at KCW from Thereza Rücker. The Atkins-Meyer encounter was almost certainly orchestrated by the extraordinary Daisy, Countess of Warwick, who lived in the castle, a flamboyant multi-faceted personality whose achievements included standing as an Independent Labour Party candidate, being the Prince of Wales's mistress, and a philanthropic devotion to many good causes, free school meals, the condition of agricultural workers and girls' education among them.

At their meeting Adèle Meyer told John Atkins about the plans KCW had to build a new hostel for women, and John Atkins told Adèle Meyer that these plans weren't nearly ambitious enough, and that they ought instead to be aiming at an entire women's college devoted to household science. Working as a GP in a poor area of West Kensington not far from KCW, Atkins was impressed by what he saw as the impact of maternal ignorance on children's well-being. His resolve to do something about this settled on the conventional solution of educating their mothers about how better to look after them. This meshed sufficiently well with the ambitions of the KCW Ladies' Committee about elevating the academic status of household science to yield a productive coalition of interests.

Following the weekend party, Atkins met the KCW Ladies *en bloc* and the plan was hatched to raise funds for a household science college. The Ladies' Committee was dissolved and replaced by a more authoritative sounding Trust Fund Committee (TFC). The legal deed supporting the TFC described its main object as 'to establish a department in connection with the University of London KCW in providing teaching of a university standard in home science and economics'. The TFC was chaired by one of Atkins's patients, Charles Paget, the Marquess of Anglesey, who promptly donated £20,000 for scientific equipment and buildings. All the members of the TFC were wealthy and well-connected: the Ladies Meyer and Rücker; another Lady, Lady Bertha Buckley, the wife of Lord Justice Buckley, who advised the TFC on legal matters; Emma Asquith, the prime minister's wife; ex-prime minister Arthur Balfour; Thomas Dewey, the chairman of the Prudential Assurance Company (another of Atkins's patients); and Eleanor, Viscountess Esher, the daughter of the Belgian ambassador, whose homoerotic husband was close to Edward VII and other monetarily well-endowed members of the monarchy. Atkins acted as Honorary Secretary, and the chemist and philanthropist Sir Richard Garton, a friend of Atkins, as Honorary Treasurer. Here was a group of elite men and women who, if anybody could, would be able to lay their hands on enough money to set up a proper household science empire.

A pamphlet advertising the need for funds to endow home science was produced and circulated widely. By the end of 1911 a further £10,000 had been raised from a succession of Dukes and Earls and Ladies. As was the habit in academic circles, the newly energised initiative spawned yet more committees and sub-committees concerned with buildings, money, curricula and the hall of residence, and an overarching Executive Committee to administer the funds. This was chaired by Henry Miers, Principal of the University of London, and included Hilda Oakeley as Warden of KCW, and the Reverend Arthur Headlam, who was Principal of King's College in the Strand. They all worked out that £100,000 was needed to achieve a separate household science college, which meant a further £70,000 in addition to the £30,000 already achieved. By January 1912 they had it all: a friend of Thomas Dewey's, Mary Woodgate Wharrie, a generous supporter of both health-care institutions and the University of London, provided £20,000 to endow the chemistry side of the work; Garton matched this with another £20,000, earmarked for the hostel, and Dewey supplied the remaining £30,000.

One noteworthy aspect of this story is that in the historiography of household science it has been framed so as to represent John Atkins and his friends as *the* founders of KCHSS.³ Yet, while the 1911–1912 fundraising was undoubtedly of great importance, so were the aspirational plans of the people, mainly women, who first placed the idea of a university education in household science in the public domain. The motives of the two groups overlapped, but were also different: the men's interest was chiefly in the efficient domestication of women, whereas the women wanted to give housework a new scientific standing. This mix of motives would thread a sometimes tortuous way though events as they unfolded.

That 'glorious goddess called domestic science'

The publicity occasioned by the fund-raising brought tensions to the fore about whether household science was an oppressor or liberator of women. At a conference on domestic science teaching in 1911, a chemistry lecturer at Newnham College, Cambridge, Ida Freund, led the public attack on the aspirations of academic household science. She poured scorn on the whole household science movement: 'From between the covers of Mrs. Beeton there is to emerge', she told her audience sarcastically, 'the embodiment of a newer and better way, the glorious goddess called *Domestic Science*; under her swey [*sic*] all that has been obscure, difficult, and slow of accomplishment is to be made clear, easy, and rapid'. Advancing to 'those temples of learning called Universities', domestic science claimed to be the equal of 'such deities as Physics, Physiology, Agriculture, Genetics'. The conception was beautiful, Freund conceded, but it wouldn't produce any practical results and it would have harmful side-effects. There wasn't enough science in household science, and couldn't be, because science took a long time to learn. What was the point of teaching what happens when jam is made – that the hydrolysing effect of the organic acid in the fruit changes the saccharose to glucose? This 'purely didactic process' simply can't yield the mental training which enables pupils to perform the central scientific task of judging whether an alleged connection between effect and cause has been established or not.⁴ Most importantly, and this was the kernel of Freund's case, the generic science teaching that was available to girls would suffer through an enlarged emphasis on *domestic* science. This part of her argument was supported by the history of domestic science teaching in girls' schools, as we saw in Chapter 3: filling the female timetable with needlework and cookery was an excuse for depriving them of 'boys' subjects.

After 25 years teaching science to Cambridge students, Ida Freund knew what she was talking about. She was a most committed and unusual teacher, circulating the streets of Cambridge and large parts of Europe on a tricycle worked with her arms following a childhood accident that had

Figure 7.1: The periodic table in cupcakes

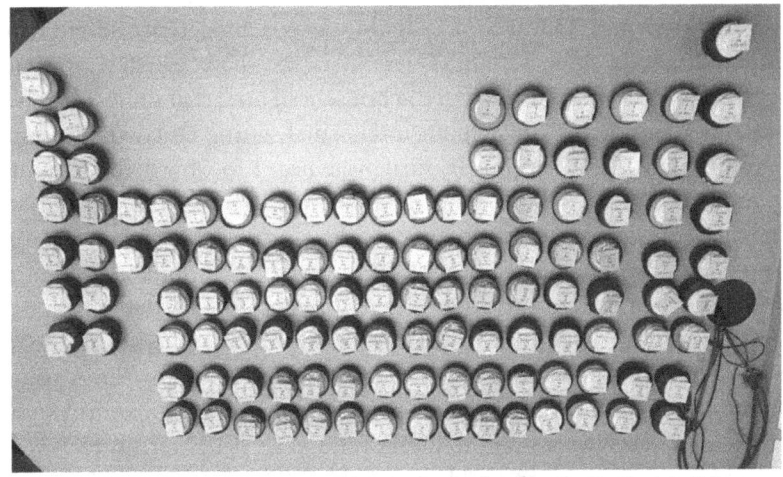

Source: Stinglehammer, Periodic Table cupcakes at Ada Lovelace Day 2017 – King's Buildings, University of Edinburgh [available under creative commons attribution CC BY-SA 4.0]

deprived her of a leg. To the surprise of some, given Freund's antagonism to housework, she herself was a fine housekeeper and cook, proving this through such exploits as fashioning a periodic table out of chocolate as a way of preparing her students for their examinations.[5] Figure 7.1 displays a modern reproduction of this methodology – the periodic table in cupcakes.

Ida Freund knew that her argument against domestic science teaching in universities would be unpopular, but it was a position she held with great passion and integrity. And so did one of KCW's household students, Rona Robinson, who contributed two vitriolic articles to the radical journal *The Freewoman* in 1912. Robinson wrote about her decision to relinquish the scholarship that had funded her place at KCW. About household science there, she said that 'a more impudent piece of charlantanry has never been perpetrated before in the history of education'. Why should women go to university to learn how to clean? The KCW course didn't provide what it claimed to, scientific teaching of a university standard, and there was nothing housewives needed to know about science anyway. Women who really wanted to know about the chemistry of foodstuffs would have to do 'an amount of real chemistry which would cause the hair of these students to turn blue and make them flee in terror'.[6]

Arthur Rücker, on behalf of the KCW initiative, took Ida Freund and her supporters to task for repeating arguments that, he said, are always heard whenever a new branch of technology or practical teaching is introduced into higher education. Engineering, for example, was at first derided as mere craft, but today the Institute of Civil Engineers is among the warmest advocates of a first-class scientific education. Does Miss Freund really believe this doesn't apply to women and housework?[7] Hilda Oakeley made the same point, and Arthur Smithells also rose to the defence of the King's household science courses. These defenders put the reasonable argument that you couldn't have a science of the household until that subject had been created as an academic unity in an intellectual setting that would nourish it appropriately. Miss Freund, in turn, was heard to object that the most vociferous of her opponents appeared to be men, who were probably not altogether conversant with the practical side of household science, although they profited from being in charge of its theory.[8] And, indeed, it was true that all the first heads of the science departments at KCW were men.

The printed communications of the debate about whether household science should be a university subject went on for more than a year. A popular song expressed disbelief in the entire enterprise: 'Don't send your daughter up to King's, Mrs Worthington/Don't send your daughter up to King's,/ They cut up poor frogs and rabbits and dogs,/Don't ask me WHAT they do./They grill and they fry, I can't think why.'[9] At a time of peak suffragist agitation it was hardly surprising that a large question mark would hover over the proposal to teach women more about housework. Nor was it surprising that this question mark should travel internationally. In Canada, the debate was led by a philosophy graduate called Evlyn [*sic*] Farris, who agreed with Freund about domestic science training for women being liable to imperil their intellectual development by depriving them of an education in science proper.[10] Farris's fiercest local opponent was the prominent British household scientist Alice Ravenhill, who had left King's College to start a second career in Vancouver, and who on the whole got the better of Farris in the Canadian debate.

An era of opulent household science

Household science in Kensington Square was cramped, and it was difficult to expand the work. Fired by their successful fund-raising, its supporters found in 1912 a much larger two-and-a-half-acre site nearby. It was part of a development of grand country-style mansions for the wealthy who wanted to live close to the city but not in it. Campden Hill rises up from Kensington High Street and then slopes down to Notting Hill Gate; it was still distinctly rural (today it contains Holland Park). The Blundell House estate on Campden Hill was purchased on a 999-year lease for an annual rental of £1,350. The cost of the lease was meant to be split equally between the general work of KCW and what the principal of the University of London described rather enviously as an 'opulent household science department'. Two reputable architects, Percy Adams and Charles Holden, were engaged to draw up plans for a new campus. Both were interested in plain functional design and the kind of close match between design and building function that would have pleased the domestic efficiency experts. Most of their previous designs had been of hospitals, and Holden would later be remembered as the creator of the University of London's Senate House, the pale modernist building that Hitler earmarked for his base in a Nazi-controlled London.

In the spring of 1913 Holden went to the United States to look at domestic science colleges there, but apparently was uninspired. He and Adams designed a simple incomplete quadrangle for Campden Hill to be built of plain red brick and white stone at right angles to Campden Hill Road. The North Wing would have a set of 'palatial' laboratories named after their benefactor, the Marquess of Anglesey: hygiene, bacteriology, physics and physiology on the ground floor, biology and chemistry above them. The West Wing would be devoted to the Household Arts Department. The South Wing would contain a refectory attached at its western end to a kitchen, scullery and servants' hall. A building that might easily have resembled a barrack thus exhibited 'the dignity of simplicity', reflected the KCW Magazine in 1920; and there was joy in such detail as the long staircase-window, the cupola of the kitchen, the common room with its 'Adams' fireplace, and the Dutch tiles in the students' rooms.[11] Figures 7.2 and 7.3 give an idea of the scale of this enterprise: we see the ornate gates at the front of the building, and the

Figure 7.2: The gates of the Campden Hill building

Source: Oxfordian Kissuth, Wikimedia Commons [available under creative commons license CC BY-SA 3.0]

Figure 7.3: Quadrangle view towards the cookery class window

Source: Courtesy of King's College London Archives, Queen Elizabeth College Photographs, Q/PH3/35

quadrangle with the bay-fronted cookery class. (Now a residential block, the building still stands today.)

It's normal for architectural plans to run out of money and this was no exception. Mrs Wharrie gave another £5,000 and the Carnegie Trust donated £5,000 for a library, conditional on its contents being made available to all classes in the community. Patron (Matron?) of the arts Mrs Samuel Courtauld's donation was for social life in the new buildings: a large hall for hosting concerts, dancing, plays and outside lectures. In its next fund-raising pamphlet the Executive Committee boasted that the value of the courses for which it was seeking support could be amply attested by the splendid range and status of the appointments KCW household science graduates were taking up: assistant to the Professor of Domestic Science,

Otago University, New Zealand; head of the Domestic Science Department at George Watson School, Edinburgh; housekeeper at the Avery Hill LCC Training College; rent collector for the Ecclesiastical Commissioners' Estate, Walworth; Board of Education inspector; and multiple posts as home science mistresses in secondary schools and lecturers in schools of domestic economy. Between 1910 and 1919 other employments listed in the reports included a bacteriological assistant at the Royal Society of Medicine; a dining room superintendent for the Bedford Hotel in London; a home science mistress at Cheltenham Ladies' College; a lecturer in hygiene and physiology at the School of Swedish Drill and Massage in Hove; a chemistry assistant at Southern Metropolitan Gas; a supervisor of factory output at Selfridges Department Store; and an administrative post for a Peace Negotiation Committee.[12]

KCW Annual Reports show that most graduates did not marry and use their skills to benefit husbands and children. About half went into teaching, and many of the rest worked in commercial laboratories. The favourite here was J. Lyons and Company, the country's largest caterer with (in 1919) 250 teashops and several restaurants; other such employers were Bovril, Heinz, Horlicks and Rowntree. KCW graduates were much in demand as hospital administrators, and later in dietetics and food science. There was clearly a lot that could be done with the pedigree of King's College household science on one's CV.

The first section of the opulent new Campden Hill set of buildings was a hostel for students finished in 1915. Named after KCW's royal patron Queen Mary, the new hostel provided 63 bed-sitting and dressing-rooms. *The Manchester Guardian* was fulsome in its praise, describing the hostel as 'perhaps the most important building of a public character' of 1915:

> The treatment of the brickwork in windows and walls is true to the Kensington traditions, and the sheer wall of five storeys relieved only by two bays and the severely restrained use of Portland stone in cornice and carved keystones shows a breadth of handling, combined with good colour effect, which is altogether excellent.[13]

Inside, the washing-cubicles benefited from hot and cold water, porcelain fittings and the marvel of a hot-air towel stand. A great attraction was that none of the rooms faced north. The initial fee for residents of 60 guineas a year included one scuttle of coal a day in winter.

The University Department of Household and Social Science on Campden Hill was a formal place, modelled on a mixture of girls' boarding schools and women's Oxbridge colleges. In the hostel a rising bell sounded at 7.15 and another for prayers (voluntary) at 7.45. A buzzer sounded at 6.30 as a warning to change for dinner. Silence was observed for two hours after dinner every evening. The students wore gowns and in the laboratories differently coloured overalls according to their year. However, the façade of opulence on Campden Hill did conceal some awkward shortcomings: the physicist Thereza Dillon had to go to King's College in the Strand to do her research on thermionic emission because the physics laboratory in Kensington had only one power plug.

A ceremony was held in the summer of 1914 to initiate all this splendour. It was attended by Princess Christian (Queen Victoria's third daughter), who laid a foundation stone. All the relevant dignitaries were there, and speeches were given, although, unfortunately, Warden Hilda Oakeley's peroration on the general purposes of the home science movement was drowned out by a terrible rainstorm. The new University Department of Household and Social Science moved to the Campden Hill site in 1916: 'With the departure from Kensington Square and the entrance into the new buildings the Department enters on a new phase of its existence' noted the prospectus for that session: 'To the past we look back with gratitude, to the future with hope.'[14]

The curious story of Haldane

The pinnacle of these achievements can only be explained by a totally unanticipated backstory, the *Report of the Royal Commission on University Education in London*, known as the Haldane Commission. It was the recommendations of this body that brought the independent King's College of Household and Social Science into existence in 1928.

The Haldane Commission had been set up mainly to sort out the relationship of the new Imperial College of Science to the University of London, but its terms were wide-ranging, and its approach was dominated by the political and administrative views of its chairman, Richard Burdon Haldane, who was interested in imposing a pattern of centralisation on the disparate parts of London University that had emerged unsynchronically over the years. The Commission's Final Report in 1913 recommended that the teaching of arts and sciences at KCW should be abandoned altogether, and that a university department devoted entirely to the study of home science and economics should be allowed to flourish entirely on its own. The arts and sciences students at KCW were to be moved elsewhere – perhaps to Bedford or University Colleges. What was left behind should, the Haldane Report suggested, be called a University Department of Household and Social Science.[15]

Thus the plans for a splendid Women's College to rise from the gardens of Campden Hill were entirely scuppered. The Haldane proposals sent shock waves through the whole household science world, and were received as shattering news by the household science department and other staff at KCW. It's not clear why the Haldane Commission reached the surprising conclusion about the future of KCW that it did. There isn't much evidence that Haldane and his colleagues – seven men and one token woman, Louise Creighton, the Bishop of London's wife – understood what household science was all about, although Louise Creighton did inscribe several sermon-like texts on topics such as *The Art of Living* and *The Economics of the Household*. Had they known more about the subject, they might have been less cavalier about cutting household science off from its feeder scientific and humanities disciplines. Quite probably the Haldane Commission found household science a bit of an uninteresting inconvenience: such a perspective would scarcely be news.

The great consternation expressed at KCW about the Haldane recommendations generated an enormous quantity of committee meetings at which the Haldane plan was deliberated, repudiated and ultimately reluctantly accepted. The Old Students' Association wrote a letter to the *Journal of Education* complaining that leaving household science to battle on its own would be a most retrograde step in women's higher education. The segregation of home science would be contrary to the spirit of a true university and would 'inevitably and unconsciously have a narrowing effect on the minds of the students'.[16] Hilda Oakeley wrote to Haldane, who refused in a gentlemanly manner to do a U-turn, and to the Archbishop of Canterbury, and to various political figures, including the Duchess of Atholl and Lord Bryce, as well as canvassing potential allies of KCW. One such was Eleanor Plumer, a former KCW student and academic administrator from an aristocratic family; Plumer managed an audience on the subject of KCW's future with the Archbishop of York: sadly, 'he was very strong on the necessity for the women to go quietly'.[17]

Hilda Oakeley herself provided a memorandum on the university education of women in London which was published as an Appendix to Volume 2 of the Haldane Report. In it she referred to the general movement to treat domestic science more scientifically than had previously been the case 'and also in closer association with historic and economic studies, and with the liberal education of a University College'. She wanted to stress that the intention was *not* (as the Ida Freund brigade had suggested) to introduce a special kind of science as more suitable for women's education:

> Although the aim is at first sight utilitarian in the narrower sense, the intention is to serve a cause of wide importance, viz, that of combating, so far as education can do so, certain modern tendencies to depreciate the work and occupations which fall to the majority of women, by revealing the importance and interest of the knowledge applicable in this field.[18]

But nobody listened; the die was cast. In January 1915 all the arts and general science students at KCW departed, not for Bedford or University College, but for the men's King's College in the Strand, where the statutes were hastily changed to admit them. The household scientists left behind, having done what they could to resist the inevitable, gathered their forces and agreed that the Department could, and would, expand so that it would eventually fill the new site. What had absolutely not been an outcome of their choosing could be seen therefore, reluctantly, in a positive light.

A degree at last

From the beginning, advocacy in Kensington of household science had been intimately tied to its imagined future as a university degree. In September 1918, the University Department of Household and Social Science on Campden Hill petitioned the University Senate for their three-year course to be given the status of a degree. The staff explained that they felt they were working at a disadvantage since, as university teachers, they had been 'brought up in the belief that the only real recognition of a University training carried to completion is the bestowal of a degree'.[19] The university resisted, citing the need for more evidence that enough people would actually *want* a degree in household science. Reading the correspondence now, one can almost hear the incredulity in the voices of the academic gentlemen who took this decision. What they were confronting was a stalwart congregation of women who weren't going to be put off. In Figure 7.4 they and their unforgiving faces are arranged in front of the cookery class window in

Figure 7.4: Staff and students of King's College for Women in 1920

Source: Courtesy of King's College London Archives, Queen Elizabeth College Photographs, Q/PH1/5

Campden Hill. It was another two years before the degree was finally agreed, and a further three before the academic gentlemen consented to allow the household science degree to be classified as either pass, or first or second class honours (rather than simply pass or fail), and thus to achieve parity with other degree subjects.

By the time of its separation from the rest of KCW, the original four departments of King's household science had expanded to 11. Bacteriology, biology, business affairs, chemistry, economics, ethics, household work, hygiene, physics, physiology and psychology: each had its individual identity and allegiances. There were 19 staff in total, nine of them women. As well as the three-year and one-year household science courses, by 1919 there were four other one-year courses providing a mix of basic and applied science: one for nurses, the 'sister tutors' course; two for health visitors and institutional administrators; and a 'special' one-year 'brides' course, which wasn't very successful. Despite the teaching being 'as elementary as possible', most of the brides failed to complete the course, being prone to prioritise their social engagements. Even replacing the science element in the course with a more easily grasped one on household electricity didn't work. As an anachronism in a mature university setting, the course was eventually ditched.

Both the two main household science courses – the three-year course, for which students had to meet the usual university admission requirements, and the one-year course catering for graduate students or those with domestic science diplomas – were unremittingly scientific in their coverage. As an indication of content, let us look at the topics covered in one of the core subjects, hygiene, in the second year of the three-year course. The term 'hygiene', meaning 'conditions or practices conducive to maintaining health and preventing disease', was absolutely crucial to the whole argument for education in household science. Taught over five hours weekly, it was made up of seven subjects. The first was Public Health (*Public Health Authorities and their Officials. Water and Water Supplies. Food. Infectious Diseases. Buildings, Houses and Housing. Refuse Collection and Disposal. Elements of Vital Statistics*). The second topic, Infant Welfare (*The care of the normal Infant; its food and clothing. Infant mortality, its chief causes, and methods of prevention*) was squeezed a little oddly after this and before the third, Domestic Hygiene (*Ventilation. Heating, Lighting, water supply. Internal Sanitary Fittings. Sanitary Construction of dwelling-house. Domestic refuse. Food storage*). Fourth was School Hygiene (*Types of School premises. Heating. Lighting. Ventilation. Sanitation. Postures and physical Exercises. Diseases which concern the school*). Personal Hygiene, fifth, was very comprehensive (*Foodstuffs. The Alimentary Canal. Teeth. Respiration. Muscular Exercise. Work. Worry. Fatigue. Rest. Sleep. Excretion. The skin. Cleanliness. Sepsis and asepsis. Clothing. The senses and education. Habit. Character*). Then came Sanitary Law (*Public Health Statutes. Orders, Memoranda*

Figure 7.5: Working in the science laboratories, 1924

Source: Courtesy of King's College London Archives, Queen Elizabeth College Photographs, Q/PH3/12

and Model By-Laws in force in the Administrative County of London); and, finally, Building Construction (*Interpretation of Plans and Sections. Materials. Local Physical Conditions*). A note attached to the latter warned that students were expected to carry out visits to such places as factories, laundries, underground dwellings and canal boats, slaughter houses and sewage works.[20]

In other words, the curriculum remained both science-based and sensitive to the everyday practical realities of housework. Students laboured in laboratories (Figure 7.5) but they also had to confront that most hated task, ironing (Figure 7.6). Were they asked to smile for the photograph? The table coverings they're using look very like those recommended by Helen Campbell back in 1896.

Since the requisite textbooks didn't exist – a similar problem in school domestic science had spurred an earlier wave of textbook writing – they had to be written. Charles Tinkler and Helen Masters, both on the staff of KCW and specialists in food chemistry, published their highly technical two-volume *Applied Chemistry* in 1920 and 1925 as a textbook for KCHSS household science. Until the 1950s, it was the standard reference work on analytical procedures for chemistry related to the home throughout the world. Another classic textbook produced for the King's household science courses was the two-volume *Economic Biology for Students of Social Science*, published in 1920 by a biologist called Philippa Esdaile. Her field of economic biology – the

Figure 7.6: The ironing room

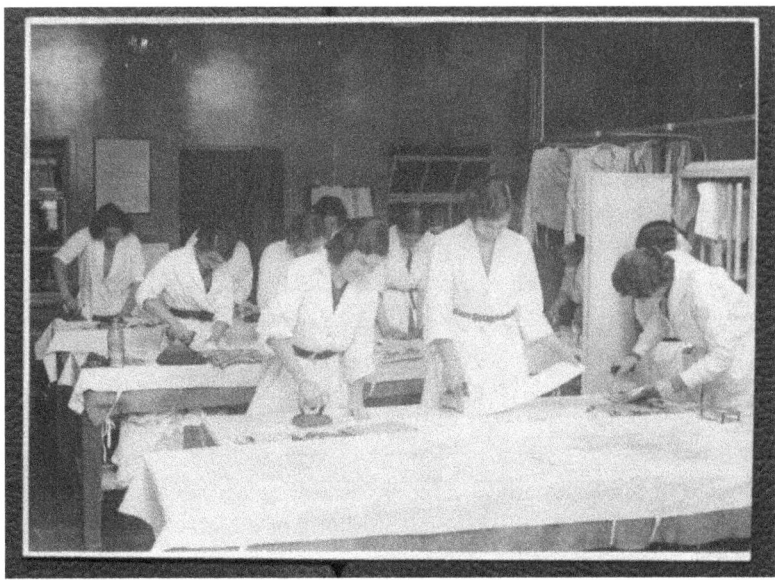

Source: Courtesy of King's College London Archives, Queen Elizabeth College Photographs, Q/PH3/15

study of how biology and economics interact – was typical of the creative interdisciplinary thinking that household science could nourish, once it was allowed to spread its university wings.

The transition from being part of a women's college to being an empire of its own wasn't easy for household science. The financial implications of being left behind on Campden Hill were huge: no one had anticipated that household science would have to pay on its own the whole rent of £1,350 *and* the costs of a 'Heating Apparatus' capable of warming all the buildings. Carving up KCW was a logistical nightmare. It was unclear which committees were responsible for which parts of what; and no one was clear about what (and who) should go where. Take, for example, the problem of the library books. Which should go the Strand and which should stay in Kensington? Some were obvious, but for others, notably psychology and ethics, the lecturers themselves would have to decide. A long list was drawn up of the physical amendments that would have to be paid for in order to accommodate KCW women in the Strand: a women's cloakroom, lavatories and common room, obviously; less obvious, but considered necessary at the time, a new separate women's entrance. All this could be funded from the sale of the Kensington Square houses, so at least that bit of the Haldane agenda was sorted.

Hilda Oakeley wasn't happy with the effect Haldane had on her own post. From being in charge of a whole women's college, and for having faithfully defended the cause of household science through contentious and personally painful times, she was now dismayed to find herself relegated to the position of Warden to the women students in the Strand. She decided to move on, to the calmer waters of running the Passmore Edwards Settlement in Bloomsbury. Her replacement at KCW, a philosopher called Rosamond Shields, had no background in household science and stayed less than two years. However, Shields's successor, a doctor called Janet Lane-Claypon, came with an outstanding scientific pedigree and a long-term interest in the health of women and children. Applying her experience, energy and vision to the management of household science on Campden Hill would take the subject to an entirely new level.

Of milk and snakes with fangs

Janet Lane-Claypon was brought up in a wealthy Lincolnshire family and educated at home. She trained in medicine at University College, where she collected various awards and scholarships, one of which enabled her to tour Europe studying preventive health-care services for mothers and babies. This exposure to other countries' methods was an important backdrop to much of her research and policy work. At the Lister Institute of Preventive Medicine in London, Lane-Claypon researched the bacteriology and biochemistry of milk. Her *Milk and its Hygienic Relations* (1916) was the first study to show conclusively that babies fed on breast milk gained more weight than those given cows' milk. Lane-Claypon also disproved the harmful, but prevalent, belief that boiling destroyed milk's nutritive value (on the contrary, boiling is needed to get rid of bad bacteria). Both the milk study and her later, post-KCW, work on breast cancer, used new statistical procedures (historical cohorts and life-table survival analysis). This marks them out as landmarks in the development of epidemiology.

Lane-Claypon first went to KCW in 1912 as a lecturer in hygiene. While her colleagues there might not have appreciated her startling methodological innovations, they would surely have warmed to her *Hygiene of Women and Children*, written when she was Dean of KCW and published in 1921. This is a volume delightfully illustrated, in true no-holds-barred household science mode, with pictures showing such matters as the methods used by flies to contaminate food; the effect of watering grass with acidulated water; an insanitary rubbish-heap; and X-rays of feet in inappropriately pointed footwear. In it Lane-Claypon argued persuasively on behalf of her subject:

> If housework is well done it is very interesting; but nothing is more dreary than attempting work of which one has no knowledge. ... The importance of a knowledge of domestic matters, expanding in

a manner compatible with that of other professions, is a real need of the present day.[21]

The new Dean did her share of publicity for the college. In *The Graphic* in December, 1919, she wrote on 'The science of housewifery', pointing out that King's College was the only university in the country that recognised 'the science which lies behind the ordinary features of daily life'.[22] Her contribution to *The Sphere* in December, 1922, was illustrated with photos showing students having a serious time wearing overalls and hats in the Teaching Kitchen; in the physiological laboratory; attending a class; in the library; and a less serious time in the refectory at lunch, and playing croquet in the quadrangle and tennis in the garden. Lane-Claypon was proud to mention that by 1919 the college had hosted students 'from every part of the world' including India, Siam, Japan, France, Norway, the West Indies and Nigeria.[23]

During the Lane-Claypon years, 1916–1923, household science at King's College laid down the foundations of its later international reputation for trail-blazing nutrition research. The KCW Report for 1918–1919 gave a foretaste in its list of ongoing projects: Miss (Helen) Masters had investigated the question of soluble lead in the glaze of casseroles, publishing her results in *The Analyst* and *The Lancet*. At the request of the Ministry of Munitions, she'd also studied different methods for cooking vegetables, and had published those results in *The Biochemical Journal*. Miss (Gladys) Hartwell had taken on the relation of diet to the secretion of milk. At the request of Dr Mary Gordon at the Home Office, Miss (Margaret) Dyer had produced suggestions for how to improve diets in Reformatories. Other research continued to run alongside the nutrition work. In the Biology Department, ongoing investigations into the habits and life-history of the clothes-moth were yielding 'interesting results', and two in-house doctoral theses were in progress on 'certain types of nudibranchiate mollusca' by a Miss Russell, and by a Mr Sarkar on 'the poison fangs and glands of higher snakes'.[24]

Of rickets and teeth

The physiologist Edward Mellanby and his wife May Mellanby were both mentioned in the 1918–1919 KCHSS Report: him for his Medical Research Council (MRC)-funded research on rickets and on alcohol and the body; her for, '[a]n extensive research on the dietetic factors responsible for the defective teeth almost universally associated with civilisation'.[25] Herein lies another fascinating side-story which illustrates the impact of academic household science on scientific knowledge generally. I'll try not to detain you with this story for too long.

Edward Mellanby did his medical training at Cambridge and joined the staff of KCW in 1913, becoming professor of physiology there in 1920. Shortly after he arrived at King's, the MRC asked him to investigate the cause of rickets and the relationship between alcohol and intoxication. Mellanby did the necessary research in the laboratories at King's (he must have particularly welcomed the new facilities on Campden Hill). Dogs were among the experimental animals that had to be housed for this research, but local residents complained about the barking; the Executive Committee asked him to remove the large dogs used for the alcohol intoxication project, and keep only the small ones required for the rickets research. But these also barked and so had to go. Some went to the Field Laboratory in Cambridge where his wife, May Mellanby, also a physiologist, continued the bone radiographs that were necessary for Edward's study. But whose study was it? All the commentaries on the Mellanby's scientific work agree that theirs was an extremely close partnership. Edward Mellanby himself acknowledged that much of the laboratory analysis undertaken for his rickets research was done by May.[26]

Edward – or May, or May and Edward – discovered that milk reduced the intoxication caused by alcohol, and this is a finding that continues to be repeated in public health advice in the 2020s. Their rickets research proved (literally) revolutionary, since it reversed then dominant theories about the causative role of infection, lack of hygiene or generally poor diet, and demonstrated that rickets was due to a deficiency of one of the 'accessory food factors' – vitamins – that were in the process of being discovered in the first decades of the 20th century. Between 1912 and 1940 European and American scientists discovered nine vitamins and 12 minerals, making an adequate diet for the first time something measurable and quantifiable. The Mellanbys were concerned with Vitamin D. They proved conclusively that this can be obtained from food and also from sunlight.[27] The experimental results in barking dogs were shown to apply to humans during trials of cod liver oil for children conducted in post-First World War Vienna; rickets as a dietary deficiency disease was rife then in Eastern Europe. This new understanding, conceived originally on Campden Hill, allowed simple preventive strategies to eliminate the disease. Textbooks today still cite Edward Mellanby as the discoverer of Vitamin D's role in rickets. Whether it was a sole or joint venture, the rickets research was a direct consequence of the idea that understanding the science behind the everyday life of people in households can make a significant difference to health.

May Mellanby noticed something else. She observed that puppies with rickets had defective teeth and that these could also be improved by the addition of cod liver oil to the diet. With MRC funding, and the help of the dogs, she found she could produce perfect canine teeth. But the dental experts all disputed her findings: oral hygiene, they insisted, was the only relevant factor. May Mellanby turned to an unlikely place for evidence, the most remote inhabited island in the world, the tiny Tristan da Cunha in the South Atlantic Ocean. The islanders, with their restricted diet of fish, potatoes and milk, had perfect teeth, but they never brushed them. It took some time to convince the disbelieving dentists, but by the 1940s the role of dietary nutrients in causing dental cavities was accepted as a result of May Mellanby's persistence (and the help of the Tristan da Cunhans).[28] This was another pathbreaking result for household science, although May Mellanby's physiological researches have never been given the credit they deserve. This continues today. While *he* has an entry in the *Oxford Dictionary of National Biography*, *she* doesn't, appearing instead in the last two paragraphs of his.[29]

Lane-Claypon as Dean was personally involved in many of these research developments, and especially with their funding. In October 1921, for instance, Professor Vernon Mottram, recently appointed to the KCW Chair in Physiology and taking over from Edward Mellanby, asked the MRC for money to continue *his* work on vitamins. Miss Hartwell needed new cages for the rats and guinea pigs who were contributing to her research on the diets of nursing mothers – the old ones had infected the animals with a nasty parasitic skin disease. And then there was Miss Clifford's work on carnosine for which she required a colorimeter; she'd been using one belonging to Professor Mellanby, but he needed it back. All these requests were granted via a correspondence between the MRC's director, Arthur Landborough Thomson, and the Dean.

The First World War disrupted the household science teaching and research in Kensington, but it also created new opportunities for it to prove its worth. During the war, student numbers increased as the accelerating disappearance of servants made studying household science more popular. The Department put on a new one-year course in home life which covered hygiene and infant welfare work; sanitary law and building construction; the use of labour-saving devices; and dust-free room furnishing. There was a run on the supply of trained workers to manage canteens, and the Ministry of Food, a constant source of requests for KCW's specialist help, appointed the college as a 'National Kitchen'. (National Kitchens were wartime restaurants set up by the Ministry of Food to provide cheap meals.) Research was required on the ideal amount of boric acid to be used as a preservative in imported bacon, and the Royal Commission on Wheat Supplies asked for experiments in connection with the cooking of Brazilian beans and the use of cotton seed oil. The Industrial Research Department requested experiments on the use of whale flesh for human consumption and the Glass Research Committee of the Ministry of Munitions enlisted KCW's help to work on methods of glass manufacture. The war also expanded the range of jobs secured by King's household science graduates: assistant inspector of canteens in Carlisle for the Liquor Control Board; manager of a canteen for the Army Pay Office Girl

Clerks; chemical work and welfare supervisor for the Ministry of Munitions; assistant lady superintendent of the National Aeroplane Factory; assistant in the Food Economy Section, Ministry of Food; inspector for the Army and Navy Canteen Board; welfare supervisor for the Air Board.[30]

As the 1920s wore on, the reputation of King's household science expanded with the new medium of radio, which offered a route for the household arts staff to reach a wide audience with a series of programmes on cookery and dietetics. In 1935 Jessie Lindsay, senior lecturer in household arts, was appointed (as the only woman) to the Ministry of Health Advisory Committee on Nutrition, and she and her King's colleagues became a recognised authority on kitchen design, including for the new Senate House in Bloomsbury.

Social science?

The years between the two world wars marked the zenith of household science's reputation and influence in the University of London and the Western world more generally. The development of connections between household science and the work of other social organisations and occupations was a sign of this maturity. Making such links was another element in Janet Lane-Claypon's contribution to life on Campden Hill.

In the summer of 1920 *The Times Educational Supplement* reported a garden party held by her that was attended by many wealthy lords and ladies. Among the attendees were Maude Lawrence (chief woman inspector of the Board of Education), and two relevant Mr and Mrs's: Mr and Mrs Cloudesley Brereton, and Mr and Mrs Graham Wallas. Maud Adeline Cloudesley Brereton was a trained teacher and engineer, an early member of the Women's Engineering Society, and an avid promoter of gas as a household aid, for which activity she stars in Chapter 9. Mr Brereton taught for a while at the London School of Economics (LSE), which was also the habitat of Ada and Graham Wallas. Graham Wallas was one of LSE's founders and a professor of political science there; Ada Wallas was an author whose clever book *Before the Bluestockings* (1929) restored a number of forgotten women to the historical record long before this had become a popular pursuit.[31]

The Wallases' presence at the KCW garden party was symbolic of the efforts that were being made to cement links with LSE. Back in 1914, Hilda Oakeley had raised the topic of joint courses offering 'social training' in London with Professor Urwick of LSE, and also with the then Principal of King's College, Ronald Burrows, who advised extreme caution because of LSE's sensitivities about the inroads KCW might be making into its ownership of UK social science. On the table for discussion here was the journey social science itself was making from an activity vaguely associated with practical social work and philanthropy to its modern career as a set of academic disciplines. At this juncture, the couplet 'household *and* social science' posed awkward territorial dilemmas.

It was the Haldane Commission which had originally suggested adding the term 'social' to 'household science' in its 1913 Report. Having decided that the university needed to support home science and economics, the Commission proposed the name of 'household and social science', as a title 'which describes better what is aimed at'. This was, however, a rather vague flourish in the direction of a group of subjects whose 'exact nature' the Commission admitted 'cannot now be determined'.[32]

The negotiations with LSE about social training concerned an issue of great substance in the attempt to academicise household science. How much science should there be in it, and if there should be as much as the King's contingent said there should be, how could this sensibly be fitted into courses of 'social' study? In October 1917, the King's Department set up jointly with LSE a one-year course for factory welfare supervisors and in October 1918 a two-year one for social and public health workers. 'The scheme is the first in the country where health subjects are combined with social study', declared the Dean of the latter in her Report, 'and it is hoped that it may become very popular'.[33] The course was composed of 30 lectures covering the 'laws of nature', and personal/domestic and municipal hygiene. The 'sanitary' side of the work was taught at KCHSS and the 'social' side was split between the two institutions. Sadly, this brave attempt to span the health and the social domains didn't last long, and it was abandoned in 1920 when the Ratan Tata Department at LSE decided to extend its own one-year scheme for social welfare workers into a two-year one. LSE was only prepared to continue working with King's if the hygiene and physiology component of the joint course were severely reduced, which Lane-Claypon resisted on the grounds that this wouldn't provide enough of the necessary science. Passions on the subject ran high, even to the extent of generating a powerful meeting in February 1920, attended by Lane-Claypon and Edward Mellanby from King's and by a contingent from LSE containing its new director, William Beveridge, as well as Professor E.J. Urwick (head of the Ratan Tata Department), Sidney Webb (a main founder of LSE), and Britain's first professor of sociology, Leonard Hobhouse. After long discussion, it was decided to let LSE go ahead on its own.[34]

The final step

When representatives of the university carried out their statutory review of the Department of Household and Social Science in London in 1926, they acknowledged its uniqueness and high level of achievement, and were 'very favourably' disposed to the work they saw in progress. They formed a 'very high opinion of the efficiency and enthusiasm of the staff', and were 'impressed by the amount of new ground that had been broken both by their research and by their teaching'. They only had a few quibbles – about the low pay of some of the lecturers and the inadequate size of the blackboard in the lecture room: 'it must be impossible at present to give a biological lecture without constantly rubbing out diagrams'. The visitors also talked to students, noting the particularly charming students' common-room, and the students' understandable desire for better sports facilities.[35]

By this time, Janet Lane-Claypon had departed because of a strained relationship with Edwin Cooper Perry, who was chairman of the Executive Committee, and Principal of the University of London from 1920 to 1926. Perry was known as a 'despot', a 'master of biting sarcasm', and a man who definitely did not respect the Dean.[36] The correspondence relating to the Perry–Lane-Claypon final fracas, on thin almost transparent papers held together with rusty paper clips, shouts of that perennial dispute men have with authoritative women. Lane-Claypon was succeeded by the short (two-year) reign of another woman doctor, Lydia Henry, the first woman to take the Bachelor of Surgery degree, and then by Helen Reynard, a quietly efficient, but not very visionary, administrator who stayed for 20 years.

The accession of KCHSS to the status of an independent College of London University on 16 May 1928, came almost as an anti-climax. There had been years of struggle, and this final apparition wasn't household science as it had originally been envisaged in Kensington – an integral part of a full-blown women's college, nourished by, and in turn feeding into, other scientific and arts and humanities subjects. After 1928, the full name bestowed by the Haldane Commission, 'King's College of Household and Social Science', proved cumbersome, and many people went on calling it 'King's College for Women'.

They celebrated, of course they celebrated. Actually they had been celebrating with a memorial dinner every year since 1923. At the memorial dinner in 1927, in anticipation of the imminent change in status, there were the usual toasts to the king, the guests, the college, and students past and present: the toast to the college was proposed by William Beveridge. They ate a menu in French, the language of haute-cuisine (the menus stayed in French until 1933): *Consommé à la Tortue, Potage aux Petits Pois, Sole à la Tyrol, Crême de Volaille, Fillet de Boeuf à la Toscane, Pommes nouvelles, Tomates farcies, Petites Glaces à la Sautage, Gateau Marquise, Friandises, Gaufrettes* and *Pyramides à la St. Gervais*, all of which must have caused quite a headache for the Household Arts Department and probably a fair amount of indigestion among the diners as well.[37]

Looking back in 1951 on the achievements of KCHSS, the college's magazine deemed it, not only a pioneer college, 'but a state of mind'. Professor Vernon Mottram recalled his own sense of excitement arriving at KCW in 1920 for his 24- year stint developing the nutrition side of KCHSS's work. He had quickly realised the outstanding calibre of KCW students. But, 'were the 1920–21 students so good because they were pioneers?' he asked. 'Times were difficult then after the First World War, but the pioneering spirit gave a radiance to King's.' Mottram lamented the decline of that radiance.

> The great difficulties now of running a home, enhanced by the rise in prices and scarcity of labour, are a challenge to us to recover that 'lost radiance,' to pioneer anew. The application of the scientific mind, of the scientific method of managing household affairs is of greater value and importance than it ever was.[38]

Elsewhere in the same issue of the magazine, students wrote optimistic ditties about the way in which KCHSS was, in fact, not only moving with the times, but shaping them:

> Oh! What a beautiful calling
> There's a course that is steadily thriving
> On equipment that's always arriving.
> They are called Dieticians who study nutritions
> Of food, in their survey of modern conditions.
> Oh! What a beautiful calling,
> Oh! What a beautiful way
> Of nationalising our feeding,
> Everything's going that way![39]

Conclusion

The Alice who stood in the marvellously and scientifically furnished kitchen designed for KCHSS could have wondered at other curiosities, not least the melée of motives and movements from which that kitchen had been created. This chapter and the previous one have followed one story of household science in London as a case-study in the struggles household science faced when it tried to claim a place in the university world. That world's theory, values, practices and people admitted household science to its echelons only grudgingly, belatedly, and, it would transpire, only temporally. The patronage of wealthy people and of patronising men is part of the story. So is the vision and persistence of those, both women and men, who refused to let go of that foundational insight, so radical in its implications, that nothing about the public world can be properly understood without a thorough understanding of what goes on in the home.

8

Transatlantic experiments

By the end of the 19th century housework was advancing into the universities of various continents in various ways. The King's College initiative in London described in the last two chapters was a bold effort to reimagine households as scientific enterprises. How the academisation of housework happened depended on place and culture. But, most of all, it depended on the spirit and energy of the people, mostly women, who pushed it forward. At King's College, Hilda Oakeley, a transatlantic traveller like many of the women encountered in this book, identified the University of Chicago as coming closest in spirit and method to their own experiments in Kensington. On one of her US trips Oakeley had stayed with Alice Freeman Palmer, a history professor who was key to establishing household science at Chicago. Oakeley had also encountered Marion Talbot, the intellectual driving force behind its life as a separate department. I would love to have overheard the conversations of these women. They would have enriched the story at the centre of this chapter of how the University of Chicago also hosted, for a few, somewhat tumultuous, decades, its own experiment in treating household science as deserving of a university home.

Tales of two cities and a few other places

In the original proposal for *The Science of Housework* I gave it the subtitle, 'a tale of two cities'. I'd been struck in my preliminary reading by the parallels between the fate of academic household science at King's College in London, and its career around the same time in Chicago. Charles Dickens's *A Tale of Two Cities* had always been one of my favourite books, especially when I learnt about the true history of Madame Defarge and the other *tricoteuses*, the women who sat and knitted red liberty bonnets while the heads of aristocrats rolled to the ground in the Place de la Révolution. The science of knitting has provided wonderful cover for all kinds of female espionage, for who would suspect an innocent knitter of anything evil? In the Second World War women in the Resistance embedded codes in their knitting with dropped stitches and misplaced purling. One of Winston Churchill's Special Operations Executives was even parachuted into France with her communication code encrypted in a woven silk hair ribbon. Domestic work, intelligently done, can be a form of sabotage.[1]

My ambition to write a detailed case-study of what happened to household science in Chicago was derailed by the COVID-19 virus and by technical difficulties of age and infirmity (mine). I was unable to visit Chicago for the purpose of rooting around in the archives there as I've done for the story of household science in London. Thus my version of the Chicago story in this chapter comes mainly from secondary sources.[2] The resulting holes in the story are packed with a few cameos of other developments in US universities where, as in Chicago, it was theoretical and analytic approaches to housework that were emphasised instead of practical skills – the endless lessons in cookery, microbe-destruction, plumbing technology and so forth that had been filling so many educational curricula from primary schools up for decades. Skipping from one academic institution to another, and featuring the profiles of eight leading American women household scientists, this chapter is a slightly taxing read because the picture it describes is a spider's web of connected threads. The challenge is to grasp the intricacy of the web without getting caught up in it. The eight women were born between 1842 and 1884, and they died between 1911 and 1968. Ellen Richards, whose dates were 1842–1911, is the outlier, the earliest, and also the most well-qualified and original of all of them. She, together with Edith Abbott (1876–1957), Sophonisba Breckinridge (1866–1948) and Marion Talbot (1858–1948) are better known than the others, but this is a relative term in a field where erasure or sidelining is the rule.

Marion Talbot's muddy start in Chicago

The trajectory of household science in the United States was heavily shaped by a piece of legislation passed in 1862 called the Morrill Land Grant Act. This offered land to state universities which would agree to offer training for rural populations in practical fields – agricultural and mechanical skills for men, home economics for women. By that date, the case for home economics in rural areas was obvious to many, including Ellen Richards, who once acutely observed that millions of dollars were spent in agricultural colleges studying the food of pigs, cows and horses, but none, until the arrival of home economics, was spent on studying the food of men (and women).[3] The land handed out by the 1862 Act, 71 million acres of it, had been expropriated, often violently, by the federal government from 245 indigenous tribal nations and repackaged into 80,000 units for redistribution.[4] This is one of many racist themes that contaminate the history of household science – see Chapter 10 for more.

By 1892, 14 land-grant universities/colleges in the United States were running degree-worthy courses called 'sanitary science', 'household administration', 'domestic science' or 'home economics'. By 1900, there were 30 departments of domestic science. Provision was uneven. Some places applied the devious cost-cutting plan known as the Mount Holyoke system (after the seminary where it was first used in the 1830s). Like some of the school domestic science provision we looked at in Chapter 3, the colleges using the Mount Holyoke system profited from the unpaid labour of household science students who were required to do daily housework for the institution itself. The history of academic housework is studded with such devices for exploiting student labour.

The subsidy provided to household science through the land-grant system in the United States helped to publicise the general case for it to be taken seriously in academic circles. But it was the new private university in Chicago funded by the oil baron John D. Rockefeller that proved to be, for a time, one of the most hospitable academic locations for science-based housework courses. The University of Chicago opened its doors in 1892 on a desolate marshy prairie that was rapidly becoming home to some of the most polluted and deprived environments in the United States. Chicago household science was led by Marion Talbot, the daughter of a fiery female educationalist mother and a father who was a practitioner of homeopathic medicine. Talbot studied with Ellen Richards at the Massachusetts Institute of Technology (MIT), and started her teaching career in sanitary science at a women's college in 1889. In her memoir *More Than Lore*, she notes that in this post she was one of the first household science teachers to focus her students' attention on the new germ theory of disease; she told them it wasn't yet generally accepted, but was worth keeping an eye on.[5] Together with Richards and other women, one of Talbot's early achievements in 1882, prompted by her campaigning mother, was inventing an influential organisation called the Association of Collegiate Alumnae (ACA, later the American Association of University Women). The ACA adopted as an early mission the debunking of the prevalent myth that labelled universities as bad for women's health. (They were and are, in the sense that unfolds in this chapter, but not in terms of the direct bodily injury argued then by rampant anti-feminists.)

A sanitary science club started by the ACA sponsored the textbook published in 1887 by Talbot and Richards called *Home Sanitation: A Manual for Housekeepers*. Figure 8.1, from their text, is a plan of the knowledge every housekeeper needs: the domestic pipe system. Decorated with those familiar pictures of U-bends and water-closets, and echoing the wonders of the peppermint plumbing test, *Home Sanitation* used the fashionable pedagogic method of asking questions at the end of every chapter to which all healthful housekeepers would answer 'yes': 'Are you careful not to throw slop-water frequently on the same spot of ground near the house?' 'Do you open your chamber-windows as soon as you are dressed?' 'If you use water from a well, has it been subjected to a chemical examination?' Standards of sanitariness and veracity were taxingly high.[6]

Figure 8.1: The domestic pipe system

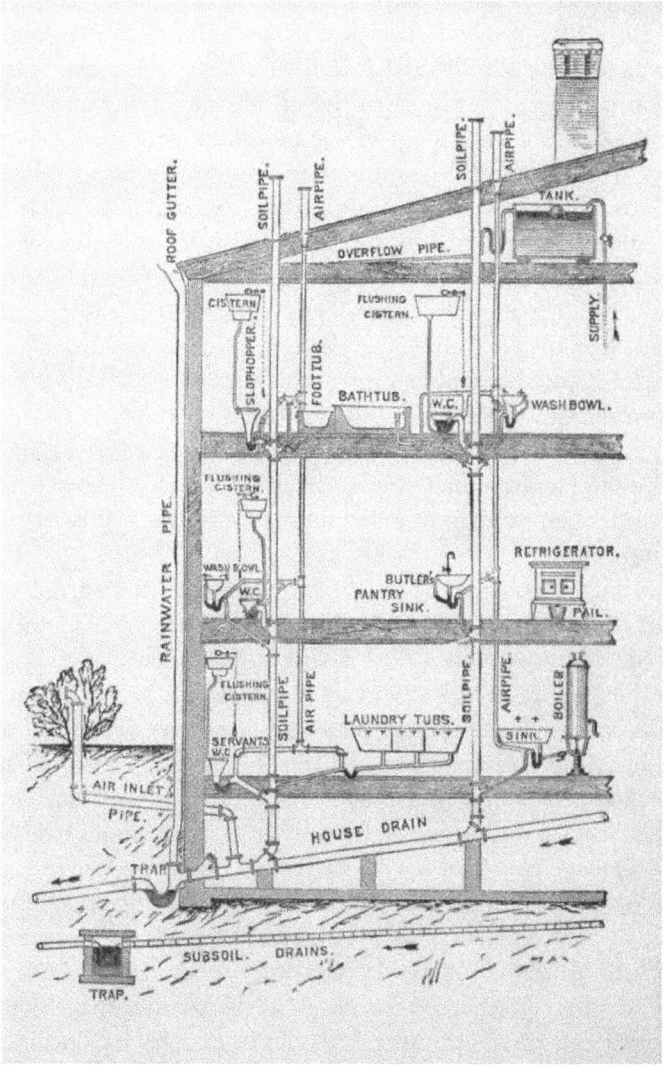

Source: Talbot, M. and Richards, E.R. (1887) *Home Sanitation: A Manual for Housekeepers*, Boston: Ticknor and Company, p 22

Talbot saw the field of sanitation as a social science that would enable experts not only to tackle dirt and poor food in homes but to deal with many central problems of urbanisation – the kind in which the new University of Chicago was itself physically mired. She put the case for the close relation between 'sanitation and sociology' as understanding the social value of individuals in terms of their health and their wellbeing and how these were shaped by material conditions: 'Clean air, sunlight, wide streets, good pavements, public parks, nourishing food, sanitary schools, public baths, adequate housing, are sanitary measures which are most effective in both sanitary and social results.'[7] In her book *The Education of Women* (1910), Talbot argued that the great transitions of industrialisation, effectively taking manufacture out of the home, were giving women the critical new function of 'directing how the products of other people's labor shall be consumed'. As much as 95 per cent of the world's consumption was controlled by women, and this responsibility demanded an altogether new training. Such training, decreed Talbot, must include 'a knowledge of fabrics and other materials, of methods of production, of laws governing industrial processes, of standards of fitness in the article and of efficiency in the workman. It should also', she continued farsightedly, 'include such an appreciation of human needs as will help determine the conditions under which goods are produced, and will demand workshops free from disease, prohibition of child labor, reasonable hours and decent wages for the workman, and simplicity, beauty, utility and genuineness in every product'.[8] What an astonishing summary to have been written over a century ago of an ambition we in the 21st century treat as a recent invention.

Marion Talbot was one of the four people who staffed the sociology department when the University of Chicago opened on 1 October 1892. Actually the department was called 'Social Science and Anthropology' for its first year, but this was a period when a variety of 'social' labels were applied fairly indiscriminately to different activities. The three other initial members of the Chicago department were Charles Henderson, a Baptist minister; Frederick Starr, an ethnologist; and Albion Small, a self-styled sociologist, the departmental head. It was Alice Freeman Palmer, with whom Hilda Oakeley of King's College had stayed, who facilitated Talbot's appointment at the University of Chicago. Talbot and Palmer had worked together at Wellesley College. The new president of the new University in Chicago, a young biblical scholar called William Rainey Harper, was a spectacularly good recruiter, a man who pursued other men with good ideas rather than having them himself. And so he recruited Alice Freeman Palmer, having failed to get her husband George, a Harvard philosophy professor, who was the one he really wanted. The University of Chicago was co-educational from the start, and Harper knew that his brave new university had to have women, although his own preference would have been to exclude them.[9] He appointed Palmer as Dean of Women, and she made it a condition of her appointment that her protégée Talbot should come too. Both women, and indeed all the women who flooded to the new university that was rising from the mud, saw it as a wonderful opportunity for their educationally disadvantaged sex.

Talbot asked Harper for a professorship to head a Department of Household Technology 'choosing the term on the analogy of departments in other fields'.[10] Her plans were aspirational: a full complement of instructors, laboratory facilities, equipment, a practice house (for teaching practical household skills), a fellowship and scholarships, and possibly even a journal. She promised Harper that home economics would come to be given 'a place among the new social sciences as honorable as that which Political Economy or the Science of Government occupies'.[11] The right noises were made by the president and his men, but funds weren't forthcoming. Instead Talbot became dean of undergraduate women and assistant professor in sanitary science in the fledgling sociology department. For a brief exciting moment therefore, the Department of Social Science and Anthropology was actually the 'Department of Social Science, Anthropology, and Sanitary Science'. The novel nature of this arrangement has to be seen in the context of the dominantly negative academic attitude to household science as a university subject. For example, when Matthew Vassar endowed his celebrated college for women in 1861, he intended domestic economy to be part of the curriculum, but Vassar's first president and its Board of Trustees decided that this subject had absolutely no place in a system of liberal education. Their attitude turned out to be a little double-faced, however; when the college had to confront an awkward sewage problem on its premises, the Board of Trustees hastily elected Ellen Richards as a member and asked her to sort it out (which she did).[12]

In 1902, the University of Chicago issued a bulletin entitled *Courses in Household Technology and Related Subjects.* This described the start of 'special courses dealing with the problems of the home and the household' that were intended 'to give men and women, as a means of liberal culture, a general view of the place of the household in society; to train men and women for the rational and scientific administration of the home as a social unit, and to prepare teachers'. There would be 'fundamental' courses in physics, chemistry, physiology, bacteriology, political economy and the study of society. The courses would provide 'a helpful foundation for future duties and interests of householders, owners, and agents of tenements, students of social reform, administrators of schools, hospitals, owners and agents of kindred institutions and practical philanthropists'.[13]

It's easy to hear Talbot's voice behind these visionary words. Her courses at Chicago followed the strictly scientific approach developed by Ellen Richards. Theory and practice were closely aligned, so much so that when the three halls of residence for women students were built, Richards was hired as an expert adviser to 'furnish a dietary' for the female students which would be high quality, properly nutritious and value for money (the male students apparently didn't benefit from this attention). We know that Talbot's sanitary science courses entailed laboratory work because of an invitation she sent out in 1895 to people whom she wanted to visit the new Sanitary Laboratory that was opening on the ground floor of one of the women's halls of residence.

The dawn of a new age?

Marion Talbot's friends were horrified at the idea of her leaving the safe enclave of a women's college for the untested waters and unfinished windy campus of the new university in Chicago. But she saw it as the dawn of a new age. Her friends gave her silverware, dishes and linen, and she bought new clothes: it was almost, she reflected later, as though she had been about to be married. The photograph in Figure 8.2, taken the year of her move to Chicago, is of someone to whom fine fashionable clothes did matter. And indeed, a great deal of nest-building was required as the university rose from

Figure 8.2: Marion Talbot in 1892

Source: Talbot, M. (1936) *More than Lore: Reminiscences of Marion Talbot, Dean of Women, The University of Chicago, 1892–1925*, Chicago: University of Chicago Press

the marshes. Harper may have been busy finding prestigious staff, but it was Alice Freeman Palmer and her assistant, Marion Talbot, who did most of the housework. I mention this because it's true, germane to the mission of this book, and a side of academic life that rarely sees the light of day. In the case of Chicago, it falls through the holes of those triumphal narratives that celebrate how the University of Chicago was the first institution anywhere in the world to give birth to the 'the first great flowering of sociology'.[14] Sociology flowered on the roots of women's domestic labour.

When Palmer and Talbot arrived in Chicago to serve the women students of the university, they, the students and a number of other staff were accommodated in an unfinished hotel building which stood in the midst of unpaved streets surrounded by deserted farm buildings. Makeshift planks led to a swampy campus. There was no electricity and the two women had to cook the first meals for 90 people. Palmer went out to buy chests of drawers, carpets and bedding for the building. President Harper saddled her with many such 'female' chores: finding bargains in linens for the dormitories; buying plates and soup tureens; training cooks and housekeepers; overseeing the construction of bathrooms. Palmer may have been Dean of Women students and responsible for her own teaching programmes, but she was also in charge of the university's academic, student, financial, social and domestic affairs. She counted on her protégée Talbot to help with all this work. This is why, on the evening before classes began in October 1892, Talbot noted, '[t]omorrow I begin my part as dear-professor instead of dear-scrubwoman'.[15]

Both Palmer and Talbot appear to have believed in President Harper's early enthusiasm for their cause, and Talbot talks about him with some affection in her memoirs. She recalls in the early days being summoned by him to play the piano in his house. She took her place at his piano armed with selections from Beethoven, Schubert and Mendelssohn, and he, stretched out on a sofa, snored to the melodious notes of a Beethoven Adagio, which she played over and over again for fear of waking him up. This deference to male authority is a little puzzling. Maybe Talbot and Palmer were playing a strategic game of being nice because they saw President Harper as guaranteeing a bright future for their subject? Or maybe he was playing a game with them?

Doing it together

Accompanying Marion Talbot in her attempts to pioneer the disciplinary rights of sanitary science was a woman whose extraordinary work in law, education and social science would make her a major contributor to American welfare policy in the 1920s and 1930s. Sophonisba Breckinridge's interests centred on citizenship, and she defined citizenship as about the application of science and evidence to the home as well as to the external world. The rights of women, children and minorities; protective legislation for employed women; public assistance for single mothers; juvenile courts – you name it and Sophonisba Breckinridge ('Nisba' to her friends) was there.

Breckinridge and Talbot met in 1893. Breckinridge had been diverted from a promising legal career by the need to care for her family after her mother's early death. Talbot found her 'a little job' at the university, assistant to the dean of women, and persuaded her to apply for graduate study in political science. In 1899 Breckinridge was signed up to teach five courses on the sanitary science and household administration programme: on the legal and economic position of women; the state and the child; modern aspects of the household; the organisation of the retail trade; and consumption. In her unpublished *Autobiography*, Breckinridge celebrated the fact that these courses 'gave an opportunity to use every kind of material of which I could make use. The legal, the economic, the historical and the social implications were all appropriately considered'.[16]

It all went swimmingly for a while, though it was never quite what the women wanted. What they wanted was a centre for research and teaching on the position of women, a centre that would simultaneously unite the health of the public and the private life of households as central concerns. On paper it looks as though a promising step was taken towards this goal when in 1904 Talbot and Breckinridge's courses were hived off from the sociology department to become their very own separate Department of Household Administration. The new department was housed in the College of Arts, Literature and Science – an oddly enormous array of subjects. The 1904 arrangement was apparently negotiated by Talbot, but we can only guess at her motives for so doing. Was this female empire-building for sanitary science, or was it something to do with the growing inhospitability of sociology to the cuckoo in its midst? By 1904 (male) academic resistance to the growing presence of women on the Chicago campus was much in evidence. The proportion of female students had risen to more than 50 per cent by 1902; women, excluded from many institutions of higher education, attached themselves excitedly to this promising place.[17] But it wasn't the utopia they expected; women staff were persistently given ranks and salaries below those of the men; they struggled to get tenured full-time appointments and to have their research and publications recognised. The separation of Talbot's courses from sociology could thus be read as a desire to corral women in a safe and separate place away from the academic centre of sociology. The new Department of Household Administration did effectively become an academic space for women, in the process losing its aspirational identity as a new social science analogous to the other more established sciences by which it was surrounded.[18]

Discouraged by the hostility of the male faculty – and also the bawdy behaviour of the male students – Palmer resigned in 1895, and Talbot took over as dean of women. In her newly segregated department, she was, however, allowed to become a full professor. Sophonisba Breckinridge was appointed as an assistant professor in household administration, and she continued with her courses on the legal and economic aspects of the home, while Talbot hung onto 'the sanitary and social aspects' – courses in social economics, dietetics and the administration of the modern household.

Talbot and Breckinridge's textbook *The Modern Household* (1912) is a product of their teaching. It was addressed to '[h]ousewives … and students of social conditions in college and elsewhere' with the aim of helping them to 'find ways by which the household of moderate income and with children may realise its possibilities as an organised group of human beings'. The book's final chapter, 'The household and the community', lays out a critical new framework for considering housekeeping as a *public* function. Homes kept clean with waste disposed of efficiently are a service to the community; so are children, the next generation, raised with due care and intelligence. Home-keepers need education in 'bacteriology, chemistry, and physics'; a command of economics and the theory of government; and a comprehensive understanding of how modern advertising works. And for all this the ballot for women is as much of a 'domestic necessity' as are the mechanical devices which lighten housework.[19] The ballot was still some years off at this point: eight years and 16 years respectively for most women in the United States and the United Kingdom.

Another leading figure in the US domestic science movement joined Talbot and Breckinridge in their quest to root sanitary science deeply in the University of Chicago's academic offerings. Alice Peloubet Norton was married to a chemist at MIT; her career in household science was the product of Mr Norton's early death, leaving her as a widow with five children to support, and of Ellen Richard's wise advice that this would be her best bet for earning a living. Domestic science fulfilled this function for many women. It provided a socially approved route for earning money when money was clearly needed.

In the Chicago Department of Household Administration, Norton was put in charge of teaching courses that involved laboratory experimentation in food and nutrition. Her text on *Food and Dietetics*, published in 1916, is no simple manual of recipes and admonitions about clean kitchens, but a crammed compendium of scientific data about the nutritive and economic value of different foods. One measure of its scientific stance is an alarming picture of a food-measuring device called 'Atwater's Respiration Calorimeter'. The Calorimeter, shown in Figure 8.3, was a box built in a laboratory to accommodate a man (it says 'a man') over a period of several days and designed so that the actual amount of heat and energy obtained from food could be calculated. It was an exercise requiring precise measurement of both input and output – the latter meaning all 'outgoings of the body'. This sounds like a tricky operation. Perhaps fortunately, not much detail is

Figure 8.3: Respiration Calorimeter, Washington, DC, circa 1915

Source: Wilbur Olin Atwater Papers. Special Collections, USDA National Agricultural Library https://www.nal.usda.gov/exhibits/speccoll/items/show/12257

given.[20] We met Wilbur Olin Atwater, its inventor, in Chapter 4: he was one of the male scientists who attended the Lake Placid conventions.

And then there was the magnificently intellectual Edith Abbott who was given a part-time appointment in the Department of Sociology by Albion Small in 1913. Part of Abbott's significance in the household science story at Chicago is her 40-year personal and professional partnership with Sophonisba Breckinridge. Together they created a model social science in which academic work and social reform were, like their own personal lives, woven seamlessly together. Around the campus of the University of Chicago the two women, diminutive and very properly dressed Victorian ladies – see Figure 8.4 – were known as 'A and B'. Abbott was an economist and

Figure 8.4: Sophonisba Breckinridge and Edith Abbott, 'A & B', undated

Source: Courtesy of Hanna Holborn Gray Special Collections Research Center, University of Chicago Library

historian whose research into the history of women's labour disputed many mistakenly held views – for example that women's entry into the labour force was something new (her first publication was an erudite piece about wages in the 12th century). The example of A and B probably didn't much help the cause of household science on the Chicago campus. In refusing to behave as though work and home are separate spheres, women in such partnerships (of which there were many examples) represented an unsettling challenge to the entire edifice of separate spheres ideology – the iron notion that work and home are both unalienably opposed and gendered. The spectacle of academic women getting on splendidly together destabilised academic heterosexism.

What the sociologists did to sanitary science

In its early years, the University of Chicago sociology department was dominated by four white men: Albion Small (1854–1926), who was there at the beginning and who founded and headed the department for over 30 years; W.I. Thomas (1863–1947), a member of the department from 1895 to 1918; Ernest Burgess (1886–1966), who joined later, in 1916; and Robert Park (1864–1944), the most celebrated, still today, as *the* founder of American sociology; Park, an ex-journalist, arrived as a lecturer in 1914. Nothing in the backgrounds of these four men predisposed them towards any interest in sanitary science, or, indeed, in women as intellectual equals. Of the four, Small was the most pro-women; he welcomed Marion Talbot into the department as a specialist in the home, whose importance for social functioning he said deserved academic study and status. W.I. Thomas, a social psychologist, wrote a PhD on sex differences in metabolism which reflected the bias of its time (1897) in characterising women as more 'atavistic' and childlike than men. From his reading of the biological data then available, Thomas concluded that men's biology predisposes them to activity and violence, while women's fits them for a more stationary life. Thomas interpreted 'stationary' as meaning a domestic life full of housework, which shows how much he understood about the kind of work housework is (particularly at the time, more than a century ago).[21]

Robert Park got his big chance in 1918 when W.I. Thomas was fired for alleged sexual misconduct.[22] Together with Ernest Burgess, Park wrote a highly influential sociology text called *Introduction to the Science of Sociology* (1921). The basic theme of Park and Burgess's text is that society is governed by the forces of competition and conflict. People fight for resources; this creates tension and prompts social dislocation. Both authors were notable anti-feminists. Burgess denigrated the work of women sociologists as without theory, order or importance. Following W.I. Thomas's line on sex differences, Park declared it a 'descriptive fact' that women 'thus far in the history of the race have generally been more instinctive, more intuitive … more emotional, more conservative than men'. He memorably remarked that the greatest damage to the city of Chicago didn't come from criminals or corrupt politicians but from the work of women reformers who were 'lower than dirt'.[23] The sexism was interwoven with racism, as in his comment that '[t]he Negro is … so to speak, the lady among the races'.[24] The strength and ramifications of Park's hostility to women in Chicago were such that when the sociologist Mary Jo Deegan tried to research it more than half a century later, she was told she would jeopardise her own future in sociology if she tried to go there.[25]

The threat hanging over Deegan's academic career as a result of her interest in probing the Chicago sociology story didn't deter her from a little detective work into Park's biography, however. Robert Park's attack on female do-gooders included his own wife, Clara Cahill Park, who, as well as raising their four children, was a social reformer and a significant figure in the creation of federal welfare programmes for women and children.[26] Her husband's scathing observation about female do-gooders was aimed at the other great school of sociology in Chicago, the Hull-House Settlement presided over by Nobel Peace Prize winner Jane Addams. Mrs Park worked closely with Hull-House where enormous amounts of scientific research and practical social reform were carried out by a group of tremendously clever women (and some men). 'Settlement sociology' dominated the universe of new ideas and intellectual careers in the early years of the university at Chicago. Sociology occupied a more peripheral position, although it was the university subject that would go on to be celebrated as 'Chicago sociology'.

These two institutions – Hull-House and the university – did sociology in different ways. At the university, the men were keen to devise theoretical frameworks for understanding social systems and problems, while the Hull-House researchers took a more pragmatic methodological approach focused on understanding urgent social questions in their ordinary community contexts – like, for example, how to introduce scientific practices in homes. One of the Hull-House women, the social reformer and specialist in child welfare, Julia Lathrop, was trained in the methods of the Rumford Kitchen which we looked at in Chapter 4. She opened a public kitchen at Hull-House in 1893 which ran for 32 years. This gave scientific demonstrations on cooking, nutrition and home sanitation, and advertised 'standard dishes made according to scientific rules'. It also offered evening classes for young working women who spent days in stores and factories, and who came to Hull-House after work to be bedecked in white aprons and caps and given lessons in how to boil potatoes and sanitise floors.[27]

In a curious and complex twist to this story, it was another branch of the settlement movement that sealed the fate of household science at the University of Chicago. A charitable organisation called the Chicago School of Civics and Philanthropy (CSCP), which was having financial trouble, was absorbed into the university in 1920 and merged with other campus divisions to become a graduate department known as the School of Social Service Administration (SSA). All the women sociologists in the Department of Sociology were moved into the SSA, and along with them went the Department of Household Administration. Most of the evidence points to the creation of the SSA as an outcome welcomed by the Chicago women social and sanitary scientists. Under Breckinridge and Abbott's committed reign it became a national centre for social research and evidence-based social policy. The SSA thus went some way to realising the women's vision of a university centre that would address public issues through meticulous social research. For several decades its staff were deeply involved with public policy in such areas as immigration, labour, child welfare and social security. In 1927 Abbott and Breckinridge launched the journal the *Social Service Review* which is still in existence today as a site for publishing academic articles on social welfare policy and practice.

Marion Talbot's household administration courses continued to be offered as a separate unit until she retired in 1925. Student numbers taking household science were dwindling by then, and courses in this subject were finally closed down in 1956. It was the CSCP's own agenda of research and training in social work practice that eventually triumphed, reducing the Household Administration Department to a mere shadow of its former self. Today the SSA survives as the Crown Family School of Social Work, Policy and Practice at the University of Chicago on a purpose-built site which includes an Edith Abbot Hall. However, Marion Talbot's emphasis on housework as a public function did linger to shape subsequent work at the University of Chicago. Hazel Kyrk, Associate Professor of Home Economics, arrived just as Talbot was leaving and for 16 years she developed the new economic framework for analysing household work we looked at in Chapter 5. The tradition of economic thinking Kyrk helped to sponsor became an integral part of domestic science teaching and research in higher education in the 1920s and 1930s. So this, at least, is a (partial) success story.

Isabel in Illinois and Agnes in California

Among the other American experiments in academic household science was one not far away from the disciplinary manoeuvres that bedevilled the subject at the University of Chicago. In 1900 one of the original land-grant colleges in the area, the University of Illinois, acquired in a woman called Isabel Bevier a leading light in the household science movement. Bevier led a domestic science programme that stood out from the usual land-grant college practical-skills approach. She had grown up on a farm, gained a philosophy degree and taught at high schools until her fiancé drowned in 1888, whereupon she decided to change the course of her life. She took classes in organic chemistry at Harvard – the only woman in a class of 11 – and met both Ellen Richards and Atwater of the Calorimeter device fame. By 1894 she was studying in Atwater's laboratory where she spent most of her time analysing food products. This was her particular area of expertise: the application of chemistry to the study of food preparation and preservation. She ran the Illinois course for 21 years, building an international reputation as a scholar and a scientist.

When Isabel Bevier moved to Illinois, she was probably in a similar pioneering frame of mind to Marion Talbot eight years earlier when Talbot had transported her pseudo-wedding gifts to the muddy acres of the new University of Chicago. Bevier spent the summer of 1900 collecting ideas, including from the local professors of chemistry and engineering, and on this basis she devised five courses in architecture, bacteriology, chemistry, economics and physiology; an entire course consisting of technical lectures on problems in home architecture and sanitation was also transferred from the College of Engineering to her department. Bevier saw household science as a valuable curriculum for men as well as women. She was angry when she found it referred to in the university prospectus for 1905 as a women's subject.[28]

Bevier's book *The House*, published in 1907, was written as the basic introductory textbook for the University of Illinois courses. 'We have been a long time in learning that housekeeping is a profession for which intelligent preparation is demanded', said Bevier. 'The woman who attempts to usurp the authority of the trained nurse in charge of the patient does so at the risk of the patient's life. Results quite as disastrous to the life of the household may be expected from the woman ignorant of the first principles of household management and care.' Bevier defined household science as embracing the agents, the materials and the phenomena of the household. A large subject, certainly, but 'Is there any good reason why the girl should not apply her knowledge of chemistry to bread, and of bacteriology to the processes of fermentation?'[29]

Bread was a central subject. Wheat is a low-cost source of protein, and 50 per cent of American bread was still made at home, so American housewives needed to know what they were doing. In 1913 Bevier composed a scientific text about bread-making: *Some Points in the Making and Judging of Bread*. It's a good example of her exacting scientific approach and commitment to the value of controlled experimentation as a methodology for household science. The text describes a series of experiments which took bread-making recipes from 12 standard cookery books to test the impact on the finished product of the varying quantities of yeast, water, shortening and salt featuring in the recipes. Three sorts of bread pans made of sheet iron, granite ware and tin were compared, as were the two varieties of 'spring' and 'winter' wheat. Results showed that the type of wheat, the container, the temperature, the time and the water needed all gave different results.[30] Figure 8.5, from these meticulous experiments, demonstrates for the keen housewife the effects different amounts of salt have on the size and texture of bread.

By 1917, the Department of Household Science at the University of Illinois had become a sizeable enterprise. Apart from Bevier as its professor and

Figure 8.5: The effect on bread of different amounts of salt

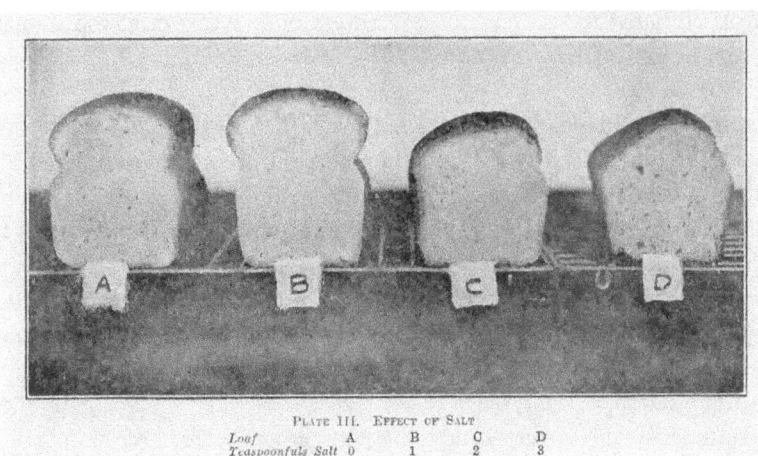

Source: Bevier, I. (1913) 'Some points in the making and judging of bread', *University of Illinois Bulletin*, 17 March, 25, p 21

director, there was an assistant professor, and another 18 women described as 'associates', 'instructors', 'assistants' and 'State leader in home economics'. They and their work were housed in a capacious purpose-built department. The basement contained a kitchen, dining room, laundry and bake shop; on the first floor were four lecture/seminar/class rooms, offices and cloakrooms; on the second floor, diet, institutional and class kitchens, small and large dining rooms, applied science and sewing laboratories, offices and store rooms; and, on the top floor, rooms for sewing, applied art, more offices and a practice apartment 'in which the concrete problems of house construction, furnishing and household administration are studied'.[31] As King's College of Household and Social Science in London carefully mapped the destinations of its graduates, so did home economics at the University of Illinois. Out of 244 graduates in the period from 1903 to 1955, 27 per cent married (and presumably busied themselves applying their household science in their marital homes), 46 per cent were teaching, and the remaining 28 per cent worked as restaurant directors or dieticians, did 'social and religious' or office work, or were engaged in further training.[32]

In her attempt to place the science of the household centrally in the academic curriculum, Isabel Bevier, like others, found herself caught between a rock and a hard place. On the one hand, there was the need to teach more up-to-date methods for *doing* housework; on the other, there was the ambition to dignify housework with the label of *science*. In Illinois, women in the rural community took Isabel Bevier's commitment to scientific principles as a betrayal of *their* practical needs: what they wanted was more *practical* courses in subjects such as dressmaking, not lectures about science. Bevier resisted, afraid that giving in would jeopardise the good name of home economics in the minds of educators. But the educators weren't very sympathetic anyway, seeing home economics as weakening the standards and reputation of the university. President Andrew Draper had appointed Bevier after it was suggested to him that a woman heading a domestic science department could also manage the campus lunchroom.[33]

The highly science-based approach introduced at the universities of Chicago, Illinois, and a handful of other US universities made these household science departments fruitful places for innovative research. This chapter closes with one final example: the University of California and a scientist called Agnes Fay Morgan, who went to the Department of Home Economics on the Berkeley campus in 1915 and turned it into a hot-house of research on nutrition.

Morgan's department was renowned for its very exacting scientific standards – too high some thought, but Morgan knew that household science deserved the same scientific status as the other sciences. Like Bevier, she carried out significant laboratory research on the nutritional composition of foods. Her special interests were the nutritional content of processed foods and the relationship between vitamins and health. As a result of her research, many processed foods became more nutritious and the nutritional effects of vitamins began to be understood for the first time. Publishing more than 250 research papers, Morgan showed, among other things, that a deficiency of pantothenic acid (vitamin B5) can damage the adrenal glands; that high doses of vitamin D can be toxic; that heating reduces the nutritional value of many proteins; and that serum cholesterol levels are related to dietary fat intake.[34] Despite this, Morgan's work was seen as making less of a contribution to science than that of her colleague Herbert Evans, whose study of hormones and the metabolism of rats almost won him a Nobel Prize.

Morgan recalled her original job interview at the University of California: the dean sent his wife and teenage daughter to conduct it. Women in such environments had to be strategic. Morgan, who was married to a football player, waited until her academic rank was secure before having a baby in 1923 – she hid her pregnancy under a long laboratory jacket.[35] Her research programme in nutrition did, however, survive. Like the nutritional research at King's College of Household and Social Science, it developed into a full-blown university department of nutritional sciences at the University of California's Berkeley campus. A year after Morgan retired in 1956, the university used the opportunity to dissolve her department and move home economics out of the high-status Berkeley campus into the lower-ranked Davis and Santa Barbara ones.

Agnes Fay Morgan's scientific legacy is only a ghostly presence in the history of science today, but, like Edith Abbott's, it haunts us architecturally. The University of California Home Economics building is known as Morgan Hall. Isabel Bevier, Sophonisba Breckinridge and Alice Freeman Palmer all have buildings named after them. Ellen Richards got only a lobby with her name on it, at the intersection of two MIT buildings, and Marion Talbot's name is attached to the foyer of a building she helped to design. Perhaps architectural memorials are easier ways of remembering than many other kinds.

Addendum: the unsettling story of Dicky Domecon

The Science of Housework isn't about motherhood but it can't be without a mention of one especially unsettling aspect of household science in America: the use of unwanted babies as student material. In Marion Talbot's original expansive plans for household science at the University of Chicago was something called 'a practice house'. Practice houses or apartments were places attached to household science departments where students could actually practise household skills. King's College for Women had one from around 1908, a flat in Observatory Gardens, Kensington, where final-year household students lived three at a time and got on scientifically with all the usual housework tasks. Practice houses took off in the United States at about the same time. But in North America this innovation acquired an unwholesome character when universities and colleges came up with the idea of using real babies for teaching scientific childcare skills alongside the household ones.

Dicky Domecon was three weeks old when his mother, having been deserted by his father, signed over parental rights to a local child welfare commissioner who loaned him to the Department of Home Economics at Cornell University, which had introduced a programme of practice babies in 1920. The arrangement was that the university could keep the baby for as long as they wanted, with the proviso that he could be returned at any time if the university staff were dissatisfied with him.[36] For more than 50 years hundreds of babies were used as tools for domestic science teaching. There were strict protocols for feeding, weighing and medical checks, and every few weeks each baby would be passed to a new group of students. The babies' birth names and identities were erased, and many were given the surname 'Domecon' for obvious reasons. All the Domecon babies were much in demand among local adoptive parents, who regarded them as superior scientific products. The custom of practising domestic science on borrowed babies came to an end only when the rise of attachment theory in psychology in the 1950s pointed to the harm this may well have done to the children themselves. In case you're wondering what happened to Dicky Domecon, Jill Christman in her book *Borrowed Babies*, who went in search of the facts, reports that he was probably returned to his mother when the Cornell students had finished with him.[37]

How to bury housework

Their work was committed, inspirational and thoroughly meticulous scientifically, but women household scientists in the United States, like their sisters in other countries, constantly faced the accusation from male academics that all they were doing was cooking. An ideological device at the time for trivialising their work, this perception is also behind household science's obliteration from the histories of those institutions that refused to make any permanent accommodation for it.

The so-called Chicago School of sociology has probably been given more attention by scholars and historians of sociology than any other sociological group or set of theoretical ideas. Until the arrival of inquisitorial feminist scholars in the 1970s, accounts of sociology's birth in the United States described a community of disinterested male scholars who classified their studies as scientific, 'objective' and entirely distinct from the female-led world of social reform.[38] This history of 'white male agency' omits, or refers disparagingly and/or fleetingly, to those fields of social research and household science in which female social scientists specialised.[39] As the sociologist Sara Delamont has put it, '[t]he women who made major contributions to research and teaching, who shared the political campaigns of the men, and the research done on women, on household work and on gender, are all grossly neglected in the modern literature'.[40]

This is true of the accounts written by both American and British male sociologists. Here are a few examples. Andrew Abbott, Professor of Sociology at the University of Chicago, published his book on the development of Chicago sociology in 1999. In it there's no reference to Marion Talbot, Alice Palmer, Edith Abbott, Sophonisba Breckinridge, Jane Addams or to the Department of Household Administration. There are, however, several mentions of 'Deegan's polemical agenda to establish female origins for ideas associated with the Chicago School' together with its apparently suspect strategy 'of close analysis of personal relations'.[41] The British sociologists do slightly better (but only slightly). In his *The Chicago School* Dennis Smith gives Talbot one reference (as a specialist in sanitary science). Like Abbott, he omits the other women and household science altogether. Martin Bulmer's *The Chicago School of Sociology* has four brief mentions of Marion Talbot. In the first she is introduced as 'the young professor of household science and later dean of women' (she was 44, compared with Albion Small's 48 and Harper's 46). The second mention refers to her as the possible basis of an unfriendly character in a campus novel. Third, Talbot appears, as Alice Palmer's 'friend' and teacher of home economics, and, lastly, and, contradictorily, as a 'teacher of social welfare administration'.[42]

The last example is the most dismissive. In his article 'Department and discipline: the Department of Sociology at the University of Chicago, 1892–1920', American historian and university administrator Steven Diner calls Marion Talbot's work 'non-academic'. He refers to Edith Abbott and Sophonisba Breckinridge as 'distinguished social workers'.[43] This seems an odd way (even with the prefatory adjective), to describe two women with four PhDs (in political science, economics and law) between them; a record of influencing the progress of evidence-based social policy at both federal and international levels; and a catalogue of more than 83 academic publications in prestigious journals such as the *American Journal of Sociology*, the *Journal of Political Economy* and *Annals of the American Academy of Political and Social Science*. Abbott and Breckinridge's publications also include 12 books published by the University of Chicago Press itself. These include *The Family and the State* (Breckinridge, 1934), *Marriage and the Civic Rights of Women* (Breckinridge, 1931), *Public Assistance* (Abbott, 1941) and *Historical Aspects of the Immigration Problem* (Abbott, 1926). They can hardly be described as social work texts.

The omission of household science from the history of social science follows from the erasure of women, and of the realities of family life, motherhood, childhood, intimacy, emotion and gender. The resulting distorted narrative has been taught to many generations of social science students (including myself in the 1960s), and it continues to dominate as a misleading 'origin myth' in sociology's history of itself.[44]

Conclusion

The instances of struggle in American universities with which we've been concerned in this chapter are witness to the birth of the 'social' academic disciplines that structure knowledge today: social policy, social work, sociology, social anthropology, social psychology: where in this list is there a place for household science? As a subject, household science struggled in what Barbara Ehrenreich and Deirdre English in their book *For Her Own Good: 150 Years of the Experts' Advice to Women* call this 'interdisciplinary mush'.[45] The American case-studies signal one particular strategy that helped to shape household science's fate in this interdisciplinary mush: classification as an 'applied' social science, and then, along with 'social work', as a non-academic female domain. The masculine academic context was crucial, infected as it was with separate spheres thinking. From their preferred role as laboratory- and evidence-based scientists cleaning up homes in order to improve public health, women domestic scientists were recast as nurturant creatures whose reforming capabilities reflected their womanhood rather than their scientific expertise.

9

Sources of power

My mother, born in 1903, possessed one cookery book, a weighty brown, gilt-engraved volume first published in 1927 to promote a new design of gas stove called 'New World'. This stove was the first to possess a thermostat, enabling the temperature of the oven to be controlled; the Radiation group of companies, which produced the cookery book, created a new term in naming it a 'regulo'. The photograph inside my mother's copy of the *Radiation Cookery Book* is an exact replica of the oven that stood in my childhood home, on which the flames would frequently and terrifyingly 'light back' in the draught from the open kitchen door: the new world of gas cooking clearly had some way to go.

This chapter looks at two of the most fundamental of all modern housework technologies: gas and electricity. Along with running water and sewerage, they form the 'technological infrastructure' of housework.[1] The story of their evolution interweaves several themes that are central to the household science movement. One is the impact of scientific-technological developments. How core is technology to the doing of scientific housework? Has technology really reduced household labour? A second theme is how such developments have helped to shape women's position as workers both inside and outside homes. Third, there is the fascinating question of the relationship between scientific understandings of housework and the modern culture of mass consumption. In the period covered by this book, but particularly in the 1920s and 1930s, household work became decisively a matter of consumption. Homes obtained and thus 'consumed' externally produced supplies and services rather than generating their own. They became essential players in a vast market of mass-produced and mass-distributed products designed to be bought and constantly replaced, and that therefore required an equally vast empire of seductive promotional advertising.

In the conversion of 'Mrs Housewife' into 'Mrs Consumer', the struggle to be clean and healthy couldn't possibly be won without buying. And to buy into a state of proper modernity, to be regarded by oneself and others as thoroughly modern, it became necessary to live in a state of highly technologised domesticity. In order to achieve its aims, the industries that sold household technology used two rhetorical devices. First, because housewives worked on their own in unsupervised jobs, the compulsion to do housework as cleanly and efficiently as possible had to be internalised: hence the advertisements had to over-persuade by over-selling what technology could do; and these messages had to be wrapped up in appeals to women's innate responsibility for housework. Second, all the tenets of household science had to be mustered to support the argument that the correct cleaning tools would eradicate germs and bacteria and infestations of all kinds. Advertisers and industry enthusiasts co-opted the labours of household scientists in laboratories and colleges and universities and turned their verifiable scientific facts into seductive, but often unverifiable, slogans. Their astute sales pitch played on the public anxiety about dirt and germs that had been enlarged, if not actually created, by the household science movement. In its extreme promotional versions, housework fuelled by modern energy sources appeared to take place 'in a fantasy land where women, resplendent in their best clothes, languidly operate appliances', as though absolutely no element of physical labour remains. Liberation from housework was never the advertiser's aim; rather, the new technological world promised reduced drudgery and increased convenience. This was 'the proletarianization' of the housewife, not her emancipation.[2]

The period from the early 1920s until after the Second World War witnessed a tense battle for custom between the promoters of gas and electricity (with solid-fuel-promoters intervening from the sidelines) to gain the attention of the overburdened consuming housewife. This was a battle in which women themselves were intimately involved. They formed three profile-raising organisations: the Electrical Association for Women (EAW) in 1924; the Women's Gas Council (WGC) in 1935; and the Women's Advisory Council on Solid Fuel in 1943. Little is known about the last of these, and not much about the second, but the EAW's archives have been extensively excavated by researchers. The three organisations differed in their promotional agility – the EAW was definitely the frontrunner. Indeed, Caroline Davidson in her *Woman's Work is Never Done* reasonably contends that the EAW is 'the only example of women actually changing the conduct of housework through collective action' over a period of three centuries.[3]

One by-product of these efforts to technologise housework was the impact on women's own technological careers. New technical training opportunities for new occupations opened up in which women could safely develop their scientific capabilities away from the critical gaze of men. Women who sought a career in engineering also found the province of domestic fuel strategically useful. These are ways in which the scientific housework movement let women into science through the back (kitchen) door.

This chapter focuses mainly on the evolution of this story as it relates to the progress of gas and electricity in the United Kingdom; the trajectory of domestic fuel's impact on housework differed in other countries (though the key themes are similar).

Out of the darkness with Cupids and hairdryers

In the first decades of the 20th century coal reigned supreme in British homes for heating and cooking. Coal fires and stoves produced immense amounts of soot, which added to housework. Cleaning was dependent on the traditional method of brooms and cloths which, as we have seen in earlier chapters, are an excellent way of spreading dirt. The whole business of laundering the household's clothes was hard labour, and its mechanisation was slow because washing depended on the rarity of adequately plumbed homes. A survey by Elsie Edwards, a member of the EAW, for a conference on scientific management in 1935 found that in three-quarters of 5,000 working-class British households water for washing was still heated using a copper, a gas boiler, or pans and kettles on the kitchen stove.[4] In rural areas, housewives also had to lay their hands on the fuel. In Ireland, for example, turf was the only fuel burnt in 60 per cent of households as late as 1920; the peat had to be cut, taken to the spreading-field, spread to allow its water content to fall, then stacked and taken back to the house.

Ironing was another awkward task. The flat irons used before mechanised ones became available were solid pieces of iron weighing between five and eight pounds; they had to be heated on a stove of some kind, and constantly reheated, and therefore carried back and forth. The following tiring and not very easy account of ironing comes from the American household economist Helen Campbell's *The Easiest Way in Housekeeping*, published in 1893:

> For ironing neatly and well, there will be required, half a dozen flat-irons, steel bottoms preferred: a skirt-board and bosom-board, both covered, first with old blanket or carpet, then with thick strong cotton-cloth, and over this a cover of lighter cloth ... it is better to use a table for all large articles, and on this the ironing-sheet can be pinned, or tied by tapes, or strips of cloth, sewed to each corner. A stand on which to set the irons, a paper and coarse cloth to rub them off on, and a bit of yellow wax tied in a cloth, and used to remove any roughness from the iron, are the requirements of the ironing-table.[5]

For lighting, many in the early 20th century had only candles; wealthier households used paraffin or oil lamps or gas mantles, all of which demanded considerable maintenance labour. Joseph Swan and Thomas Edison brought their electric lightbulb onto the market in the late 1870s, but this was of no use to the 94 per cent of British households that still had no electric wiring by the end of the First World War. And gas lighting, although hot, smelly and dirty, did offer a gentle and localised glow that helped to hide the unhygienic evils of Victorian homes. By contrast, the bright light cast by electricity was less forgiving and more suggestive of the need for scrupulous and continuous cleaning.

One of the earliest British advocates of domestic electric lighting was Alice Gordon, who wrote under the name 'Mrs J. E. Gordon' gushingly about the uses to which the new illuminant could be put if you had the money. Her husband was an electrical engineer; like many wives, she worked as his 'assistant' and learnt a great deal in the process about the trade, so much so that she was able to manage single-handedly, in his absence, the new electrical lighting and power installation he had designed in 1886 for Paddington Railway Station. The Gordons' own houses in Dorking and London were immodest exhibitions of what electric lighting could do. Alice's book *Decorative Electricity*, published in 1891, extols the virtues of 'the scientific imagination' in dressing a home with exotic lights, shades and electrical devices. For the dining room, '[a] suspended light wire frame, round or eight-sided, covered with silk and edged with a frill' was recommended; for the boudoir, '[a] flying Cupid in Italian carved woodwork, holding an electric lamp'. Light shades, like clothes, should be changed regularly, and each lamp should have three sets of clothes: the best one for parties; another for summer visitors and bright weather; and a third 'common one for London fogs'. The switches for the drawing-room lights ought to be placed inside a little wooden cupboard, 'the panel ornamented with Japanese work, a photograph, piece of brocade, or any other decoration to suit the room'.[6] The mistress of the house should keep the key of this cupboard and only unlock it when lights were needed. This piece of advice highlights how the management of domestic fuel, from the cutting of peat to the operation of light switches, was inescapably women's business. Women were the 'energy managers'.

Another of the many texts of the period celebrating the domestic wonders of electricity was published in 1914 by another engineer's wife, Maud Lancaster, who offered another reason why domestic electricity was a good idea: 'The hard-working husband also will find that things have changed for the better', she counselled,

> for instead of finding on his return home a 'neurotic' wife, worn out with the worries of housekeeping and domestic troubles, he will be welcomed by a loving woman, bubbling over with mirth and joy, a sure antidote for all the worries and trials which each man, more or less, has daily to encounter.[7]

The drawing in Figure 9.1 of an impossibly thin-waisted woman cheerfully drying her hair (with a remarkably modern-looking hairdryer) was one of the illustrations Lancaster used to prove her point that electrical women are happy ones. She didn't mention the reality, which was that hairdryers were heavy, not very warm appliances (100 watts compared with circa 2,000 today), prone to frequent overheating and actually sometimes guilty of electrocuting the user.[8]

Early advertisements for electricity often depicted servants who wore black dresses, white pinafores and caps. For Maud Lancaster, electricity itself was

Figure 9.1: The new electric hairdryer

Source: Lancaster, M. (ed E.W. Lancaster) (1914) *Electric Cooking Heating Cleaning etc Being a Manual of Electricity in the Service of the Home by 'housewife' (Maud Lancaster)*, London: Constable & Company, p 256

a servant, and this was a very significant point in those days when working-class women were increasingly choosing factory work over domestic service. 'In its capacity as a servant', Lancaster advised,

> [electricity] is always at hand; *always willing* to do its allotted task and to do it perfectly, *silently*, swiftly and without mess; never wants a day off; never answers back; is never laid up; never asks for a rise; in fact, it is often willing to work for less money; never gives notice and does not mind working overtime; it has no prejudices and is prepared to undertake any duties for which it is adapted; it costs nothing when not actually doing useful work.[9]

This gives us some idea of what middle-class housekeepers expected of their vanishing servants. And the sad truth was that servants at this time were cheaper than electricity.

As the cost of electricity became more competitive, human servants disappeared from the advertisements and were replaced by the 'silent servants' of electrical aids. One 1928 advertisement for a company called 'Met-Vick' was headed 'Your Silent Servants'. It claimed (ungrammatically) that '[m]ost household duties can now be performed easier, quicker, and more efficiently' through the medium of electricity and dependable electric home helps (a vacuum cleaner, a washer, an iron, a fire and a cooker were all lined up in the advertisement).[10] The women who were shown using these modern appliances were invariably well-dressed and smiling, like the one in Figure 9.2 who scarcely looks dressed for housework (the point being of course that modern housework didn't require one to be dressed for it at all). Indeed, the adjective 'smiling' became a generic descriptor for women who had successfully embraced the new technology of electricity. 'The woman in the Canadian home sits down to her ironing with a *smiling* face', enthused Lady

Figure 9.2: Woman with vacuum cleaner smiling

Source: *The Electrical Age for Women*, 1(2), 1926, p 64

Figure 9.3: Annie confused

Source: *The Yorkshire Evening Post*, 11 March 1929

Cowan, the EAW's vice-president. 'She sits down to do the ironing, with a *smiling* face, at a wonderful ironing machine' [italics added].[11] These were times when it was easy to be confused about which button to press when. A cartoon in *The Yorkshire Post* in November 1929 made fun of a puzzled housewife who is attempting to fry bacon on a loudspeaker (Figure 9.3).

A slow business

Until the 1880s in Britain, the main use of electricity was to drive locomotives, to plate silver and illuminate lighthouses. Factories, business premises, public buildings and streets were all powered by gas. In fact, both the electricity and gas industries were amazingly slow to apply any of their innovations to the private world of housework for the familiar reason that housework was seen as something private and unimportant. One consequence was that most women in the 1930s didn't have access to even the most basic appliances. Refrigerators, washing machines, water heaters and vacuum cleaners – all these took decades to find a place in most British homes. This is in stark contrast to durables for leisure (radios, televisions, and so on) where the take-up was rapid. For example, it took 40 years for vacuum cleaners but only nine years for televisions to reach 50 per cent of British households.[12] The exception was irons, for the good reason that ironing was an awful task and irons were relatively cheap. By 1939 over 50 per cent of British households used an electric iron; by 1948, this had become 86 per cent. But in that latter year, only 40 per cent had a vacuum cleaner, and, far fewer, 4 per cent a washing machine, and 2 per cent a refrigerator.[13]

The mass domestic use of electricity is a surprisingly recent occurrence – surprising, that is, to younger people who have difficulty imagining non-mechanised homes. It's not that surprising to older generations who grew up in them. The house in Acton where the New World cooker frightened the life out of me had no central heating, a coal fire, a gas refrigerator and no washing machine until the late 1960s. In the United Kingdom electricity didn't reach most households until the 1950s. Among the many reasons for this slow progress was the chaotic nature of supply: until the standardisation introduced by the Electricity (Supply) Act in 1926, electricity was produced by an uncoordinated collection of small generating stations using 44 different voltages and seven different frequencies. Hence an appliance that worked in one home might well not work in another, so even people who could afford them were reluctant to buy them. Many of the earliest electric domestic appliances were rented. Another obstacle to change was that power sockets took some time to arrive on the scene, so early users of electric devices found themselves taking lightbulbs out in order to get the ironing or vacuum cleaning done.

An electrical age for women?

Caroline Haslett, born in 1895 – a woman of 'immense charm and extraordinary energy' – led a life of relentless commitment to the electrical world.[14] Haslett's interest in electricity was inspired by her failure to excel in her girls' school's version of domestic science (she couldn't for the life of her (like me) manage to sew a buttonhole), and by an appreciation of exactly how laborious housework can be. In the well-resourced middle-class household of Haslett's childhood:

> The kitchen stove burnt coal which had to be brought in buckets from the outhouse, and the flues had to be cleaned and the stove itself

polished with blacklead by hand. On washing days the scullery copper was lit and it took all day to get the piles of dirty linen washed. The frilly white underclothes and also the heavily embroidered cotton garments, which were worn at that time, needed heavy starching and ironing, and so the work of the house went on, sweeping, scrubbing, polishing and dusting, all done by hand.[15]

It was hardly surprising that her mother complained of tiredness. Caroline decided she didn't want to waste her life like that.

And so she didn't. Instead she negotiated for herself a training with a boiler-making company in Scotland, and at the age of 24 she became the first secretary of the recently formed Women's Engineering Society (WES). She went on to be the leading founder of the EAW, a journal called *The Woman Engineer* (still in existence today) and another optimistically entitled *The Electrical Age for Women* (later reduced to *The Electrical Age*). She never married, although she did maintain a long intimate relationship with one Frederick Stephen Button, an electrical engineer of radical persuasion.

The story of how the EAW came about involves another ground-breaking female electrical engineer, Mabel Matthews. (This proliferation of forgotten female technologists is why Henrietta Heald called her book about them *Magnificent Women and their Revolutionary Machines*.) Matthews ran the electrical department of an outfit called the Consolidated Pneumatic Tool Company. In 1924 she presented to the male-led Institute of Electrical Engineers (IEE) and the Electrical Development Association (EDA) (an organisation that represented electricity suppliers), a paper entitled 'The development of women's interest in the domestic use of electricity'. Matthews's paper argued in favour of a new organisation that would publicise the capacity of electricity to lighten housework and bring enormous benefits in terms of health, hygiene and comfort (to everyone, not merely the harassed businessman and his neurotic wife). According to the well-established male engineering tradition that saw everything domestic as beyond the pale, both the IEE and the EDA turned down Matthews's scheme. The WES, of which Matthews was a member, was more receptive, and thus it was under their auspices that the EAW was born.[16]

These two organisations, the WES and the EAW, worked closely together, sharing office space, staff, budgets and ideas, and the electrifying persona of Caroline Haslett who was secretary of one organisation and director of the other. In the EAW's founding year, Haslett had attended the World Power Conference in London, and there had met Lillian Gilbreth of scientific efficiency in the home fame (see Chapter 5). I can't avoid mentioning, in one of those intrusive but intriguing asides, that at the next World Power Conference in Berlin in 1930, Haslett encountered Albert Einstein. She told the *Berliner Stadtblatt* that brilliant inventors were rarely good teachers, so there was a great need for women to explain to women how to use electrical inventions. This was the basic model of the EAW. Her visit to Berlin prompted the formation of a German Women's Engineering Society, which was closed down by the Nazis in 1933. Women engineers can only be a subversive breed.[17]

Selling science

The EAW, founded in 1924, placed much emphasis on science as guaranteeing women liberation from exhausting and old-fashioned methods of managing homes. Its slogan, 'emancipation from drudgery', was Haslett's own guiding aim. The purposes of the organisation were spelt out as

> to make provision for the education of, and to give instruction and training to women and others [about] electrical energy … domestic science, hygiene and social welfare; to promote, encourage and further education and research relating to the use of electrical energy in connection with matters of particular interest to women … [and] to examine persons as to their knowledge with respect to electrical energy and [its] use.[18]

For 62 years until 1986 when it was finally closed down, the EAW brought the manufacturers, suppliers and users of domestic electricity into an alliance that had a huge impact on how domestic electricity developed. It provided electrical education classes for housewives; advice to government and industry; and training for demonstrators and domestic science teachers. It published a series of 'How it Works' leaflets for household appliances, and devised and carried out numerous campaigns. The first was the 'Outlet' campaign of 1928 geared to achieving more socket outlets in homes on new housing estates. An Electrical Housecraft Course, awarding either a certificate or a diploma, began in 1931. Housewives and students could take a Home Worker's Certificate covering electricity generation and transmission; the home installation of meters, fuses and switches; and how to cook, refrigerate, plan kitchens and all the rest of it so as to make the best use of electricity.

Because (again) there was no suitable textbook, the EAW wrote one, under the tireless editorship of Haslett. *The Electrical Handbook for Women* was widely used for several decades, and is a daunting mix of highly technical detail (what electricity is, how it's supplied and paid for, how to trace and repair electrical faults) and practical information about specific domestic appliances. There are sections on how to teach and demonstrate electrical housecraft, and pages of illustrations, many of which demand a fair level of comprehension: take, for example, 'Section of 132,000 volt single core, oil-filled, underground cable' or 'Diagram of shunt, series and compound wound fields'.[19] Most strikingly, and as can be gathered from these examples, the text of the *Handbook* treated women as intelligent and capable of understanding matters that were commonly regarded as beyond them.

Largely as a result of the EAW's fierce campaigning, the subject of Electrical Housecraft quickly leaked its way into household science curricula. In London, both Chelsea and Battersea Polytechnics introduced specialist courses in electrical science in 1927, and King's College of Household and Social Science (KCHSS) followed suit in 1928. The new link between technical mastery (mistressy?) and femininity created by the household science movement flowed smoothly into the production of further educational courses devoted specifically to explaining the array of household appliances that were entering the market. In the United States, the home economics department of Iowa State College was the pioneer of something called 'equipment education'; the college launched an undergraduate major in household equipment in 1929, and by the 1950s hundreds of BSc and MSc degrees in household equipment had been awarded.

In both the United States and the United Kingdom manufacturers were keen to capitalise on the new educational initiatives, and so offered their appliances to academic institutions free or at reduced rents. This practice continued well into the 1940s and 1950s. For example, in 1947 the EDA, acting on behalf of appliance suppliers, made the 'very generous gifts' of a 'single deck pastry oven, 1 R.22 Revo cooker, 2 series N Jackson cookers, 1 GEC cooker, and 1 large size Frigidaire unit' to the Household Arts Department at KCHSS; the Physics Department got a Baby Belling cooker and two Belling fires.[20] These electrical devices replaced the gas-fuelled ones that had, equally generously, been provided on the same basis by the Gas Light and Coke Company.

Anticipating the consumer organisation *Which*, the EAW tested devices for safety, convenience and efficiency, and solicited information from users on the design and performance of domestic electrical appliances. This information was fed to relevant industry bodies. Both in the range of its activities and its sisterhood (Haslett was a committed suffragette), the EAW functioned very differently from most industrial organisations: 'My staff work with me, not for me', declared Haslett.[21] Although run centrally from various appropriately electrified offices in London, the EAW devolved considerable autonomy to local branches. By 1934 there were 47 of these; in 1971, 272. The branches were often managed by the wives of the electrical engineers who ran local electricity supply companies.[22]

What gas can do in capable hands

'What gas can do in capable hands' is the title of a chapter in Maud Cloudesley Brereton's persuasive volume *Cooking by Gas*. The book was published around 1930 by the British Commercial Gas Association (BCGA) with the scientific help of Margaret McKillop of KCHSS. Its red, black and beige cover shows a woman wearing bright lipstick and rouge stirring a saucepan with a gas cooker in the background, and the outline of what appears to be a man in chef's uniform also stirring a saucepan. Brereton was the British gas industry's public relations specialist, the editor of the BCGA's journal and author of its promotional material, a leading figure in the campaign for gas rather than electricity to be the main source of domestic power: the gas counterpart of Caroline Haslett, in other words. Maud Cloudesley Brereton was a member of the WES and the Royal Institute of Public Health and the first honorary female member of the Institution of Sanitary Engineers; she was decorated in 1907 by the French government for her services to international public health. Yet none of these achievements apparently qualifies her to be remembered in most histories of the sanitary reform movement.

Cooking by Gas stirred together a pungent casserole of reassuring remarks about the safety and efficiency of gas and its superiority to electricity – it was cheaper and the user had more control over a gas flame than an electric cooker – with instructions about the cleaning and maintenance of gas appliances. A further ingredient was a repertoire of healthy gas-cooked menus for different seasons and days of the week. For a Monday in summer, for instance, Brereton advised a filling menu of rabbit pie, salad, junket, fruit and cheese for lunch, and milk soup, roast veal, cauliflower, potatoes and currant tart with cream for dinner.[23]

Brereton trained and worked as a teacher, and had five children in two marriages, the second to an educationalist and schools inspector called Cloudesley Brereton. For her, the technology of domestic gas offered a direct route to health improvement. She argued that gas cookers, gas water boilers and gas fires could potentially improve housing and nutrition and save lives. In her view a correctly technologised home would benefit health, the infant mortality rate, 'and all the issues of life'.[24] In addition, women would have their domestic labours reduced in both time and effort. They would therefore have an enlarged capacity for work or voluntary service outside the home. Domestic technology was, for Brereton, what it often, in other promotional texts, was not – a matter of enlarging women's role in the public sphere, not simply of freeing up a few hours for leisure, or the occasional improving lecture. Efficient, clean homes are a matter of women's rights, just as factory workers are entitled to safe, healthy workplaces. Like Haslett, Brereton pushed gas company managers to listen to women, and suggested they should consult with 'well-educated lady advisors' in adapting gas technology to the home.

Switch on to health

Women like Maud Cloudesley Brereton, Caroline Haslett, Alice Gordon and Maud Lancaster all stressed the intrinsically healthy nature of modern domestic fuels, compared with coal or other solid fuels. The health argument was particularly relevant to refrigerators, both electric and gas, because only safe food storage would enable housewives to fulfil their duties as providers of safe food. Advertisements for the British Thomson-Houston Company's electric refrigerator claimed that it was simply the most wonderful health safeguard in the world. It was automatic, silent, spacious, simple and easily cleaned – and it shared the fashionable cabriole legs of the new gas and electric cookers (Figure 9.4). Thus all these new mechanical aids were

Figure 9.4: 'The most wonderful health safeguard'

Source: *The Electrical Age for Women*, 1(13), 1929, p 512

able to masquerade as familiar-looking furniture. In the United States the Bohn Syphon Refrigerator Company announced equally boldly that 'infant mortality would be greatly reduced' by purchase of its product.[25] 'For Health's sake use electricity' and 'switch on to health' were the constant messages.[26] In her book *Household Electricity*, Haslett conjectured that 'perhaps the comfort and convenience of an all-electric home have no small part in eliminating illness, or at any rate in reducing the bills of oculists and doctors to a minimum. … The improved mental health of women with all-electric homes would make a fascinating subject of research'.[27] This is reminiscent of Harriette Plunkett's case that proper plumbing would reduce the need for doctors (see Chapter 4). Indeed, the power of self-help health care (or at least woman-helped health care) to do doctors out of business is another way of phrasing the entire rationale of household science.

The effort to modernise fuel sources in households encountered resistances. One was fear. In the early days of electric lighting, notices hung on the walls of wired homes warned that there was no need to use a match in order to put a light on; underneath in small print it was noted that, 'The use of Electricity for lighting is in no way harmful to health, nor does it affect the soundness of sleep.'[28] Lady Thereza Rücker, doyenne of the KCHSS story recounted in Chapters 6 and 7, shared in this general anxiety about what electricity might do. At least you could *see* the flame of gas, but electricity was invisible, which is why Lady Rücker put plugs in the idle electrical sockets in her home to prevent it escaping and damaging her carpets. Might food cooked with electricity actually be poisonous? The same had once been feared of gas, even by some doctors in the late 19th century. In her manual, *Cooking by Gas*, Maud Cloudesley Brereton addressed the concern that gas might injure food by inviting her readers to cook a milk pudding, onions and herring in the same oven and see if they shared their flavours (even if I had a gas oven I don't think I'd be tempted to try this). Caroline Haslett understood that confidence was important.

> Once a woman realises that a fuse is a sort of safety valve, her fear vanishes. When the electric iron goes wrong or the fiddly parts of a light fitting get loose, what a relief it will be to have the remedy on one's own finger tips, and not to have to wait patiently till a man comes along.[29]

In Figure 9.5, from *The Electrical Handbook*, a woman, unafraid of fuses, is competently fixing one. Nonetheless, there was logic to the women's anxiety. These new machines often did go wrong. Gas leaks and explosions were common.

The double motive of improving national health and making a healthy profit could be illustrated by taking the career of many different appliances/

Figure 9.5: Woman mending fuse

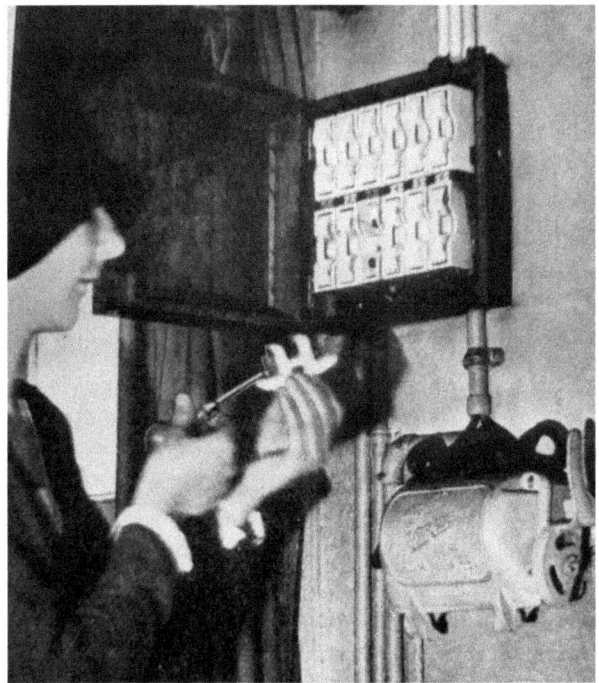

Source: Haslett, C.H. (ed) (1934) *The Electrical Handbook for Women*, London: Hodder & Stoughton Limited, facing p 158

devices, but here is just one: Mr Booth's vacuum cleaner. The prototype of the modern electric vacuum cleaner came to Britain in 1901 when an engineer called Hubert Cecil Booth set up the British Vacuum Cleaner Company. He had been impressed by the demonstration at St Pancras Station of an American machine that blew dust out of railway carriages. Booth's much more sensible idea was to build a filter that would keep the dust inside the machine. He went home and tested this notion by sucking on a damp cloth he had put on the arm of a chair: when he turned the cloth over it was filthy with dust.[30] This was a critical eureka moment for the science of housework (as well as possibly a rather unpleasant one for Booth himself). Suction, and containment of the results in a bag that could be emptied, was an efficient way to remove bacteria and germs from the home and therefore to promote health.

Booth proved this by commissioning a study that was carried out at the Clinical and Bacteriological Research Laboratory in Bristol in 1910. A sample of one gram of house dust from the home of the Princess of Wales was shown to contain some 355,500,000 living organisms, including diphtheria.[31] The royal family had enthusiastically embraced the new invention of the sucking vacuum cleaner after King Edward VII had observed its use on the carpet in Westminster Abbey prior to his Coronation in 1902. Wealthy society ladies threw 'vacuum cleaner parties' at which they sipped their tea and lifted their feet for Booth's uniformed men to get at the carpets. These early machines were large petrol-driven and horse-drawn units that were parked outside the building to be cleaned and had long hoses that snaked through the windows. They were expensive, at £350 – around £55,040 at 2024 prices. The British Vacuum Cleaner Company was awarded a Gold Medal by the Royal Sanitary Institute after one of its machines was said to have stopped an epidemic of a tick-borne fever among soldiers stationed at Crystal Palace during the First World War. Advertisements for somewhat more compact versions of the vacuum cleaner boasted unrealistically about its capacity to solve 'every cleaning problem'.[32]

Lady demons

Booth used men to demonstrate his fancy machines, but the fight for control of the domestic fuel empire spawned a new occupation that was mainly for women: that of 'lady demonstrator', also colloquially (and tellingly) called 'lady demons'. Demonstrators were hired by local energy companies to show how domestic machines were operated and to spread the message of how easy it was to prepare elaborate three-course meals, launder linens and clean carpets once you had the right source of power and the right device to help you.

The practice of deploying women to demonstrate, and thus hopefully sell, domestic technology had begun with sewing machines. In the early 1860s Isaac Singer in New York employed 'attractive young women' to operate sewing machines in the window of his shop. An entrepreneurial gas salesman called Edmund Richmond followed suit in the United Kingdom in the 1880s by hiring 'lady lecturers' to help his business. They gave demonstrations and lectures with lantern slides to illustrate the use of solid cast-iron gas cookers, and they called at gas customers' homes to give personalised advice. Richmond found women to be much more effective sellers than men.[33]

All professions require proper methods of accreditation, and the lady demons were no exception. In 1931 the EAW launched a Diploma for Demonstrators and Saleswomen. This required an examination, four years' experience in a showroom and a test demonstration in front of an audience. By the end of 1932 nearly 100 diplomas had been awarded in England and the graduands had taken jobs in industry, in electrical showrooms and elsewhere; for example, one was hired to demonstrate a new waffle iron in Harrods department store. The role of demonstrator was a career option offering women a gateway to a semi-technical position without the threat of being accused of taking a man's job. To the electrical industry, lady demonstrators may have been saleswomen, but the EAW saw them, and treated them, as novice engineers. 'Here is a promising profession for women, which, while not needing full technical training, may be said to be on the fringe of the Technical World', proclaimed Caroline Haslett in a report for the WES in 1919.[34] Hilda Dover, who attended one of the early demonstrator courses, counselled that:

> Women who are thinking of taking up a career in Electrical Showrooms as Saleswoman must one and all possess a pleasing personality, for however great one's technical knowledge, practical or artistic bent, it is the customer's interest which is required first before advice can be given or a sale effected.

This was potently shown, Dover reported, by one Miss Gladys Burlton who demonstrated how a customer would respond (very differently) to a 'self-opiniated, highly technical salesman' on the one hand, and a 'charming sympathetic saleswoman' on the other.[35] But the lady demons had to be careful. Their semi-professional role alerted the anxieties of the men who worked in the gas and electrical industries; male inspectors and stove fitters were adamant that the lady demons shouldn't be allowed to carry tools or undertake repairs; their role should be decorative – pleasing – and definitely not technical.

Demonstrators are another group which has been overlooked in histories of engineering and energy because male-dominated industry saw them as low-status and marginal. Therefore, we don't know much about who they were or what they actually did. But some aspects at least of their legacy can be recovered today. The celebrated British television cooks Mary Berry, Fanny Cradock, Marguerite Pattern and Zena Skinner all had jobs as demonstrators early in their careers. Mary Berry worked for Bath Electricity Board and she conducted home visits to educate women in the proper use of their new electric ovens by making endless Victoria sponges.[36] Fanny Cradock worked for the Gas Council after a spell selling encyclopaedias and vacuum cleaners door-to-door, having locked her toddler son in a room at home while she did so. ('Everything about Fanny Cradock was preposterous'.[37]) Marguerite Pattern wanted to be an actress but couldn't afford the fees at the Royal Academy of Dramatic Art, so she took a job in Barnet with the North Metropolitan Electric Power Supply Company where her dramatic talents came in useful.[38] In the 1940s, Zena Skinner got her demonstrator training at an establishment called the London School of Electrical Domestic Science and then worked for the Eastern Electricity Board at one of its Hertfordshire showrooms.[39] The London School of Electrical Domestic Science was based in Knightsbridge and flourished in the early 1930s, although it appears not to have lasted very long. It advertised 'interesting, inexpensive courses' leading to a diploma for 'ambitious young ladies', who would thereby be destined to take up 'remunerative careers' as qualified demonstrators.[40]

All-electric homes

In all the rhetoric, propaganda and science written about the modernisation of domestic fuel in the period from 1880 to 1940, the two goals of greater cleanliness and reduced labour are the leitmotifs, the calls to action, the hooks on which everything else could be, and was, hung. But these new machines had, or were advertised as having, an aesthetic appeal as well. 'Not the least of the virtues of domestic electric equipment is its beauty', asserted one of the regular information sections in the journal *The Electrical Age for Women* in 1930. 'Few women can without a thrill gaze on the latest kettles, toasters and other handy electrical devices.'[41] There was, too, the almost-science-fiction allure possessed by all new technological devices. An 'electric moth destroyer' – a hand-held non-sucking vacuum cleaner – blew the poisonous chemical dichloride over everything, and for small children there was an 'Electrical Lullaby', beginning, 'Hushaby! Baby. Mother is near,/Don't you cry precious, take an ampere/Cuddle down, sweet, near the dynamo's brush,/The current will put you to sleep with a rush.'[42] And for the animals: a Mrs Walter Lawson, a regular writer on electricity, turned her attention to 'electricity at the zoo' in an article in 1928. The new Reptile House, the Monkey House and the Baboon Terrace were completely electric, the Monkey House even having its own ultraviolet ray lamp above a swinging perch, while the hippopotami had 'electrically heated baths to disport themselves in'.[43]

Behind all this was the appeal to modernity. To be electric was to be connected to the most up-to-date cultural developments. Thus it wasn't simply the machines that had to be demonstrated but all their connected material contexts. Practising what she preached, in 1925 Caroline Haslett moved into a small flat at 69 Abbey Road, St John's Wood, which she and her engineering friend Margaret Partridge ensured was as electric as it could be. The *Westminster Gazette* published a long article about this venture under the by-line, 'An interview with "Miss All-Alone" COSY FLAT FOR ONE'.[44] The paper seemed more impressed by the spectacle of a career woman living on her own than by her novel electric mode of living.

These were the days when bachelor girls made the news. An 'Electric Flat for Bachelor Girls' was designed by the first female professional architect in Britain, Edna Mosley, for the EAW. It was exhibited at something called the Bachelor Girls' Exhibition in London in 1930. The model flat was small: one bedroom; a sitting room with a dining recess; much built-in furniture and lots of electrical gadgets; rubber bathroom walls; cupboards that illuminated themselves when the doors were opened; and, most wondrous of all, a verandah, 'where the Bachelor Girl can indulge in her love of flowers and where she can enjoy real sunshine in the Summer and artificial sunlight in the Winter'.[45] The promotional material for these manifestations of the new electrical age highlighted their design *by* women *for* women. This point was emphasised at the Exhibition by an unusual notice excluding from the exhibition any man unless accompanied by a woman. The insistence that housework-efficient electric living should be part of house design and construction, rather than an afterthought, connects directly to the protests made about the idiocies of male-led house design we looked at in Chapter 5.

An even more ambitious and much-written about feat was the All-Electric House which was commissioned by the Bristol Branch of the EAW in 1935 by another vigorous electricity campaigner and electric wife, Dorothy Newman, who was married to the Chief Engineer of the Bristol Corporation Electricity Department. The Bristol All-Electric House would definitely have been very easy to look after compared to many cramped, poorly maintained or alternatively grossly over-decorated homes of the time. Its flat, square modernist exterior was matched by a minimalist interior with recessed lighting; more automatically lit fitted cupboards; tubular heating; steel furniture; a staircase balustrade solidly constructed to avoid the accumulation of dust; waist-high electrical outlets to prevent stooping; and absolutely no mantelpieces or other dust-catching surfaces. The kitchen was arranged according to scientific management principles that were guaranteed to reduce the housewife's steps to a minimum, and with a built-in refrigerator and ironing board, a pull-down table and no mouldings that would need dusting. Naturally, the house was laden with electric objects: electric clocks; an electric airing cupboard; a heated towel rail; built-in electric fires; an electric cooker, water heater and wash boiler; and even a small incinerator for disposing of personal papers. Long queues of people came to see it, men as well as women; the men were thought to be mainly interested in the financial side. The house cost £1,000, a sum well-off middle-class families could afford, and it sold within a week. Although intended as a prototype to be copied in other places, this ambition didn't work out as building elsewhere proved too costly. The Bristol house, however, survived, and is still inhabited today (Figure 9.6).[46]

The All-Electric House was in an urban area: rural electrification posed an even more obdurate problem. Margaret Partridge, who helped to electrify Caroline Haslett's London flat, turned to this challenge when ejected at the end of the First World War from her engineering job testing technical equipment for the army (searchlights, X-ray sets, dynamos, and so forth). She set up her own engineering business, 'M. Partridge and Co, Domestic Engineers', and acquired a reputation for not only handling live wires, but being one herself.[47] In Devon, her home county, Partridge exhibited labour-saving electrical appliances to show how rural housework could be

Figure 9.6: The Bristol All-Electric House, 1935

An exterior view of the house, a portion of the roof is paved for sun bathing and surrounding steel rails provided for the erection of an awning

Source: *Design Today* © Courtesy of The Stradling Collection, Bristol

transformed. She was commissioned to install it in many private houses (and three churches). More ambitiously, she established small generating stations that could electrify whole villages. The 737 residents of a village in Devon called Thorverton were the first to benefit, being lit up by Partridge in 1925. It was exciting and hazardous work: cows attacked the electric wires; birds killed themselves on the overhead cables; people fell into the holes dug for telegraph poles; and a factory inspector came across one of Partridge's female apprentices doing maintenance work in a power station late one evening, which contravened the law on women's working hours. But what were you supposed to do when there was essential work to be done and no man to do it? After some struggle, the WES got the law changed to exempt women in managerial positions from the ruling about night work.[48]

What was the point of it all?

When I wrote my book *The Sociology of Housework* in 1974 I could locate only 11 studies that had looked at the working hours of housewives. These studies, carried out in three countries between 1929 and 1958, had come up with varying totals between 51 and 82 for housewives' average working week, which compared with the 77 hours I found among the 40 women I interviewed in London. Of course these were the days before the internet, which would have enabled me to find much more research: a Google search for 'housework hours' done in June 2023 turned up some 23,500 references. Perusing the first few pages of these showed that many were concerned with the endlessly diverting topic of how much housework is done by men.

In her 1935 report on electricity in working-class homes, Elsie Edwards demonstrated that housework in an all-electric home took little more than a quarter of the time it occupied in a non-electric one. Some tasks (cleaning and filling paraffin lamps, making fires) simply disappeared, while others took half the time when mechanised help was available. Yet the question of whether technology was transformative in the sense envisaged by its early protagonists is much more complicated. It is also an area that has benefited from considerable modern scholarship: from detailed analyses of large and small quantitative and qualitative datasets to more popular works such as the American historian Ruth Schwartz Cowan's *More Work for Mother*, published in 1983. Cowan is convincing on the impact new domestic technology has had on housework: the creation of new and more regular and frequent forms of housework – washing and cleaning every day, for example, instead of once a week or less often. Technology also creates its own tasks of administration and maintenance. My own battle with a dishwasher malfunction in the Prologue is one of many such events that delayed progress on this book.

Louise Peet, who started the household equipment course at Iowa State College in the United States in 1928, admitted in the 6th edition of her *Household Equipment* manual in 1970 to great disappointment that there appeared to have been little or no effect on homemakers' working hours.[49] Caroline Haslett, Maud Cloudesley Brereton, their colleagues in the EAW, the WES, the BCGA and the WGC, and all the lady demons with their concealed tools and technical erudition would probably feel the same. While vacuum cleaners, refrigerators, toasters, electric moth destroyers and all the rest were taking their time to become part of housework, ideas about homes and human bodies were shifting to create an even bigger marketplace for 'an endlessly regenerating inventory of products'. There are whole other histories here: of the bathroom, for example, as a newly equipped space for bodily care, 'a laboratory for the management of biological waste, from urine and feces to hair, perspiration, dead skin, bad breath, finger nails, and other bodily excretions'.[50] For the woman in the home, the mapping of the human body as a mass of danger zones added to the hazards of the architectural body, the home.

Conclusion

In a speech to the EAW in 1934, the Labour Party politician Ellen Wilkinson declared that the twin keys to women's earthly paradise were the vote and electricity.[51] Sadly, it wasn't as simple as that – in the case either of the vote or of electricity. Neither political emancipation nor mechanised housework has succeeded in dismantling those beliefs and values about family and personal life that associate women with the moral and actual responsibility for domestic labour. Because the underlying gender schema didn't change (and the household science movement did little directly to effect this), those sources of power that might have abbreviated housework delivered instead new reasons to fill the time available. Yet, like the household science movement in general, the introduction into housework of modern fuels did enable women to claim a new technical competence. With this they were able to challenge male engineers and architects to see homes, housework and women as a domain to which the benefits of science ought to be applied.

There was another legacy, too: the obsession with whiteness. As advertisers of new household appliances trumpeted their power to remove all traces of dirt, so whiteness – of surfaces, machines, clothes, linen, bodies – became, in the early 20th century, the standard to which scientifically-minded housewives should aspire. This spawned a multifunctional existence for whiteness as a bleached sanitary ambition, a moral quality, and an imperialist ideal, as we shall see in the next chapter.

10

White subjects: domestic science in the colonies and other places

Classism is the most obvious 'ism' to plague the domestic science story. The domestic science movement *was* undeniably, to some extent and in certain quarters, about putting working-class women in their place. Imposing middle-class values on 'an unruly, unkempt and ultimately unfit working class' was a poorly thought out route to solving many problems of industrialisation and urbanisation: crime, drinking, poor nutrition, high infant mortality.[1] But classism and sexism are linked to other 'isms'. This chapter focuses on racism, imperialism and colonialism as creeds that have done their part in afflicting the domestic science movement. The chapter is also about the wide reach of the Euro-American ideology and practice of home science: how it was exported to other places, including Japan, Canada, New Zealand and other territories of what used to be the British Empire. The story in this chapter features a multi-faceted cast of characters: two Japanese women advocates of household science, Sumi Miyakawa and Hideko Inoue; the British household scientist Alice Ravenhill (again); a wealthy Canadian called Lillian Massey Treble; two clever Canadian food chemists, Annie Laird and Clara Benson; three British women who developed household science in New Zealand, Winifred Boys-Smith, Helen Rawson and Margaret Dyer; and two very different male characters, John Studholme, a philanthropic landowner, who thought women needed to be educated for their work at home; and an enthusiastically reformist Indian royal, the Maharaja of Gaekwad, who wanted a scientific woman to modernise his palaces. Household science was nothing if not versatile in adjusting to different cultural contexts. However what was versatile could also be inflexible. The same Euro-American-derived values and practices didn't necessary agree with the habits of the cultures into which attempts were made to insert them.

Why whiteness?

In 2001 a Canadian home economics teacher, Mary Leah de Zwart, was asked a testing question by one of her students: 'White flour, white sugar, white sauce, white table manners, why is it that everything we do is *white*?'[2] The student might have added to her (it was almost certainly a her) list of white subjects the overwhelming emphasis on whiteness and how to achieve it that has habitually haunted the laundry sections of domestic science manuals and classes, and that more than linger in our consumer industry today. Why *should* everything be white? What's wrong with off-white, grey, brown or even black?

The student's question made the teacher think. De Zwart thought about the association between whiteness in home economics education and White imperial practices, about the resonances hiding in the awkward land of home economics ideology and the cultural colonisation of other nations. She went on to write a PhD about domestic science education in the 'settler country' of Canada in the early 20th century. Using the example of two home science textbooks written for Canadian students, De Zwart asked how these texts and the subject in general had come to be so thoroughly drenched in White cultural practices. She took as a metaphor for describing the state of home economics education the making of white sauce. This 'bland and textureless' substance occupied so many cookery lessons as the basis of so many other dishes (soup, soufflés, pasta bakes, pies, and so on). Most importantly, white sauce was/is capable of covering up 'many sins, culinary and otherwise'.[3]

Many years ago, sometime in the 1980s, I was at an academic meeting with one female and many male colleagues (the sex ratio wasn't unusual at the time). I don't remember what the meeting was about, but I do remember the men engaging in some commonly used metaphor that was derived from cricket. My female colleague and I didn't understand what the men meant, because we'd never played cricket. So we quietly conspired with one another and slipped a different metaphor into the discussion, one that referred to the making of white sauce. We particularly mentioned the difficult stage in which you add milk to a flour and butter mixture, and if you don't get this right, you'll end up with an extremely lumpy product rather than the smooth glistening white mixture which is the aim of the exercise. The men at the academic meeting stared at us uncomprehendingly (they evidently had never made white sauce).

The starkest and most shocking demonstration of how the rhetoric of whiteness has inhabited and contaminated the household science movement is conveyed in Figure 10.1. In an advertisement from the 1880s, a Black child is being washed clean (white) with Dingman's 'electric soap'. There was nothing electric about the soap: it was a laundry detergent in bar form, not intended for use on the skin, except for skins like this one. Pugsley, Dingman & Co. were soap manufacturers based in Toronto who used racist images in their advertising. Pears' Soap in Britain was another such offender.[4]

Whiteness was both actually and symbolically important. In Japan, where we will go in a moment, the qualifying examinations for Japanese domestic science instructors much emphasised the bleaching of clothes and general use of bleach powders, and the substitution of white sheets for traditional non-white Japanese bedding. In the reformed Japanese kitchen, women wore white aprons to prove their cleanliness. This was in direct contrast to the

Figure 10.1: Dingman's Electric Soap, advertisement, c 1880–1889

Source: It am de stuff: Dingman's Electric Soap / [Pugsley, Dingman & Co.]. Wellcome Collection. https://wellcomecollection.org/works/crbxm7tm

customary role of white clothing in Japan, which was only used on sacred and ceremonial occasions, and was the colour that symbolised mourning and death.

Antimacassars and knives and forks

Training girls in housework and European concepts of domesticity was entrenched in the British colonial educational system. A Board of Education report dated 1905 noted that in the mission schools of the African Gold Coast (now Ghana) it was usually the task of the headteacher's wife to provide girls with 'a Christian training of such a kind as to fit them to be useful wives and mothers'.[5] Needlework was a high priority, perhaps because, as we noted earlier, you need few resources in order to teach sewing. Girls learnt how to make shirts, frocks and drawers; pillow cases and babies' garments; socks, stockings and antimacassars. In Trinidad and Tobago, girls aged seven to nine had to do hemming, buttonholing, patching, darning and herringbone stitches on canvas or flannel, much as I was taught in my London girls' school in the 1950s. While I wondered at the time about the usefulness of herringbone stitches, these mission schoolgirls must have been truly puzzled by its irrelevance to their daily lives (I won't comment on the antimacassars).

Before Mary de Zwart turned her attention to white sauce, she worked in Malawi (then Nyasaland) on the home economics curriculum there. It was heavily based on the British curriculum, requiring students to demonstrate how to make cakes and pastry, how to do laundry using soap flakes, and how to lay tables 'properly' with sets of knives, forks and spoons. And all this despite the fact that wheat flour was unaffordable for most Malawians, few of whom had ovens, cake tins or measuring devices; soap flakes weren't available, and washing was done by the village pump or in the river; and meals involved eating tidily with one's hands. The conflict between the curriculum of scientific home economics and indigenous student experience is aptly recalled by Mildred Barnes Griggs who was the first African American to rise through the ranks as a teacher of home economics in the 1970s at Isabel Bevier's University of Illinois. During her time as a student, Griggs lied about the food her family ate at home when called upon to report it in a nutrition class, 'because our food, collards, turnip greens, butterbeans, teacakes, molasses, catfish, sweet potato pie, etc. were never mentioned in our books'. Instead, she simply copied out some of the items in the class textbooks they were using.[6]

Housework as a modernising project

The idiocy of assuming that other cultures housekeep in the manner of Europeans or Americans is well-illustrated in the fascinating case-study of scientific housework education in Japan. The Japanese had no word for 'housewife' until the 1870s when American and British books about home economics began to be translated. The term *shufu*, meaning 'the economic manager of the household and supervisor of domestic affairs', was created to fill this gap.[7] Christine Frederick's ideas of efficiency had permeated domestic science education in Japan by the 1920s, and had assumed a key role in a much larger agenda of national modernisation that was being promoted by intellectuals and political leaders. Before the Meiji era (1868–1912), there was no state education for girls and women. When girls' schools started to be introduced in the 1870s, they were organised on the 'good wife and wise mother' principle: state-sanctioned gender inequality. A huge publicity stunt called the Japan-British Exhibition that was held in London for five months in 1910 effectively advertised this. The exhibition site gave its name to an area called 'White City' (because of its white-painted steel and concrete buildings).

Housekeeping in Japan was a matter of elaborate tea ceremonies and flower-arranging. It was a vehicle for the reiteration of traditional values and customs. Being a good wife and wise mother was an onerous business that was definitely not catered for in the housework manuals written by European and American household scientists. Caring for the household's clothes, for example, meant the cleaning of kimonos, but these had to be taken apart for washing and then re-sewn for wearing, which didn't happen to European clothes. The sort of domestic technology that was being avidly promoted in the early 20th century in the West didn't mesh well with Japanese habits. Much housework in Japan, including cooking, was done from kneeling or squatting positions. Thus technology companies, ever inventive in their pursuit of profit, had to design gas equipment for Japanese kitchens that could be set low on the floor, and they had to promote gas-burning rice cookers in place of the large Western-style gas ovens that didn't suit Japanese culinary customs.

Two Japanese pioneers

Among the Japanese educators who grappled with the kimono problem were two astonishing women, Sumi Miyakawa and Hideko Inoue, who were both born in 1875.[8] Miyakawa came from a peasant family and had the misfortune of a large birthmark on her left cheek which was said to make her unmarriageable. She wanted to be a doctor, but her brother, who was one, told her this was too difficult for women, so she trained to be a teacher instead. An Act of 1899 required all Japanese secondary schools to have a new subject called household affairs. Miyakawa started teaching this, and in 1902 she won a government scholarship to travel and find out more about the teaching of domestic science in other countries. For this, she arrived first in London, and later took in Belgium, France, Germany and Holland. Hideko Inoue's background was quite different, though she was equally passionate about the teaching of household affairs and equally well-travelled: Inoue came from an elite family, and went to a boarding school. She became friendly with two founders of the Japan Women's University which opened in 1901 with three departments covering English and Japanese lierature and home economics. By then married and a mother, Inoue enrolled as one of the first home economics students. When she graduated and expressed a desire to study the teaching of domestic science abroad, it was suggested that she do this in the United States, at Teachers College, Columbia University, and in Chicago.

Hideko Inoue

Hideko Inoue's work demonstrates the internationalism of the household science movement particularly well, and also its links to other female reform initiatives such as the international peace movement. The photograph in

Figure 10.2: Marian Irwin and Hideko Inoue at a peace conference in 1921

Source: National Photo Company, Library of Congress, Prints & Photographs Division, https://www.loc.gov/pictures/item/2016831797/

Figure 10.2 captures Inoue, demure in thoroughly Western costume as a retreat from the time-consuming kimonos, together with her secretary, Marian Irwin, a science graduate of Bryn Mawr College in the United States. They look unsmilingly at the photographer in a moment snatched from their attendance at the Women's World Conference on Arms Limitation in Washington, DC in 1921.

Hideko Inoue believed that women had a distinctive part to play in social reform, and she saw home economics as a gender-specific subject that would enhance Japan's progress to modernity. Her first trip to the United States was in 1908. At Teachers College, Columbia University, she investigated the nutritional value of foodstuffs and took a household chemistry course and a course on housekeeping in institutional settings. She was one of the 143 home economists who attended the first meeting of the American Home Economics Association that same year, and this was what finally convinced her of the great future home economics could have in academia. The advanced scientific level of the US courses impressed her – the emphasis on observation and experiment, the reliance on inductive reasoning. She deemed this approach unimaginable in Japan and therefore an imperative aim for the future.

Among the University of Chicago courses Inoue took in order to learn about American household science was one called 'contemporary society in the United States' with George Vincent, a sociologist and one of the male minority who had attended the original Lake Placid conferences. There's no mention in the available sources of Hideko Inoue having met Marion Talbot, the leader of household science on the University of Chicago campus, during her time there, but she surely must have done. That year, 1908, was when Talbot withdrew her Household Administration enterprise from the Department of Sociology and Anthropology, an event that would have been a topic of conversation between the two women. Inoue also visited some of the elite women's colleges in the Eastern United States, such as Vassar, recording the 'disrespectful ridicule' of the staff at such places once they discovered her concern for domestic science as a university subject: 'It was unthinkable for them to include domestic science in their curriculum since they assumed that it would irrevocably degrade the institutional prestige.'[9]

As a result of her visit to the United States, Inoue acquired a sociological understanding of how women's household work changed with industrialisation: how it is shaped by external material conditions; and how the health and welfare of modern nation-states requires it to be done much more scientifically. Also in this period, Inoue travelled to the United Kingdom, France, Germany and Russia. British domestic science education didn't impress her with its focus on manual training and a decided scarcity of scientific theorisation. But all these other countries offered women what Japan didn't: access to university education. For Inoue, then, issues about women's opportunities in the public world were deeply embroiled in the mission to scientise domestic work, and both these concerns were in turn part of the greater ambition to reform world politics so as to make it more woman-friendly, less war-prone and more aligned with international welfare and well-being goals. She thus saw home economics as 'an interdisciplinary science of human living activities'. In her book *Household Administration* (1928), the first such to be published in Japan, she wrote about systematising and rationalising households through 'a total coordination of not only clothing, food and shelter, but also family members' labors and social lives'.[10]

Returning to Japan in 1910, Inoue worked as a professor and head of the home economics department at the Japan Women's University. There she invented a 'domestic affairs' curriculum which taught cookery, clothing and shelter through the basic sciences. This was the first such university-level course in the country. She also founded a Home Economics Research Institute with laboratories for cooking, laundry and sewing. She built herself a Western-style house with three stories and 13 rooms in order to demonstrate her own personal break with tradition. Her second trip to the United States (which also took in Europe and China), motivated Inoue to propose that her home economics courses should be renamed a Faculty of Science, with two programmes devoted to food science and child development – the two areas where she'd observed on her return visit to the United States that real progress was being made.

Hideko Inoue struggled for years to get her approach to household science accepted in the Japanese higher education system. The extreme conservatism of Japanese society and the state with respect to women's position were obstacles household science in Europe and America didn't have to face in quite the same way. But Inoue kept going. In 1954, at the age of 79, she was back in the United States touring home economics departments and picking up ideas about how to integrate the physical sciences, information about new household appliances, and modern audio-visual materials into Japanese home economics teaching.

Sumi Miyakawa

Sumi Miyakawa similarly benefited from the turn-of-the-century policy in Japan to include the subject of household affairs in all female secondary school curricula. She taught the subject at the Women's Higher Normal School in Tokyo and won a three-year government scholarship to research the subject in the United Kingdom. Arriving in London in 1902, six years before Hideko Inoue, she expected to find home economics thoroughly embedded in the British university system and was surprised to find it missing. She went to Bedford College to study hygiene teaching for the first few months, and she also attended training courses in laundry, cookery and sewing at Shoreditch Technical Institute. Next, Miyakawa enrolled on a course to train domestic science teachers at Battersea Polytechnic Training School of Domestic Economy. There the subject was treated largely as a practical discipline: three-quarters of the curriculum was occupied by cookery, laundry and needlework as manual skills. Unable to return to Japan at the end of the three years because of the Russo-Japanese War, Miyakawa stayed in Europe for a further year. Like Inoue, she went to find out what they were doing in other European countries. On her return to the United Kingdom she went back to Bedford College which prepared women for work as sanitary inspectors. Here she got a thoroughly scientific education – chemistry, physics, bacteriology and physiology – of the sort that was beginning to be provided at King's College for Women (KCW) in Kensington. After acquiring her sanitary inspector's certificate, Miyakawa worked as one for a while before returning in 1907 to her project of modernising domestic science teaching in Japan.

Back in Tokyo, she was appointed as a professor in the Department of Arts and Crafts at the Women's Higher Normal School. What followed was a period of increasing dissatisfaction with the institution, as her requests for resources (metal basins for laundry instruction, a drying room) were rejected by the all-male school administrators and professors as unnecessary, and likely to lead to trouble, were students to compare such facilities with their own under-equipped homes. Miyakawa published several domestic science texts between 1910 and 1917 which capably meshed Japanese tradition with Western ideas about housing and clean homes. How to clean carpets was covered, for example, as these were beginning to infiltrate elite Japanese homes, although most would still have used *tatami* (rush mats) as flooring. In her second book, she outlined her view of the role scientifically managed households had to play in national prosperity: 'The household is a fundamental component of the state,' she wrote. 'Accordingly, national expansion, strength, and prosperity totally depend on efficient management of every single household.'[11]

In the middle of all this, Miyakawa defied her family's prediction of her unmarriageability and acquired as a husband a widower in the Imperial Guard of Japan. This enabled her to write her textbooks from the new highly respected perspective of a married *shufu*. But sadly she had only six years in this role before her husband died of pneumonia. At this point, she gave up on the Women's Higher Normal School's reluctance to support her domestic science project, and in 1923 she started a private academy, an Institute of Domestic Science, in her own home.

The new Institute prospered when Miyakawa was able to purchase a plot of land for a purpose-built domestic science college. Here she installed model kitchens, being careful to adapt the British model to cater for Japanese customs. But she actively contested the traditional sitting, kneeling and squatting positions for housework, arguing that they were both inefficient and unhygienic. Her Institute of Domestic Science, which opened in 1925, had professors of nutrition, architecture, chemistry and psychology from the Tokyo Imperial University teaching in it, as well as instructors with 'professional housewife experiences'.[12]

Like KCW in London, Miyakawa's Institute of Domestic Science catered for at least two distinct groups of students: women who planned teaching careers and those whose aspirations were to be more effective housewives. The former could take a three-year teaching programme, while for the latter she provided shorter courses that were very popular with parents who wanted more marriageable daughters. A fascination with domestic technology accompanied Miyakawa's focus on practical skills. She imported an electric washing machine from the United States in 1928, and, believing that efficient housekeeping entailed being able to drive, she bought a second-hand Nissan car the following year so she could give her students driving lessons. A particularly successful aspect of her Institute's curriculum was the sewing course which catered for the change in female employment in Japan. The expansion in numbers of women teachers, nurses, telephone operators, department store clerks and so forth meant much more demand for Western-style clothes. Like Hideko Inoue, Sumi Miyakawa persisted in her ambition to modernise Japanese housework for as long as she could, in fact until a massive bombing raid on Tokyo by the United States in March 1945 destroyed her Institute.

Domestic science in the settler colonies of Canada and New Zealand

Personal reasons were responsible for another international export of British household science teaching – to Canada. The unflagging advocate of academic household science, Alice Ravenhill, moved there together with her sister, Edith, in 1910, in order to help her divorced brother and his son reinvent themselves as farmers. Alice and Edith took their furniture, pictures, silver, glass, china, a small grand piano and 1,000 books to Vancouver Island via the Panama Canal route. They also took a fruit and vegetable presser, a steam pressure cooker and a vacuum cleaner, expecting Canada to provide an empire of other household devices, but being surprised, when they got there, at the total absence in Canada of a housewares industry.

The arrival in Canada of an internationally renowned expert with a lifelong commitment to improving the efficiency and health of the home proved very welcome. Alice Ravenhill soon found herself much in demand as a speaker to women's organisations and as a writer of government domestic science propaganda. The pamphlets she wrote for the Women's Institutes and the British Columbia Department of Agriculture repeated the educational messages she had spread in her home economics work in Britain: invaluable tips such as leaving windows open to encourage air circulation; washing one's hair every two or three weeks (only!) with rain-water and good quality soap; thoroughly masticating food to prevent tooth decay; and dosing children with rhubarb to avoid constipation, 'the chief physical sin of women'. These items of advice were mixed with extremely specific instructions about how to make an earth-closet and how to use the results to grow cabbages.[13]

Building on her KCW experience, Ravenhill worked towards creating the first home economics degree at the University of British Columbia in 1943. After that, she turned to a different project to occupy the last decades of her life. Performing an important service for Canada's native Indian culture, she taught herself all about indigenous arts and crafts and took on the task of incorporating these in the educational curriculum. She wrote two books, *The Native Tribes of British Columbia* (1938) and *A Corner Stone of Canadian Culture: An Outline of the Arts and Crafts of the Indian Tribes of British Columbia* (1944). Lady Tweedsmuir, the wife of Canada's Governor-General and a friend of Ravenhill, gave a copy of Ravenhill's *The Native Tribes of British Columbia* to the Queen Consort of Great Britain. The royal stamp of approval which was so marked in the early stages of the household science movement in England had no difficulty crossing national borders.

Housework in stained glass windows

One of the things Alice Ravenhill was asked to do in Canada was to speak in January 1913, at the official opening of a new household science building at the University of Toronto. The building still stands there today, an imposing mock-classical affair with the words 'DEPARTMENT OF HOUSEHOLD SCIENCE' inscribed behind its huge iconic columns. Today the building houses the Department of Classics and the Centre for Medieval Studies, with (appropriately) a shopping centre in the basement. In 1913, when it opened, it was plausibly the grandest building in the world devoted to this challenging subject of housework. In it were classrooms, offices and laboratories, and, serving the general cause of women's education, a gymnasium and a pool for female students who weren't allowed to access the main university facilities until the 1970s.

The most remarkable architectural aspect of the Department of Household Science building in Toronto was the three brightly coloured stained glass windows that greeted you above the main staircase in the entrance hall. They were designed by the British pre-Raphaelite artist Henry Holiday, who is also responsible for the stained glass figures in the famous Brunel memorial window in Westminster Abbey. His three panels in Toronto feature housework, which is unusual for stained glass windows. Stylised Egyptian figures perform the household activities of food production, textile manufacture and clothing care. The ratio of men to women in these is possibly a little unrealistic: in the food window, two men are cooking a goose, and in the clothes window a man and a woman are washing linen together while two other men are ringing out the wet linen. Nonetheless, the magnificence of the windows is arresting. As you mount the central staircase, it's a portent of the architectural splendours to come (see Nile Scribes: https://nilescribes.org/2017/10/21/stained-egyptian-glass-wind ows-at-lillian-massey-building/).

For all of this grandeur, the University of Toronto had a woman called Lillian Massey Treble (usually referred to as 'Lillian Massey') to thank. She paid for the building out of money inherited from her wealthy industrialist father. Getting household science finally incorporated in the university curriculum was as much her ambition as it was Sumi Miyakawa's or Hideko Inoue's or Marion Talbot's or Alice Ravenhill's. The four-year BSc in household science that she worked to introduce at the University of Toronto in 1902 had its origins in Massey's own (literally) kitchen-garden philanthropy, which had provided gardening, cooking and sewing classes for working-class girls in Toronto. Since these failed to have the impact Massey desired (here, as elsewhere, the poor didn't take kindly to the sermons of the rich), she moved on to set up the Lillian Massey School of Household Science, and it was this that formed the basis of the faculty inhabiting the grand building with the gender-misleading stained glass windows.[14]

Like other university departments of domestic science, the one in Toronto was the first in the university to have any female professors. Two outstanding women scientists were hired to run the household science courses, Annie Laird and Clara Benson. Laird did her job as director for a magnificent 34 years and Benson, who headed the food chemistry section, held onto hers for 20. In 1920 they succeeded in introducing a master's degree in nutrition which marked the path the faculty was taking to specialise in nutrition, a path that paralleled the disciplinary journey of KCW in London.

In 1915, Annie Laird was interviewed for the magazine *Maclean's*. The interview took place in her 'pleasant apartment', with 'the best and latest textbooks' on the shelves. 'Miss Laird', wrote the interviewer, 'is still a young woman [she was 45], and of a very lovely presence, over medium height, with the gentle voice and manner associated with some strong and tenacious natures'. Clara Benson was also present at the interview, a 'tall, handsome, capable, versatile, agreeable' woman, and a 'Miss E. M. Eadie, who is described as a lecturer in household science in the department' with the background of a year spent at KCW in London.[15]

The Toronto household science degree was just as scientific as the one KCW developed. Both stressed the science behind housework through dietary studies and experimental laboratory work. Laird was proud of the fact that the whole south wing of the Lillian Massey building was devoted to laboratories, for, 'it is just as impossible to teach household science without laboratory work as to teach physics and chemistry without it'.[16] In an ideal world, neither she nor Benson would have been tucked away in a household science department. They were both distinguished food scientists. Laird began her training at the Drexel Institute in Philadelphia, and then, after her first degree at the University of Toronto, she moved straight to a PhD on the erudite topic of *The Rates of the Reactions in Solutions Containing Ferrous Sulphate, Potassium Iodide, and Chromic Acid*. Unable, as a woman, to find work as a physical chemist, Benson joined Laird initially as a food science demonstrator at the Lillian Massey School of Domestic Science. In 1906 she was the sole female founder of the American Society for Biological Chemistry (now the American Society for Biochemistry and Molecular Biology). At the Faculty of Household Science, where she rose to head her own Department of Food Chemistry, Benson specialised in the chemistry of seafood. She was part of a group that carried out groundbreaking investigations into fish and fish products for the Biological Board of Canada. Her strong research and public service record won her a place in various editions of the encyclopaedic *American Men of Science*, although she was neither American nor a man (women were added to the title in 1971).[17] Clara Benson is remembered chiefly for an unlikely discovery, made during the First World War, that the same process can be used to analyse the chemical properties of food and explosives. It does seem peculiar that a tomato and mortar powder have anything in common, but her disclosure was rapidly taken up by munitions laboratories which found it helpful.

Tactful woman wanted

In New Zealand household science arrived in the early 1910s courtesy of three British women: Winifred Boys-Smith, a Cambridge-educated natural scientist, and two women who had studied and taught at King's College of Household and Social Science (KCHSS), Helen Rawson and Margaret Dyer. The site for Boys-Smith and Rawson's work was Otago, one of the four constituent colleges that made up the University of New Zealand. Dyer, who had headed the Department of Household Arts at KCHSS, joined them in 1924 as New Zealand's first Inspector of Domestic Subjects.

As with the story of how KCHSS developed, male support played a crucial role in the early stages of the New Zealand initiative. A wealthy farmer and philanthropist, John Studholme, shared with his friends, Dr Frederick Truby King of baby-care fame, and Ferdinand Batchelor, a surgeon, the same belief that had motivated Dr John Atkins to fund-raise for domestic science in Kensington: that training in household science would lead to the better management of homes, more successful child-rearing and general improvements in the national health. In 1909, Studholme offered to fund a university domestic science department in New Zealand at the rate of £300 a year for the first four years, plus £75 for a laboratory.

There were two immediate problems. One was the usual obstacle of academic opposition – the men who argued that domestic science belonged in technical schools, not in universities. The second problem was that New Zealand lacked a suitable woman (they thought it should be a woman) to head this enterprise. In a letter to the chancellor of Otago University, which would house the new department, Studholme spelt out what the ideal candidate for the post would need: a background in all the basic sciences, and expert knowledge in all the relevant subjects (household chemistry, food production, manufacture, and preparation, nutrition and dietetics, domestic hygiene, textiles and needlework, house structure and sanitation). In addition, said Studholme, perhaps sensing the battles ahead:

> [S]he must have considerable force of character, the power of organisation and initiation, a temperament that will be braced rather than depressed by opposition, a pleasing personality, a considerable amount of tact, and adaptability, facility in public speaking, and lastly if she is to convince others of the value of her work she must herself have vision and enthusiasm and an intense conviction of its value.[18]

In other words, she needed to tick an awful lot of boxes. But Studholme's formula for the ideal candidate does describe most of the women household scientists who populate *The Science of Housework*.

John Studholme went to the United States in 1907 to search for the right woman to launch domestic science as a university subject in New Zealand. There he coincided with Winifred Boys-Smith, who had won a travelling scholarship to visit domestic science departments in the United States. Since she presumably met the stringent criteria Studholme outlined in his letter to the chancellor, Boys-Smith sailed to New Zealand in 1910 to settle in the socially conservative community of Dunedin on the South Island, together with her partner, Mary Jenkins, who is described as her 'companion-secretary',[19] providing another opportunity for the men to get upset by successful female partnerships. Boys-Smith took her post, of professor of home science and the domestic arts, at £500 a year, £350 less than the men were paid.

Boys-Smith, the first female university professor in New Zealand, introduced both a diploma and degree course in home science in 1911. These were housed initially in a tin shed that had belonged to the School of Mines. The curriculum for both courses was thoroughly scientific, on the British model, with lessons in science, food and nutrition, cookery, needlework, hygiene, and home and institutional management. Professors from the medical school taught the same science courses in the home science department as they did for the intermediate examination in medicine – physics, inorganic chemistry, bacteriology, biology, physiology and public health. There were 26 students at the beginning; by 1920, 71 were studying for the home science degree. Boys-Smith's deliberate emphasis on science derived both from her genuine conviction that home management needed to be more scientific, and from her pragmatic desire to silence those male academic critics who thought the home totally inappropriate as a university subject. For this it was essential to make the same points over and over again, that household science was a science like any other, and that the academic women who taught it weren't on campus merely to cook and generally make life comfortable for the other staff and students.

Soon after arriving, Boys-Smith was joined by Helen Rawson as an assistant lecturer at £250 a year. Rawson, a cotton-spinner's daughter from Yorkshire, came fresh from her postgraduate diploma in home science at KCHSS. She was hired to teach applied chemistry and household and social economics and she took over as head of the Home Science Department when Boys-Smith left in 1920. The reasons for Boys-Smith's departure are unclear, though there are references to her having to face 'considerable academic opposition'.[20] The university administrators were inflexible, persisting in treating home science as an inferior subject, and starving it of resources. In addition, imposed on all these scholarly women was the extra burden of looking after the moral and social lives of their female students. The opening of a residential hostel for female students meant that both Boys-Smith and Rawson wasted hours of time petitioning and arranging for hot water, fittings, equipment, and so forth, in an echo of Marion Talbot and Alice Peloubet Norton's lives at the infant University of Chicago in 1892.

Under Rawson's regime the Department of Home Science was elevated to the status of a faculty; a four-year Bachelor of Home Science degree was established in 1922. She herself disappeared from the university domestic science scene the following year when she married a geology professor. The marriage bar deprived academia of her services as it did other women who punctuate the pages of *The Science of Housework*, including Janet Lane-Claypon, who had steered KCHSS so steadfastly in a scientific direction.

Helen Rawson's replacement at Otago was a woman whom John Studholme had initially wanted as the founder of university home science in New Zealand, an American called Ann Gilchrist Strong.

Home science with the Maharaja of Gaekwad

If a feeling of fatigue is creeping over you at this moment, it will echo the one I sometimes felt when researching and writing this book. It is just impossible to tell the story of scientific housework without encountering a host of tenaciously clever and inspiring women. I do promise you that Ann Gilchrist Strong is very nearly the last such woman you will meet in this book.

A middle-class American schoolteacher, Strong conceived the ambition to specialise in home science after a period of teaching what were then called 'delinquent' children: she saw home science as a way to prevent delinquency altogether. She was a Lake Placid pioneer and a founding member of the American Home Economics Association. After taking a home economics degree at Teachers College, Columbia (where she quite possibly would have met Hideko Inoue who was visiting at the time), Strong started a department at the University of Tennessee. It was there that John Studholme encountered her and tried to persuade her to move to New Zealand. Instead, she stepped sideways and married Mr Strong, a wealthy, much older, businessman. The marriage didn't work out, so in 1917 Ann was free to work outside the home again. She went to India at the invitation of the Maharaja of Gaekwad to familiarise Indians with Western ideas about domestic science.

Maharaja Sayajirao Gaekwad, a dashing young man when appointed King of Baroda in Western India by the British in 1881, was responsible for a large modernisation programme in India. This included legislative reform; the building of railways; the founding of libraries and banks; the introduction of universal primary education; and borrowing from the West the tradition of teaching girls and women how to do housework properly. His motives in recruiting Ann Gilchrist Strong were rather mixed. What he wanted was a scientifically trained Western woman to reorganise his 15 palaces and train his servants, but, in order to make the position more academically appealing, he added the task of setting up home economics courses in schools and colleges. This latter commission entailed the organisation of a graduate course in home science at what was then the Baroda College of Science (and is today Maharaja Sayajirao University). The seriousness of the educational challenge is demonstrated in the severe expressions of Strong and her Baroda students in Figure 10.3. Not even the (unhygienic?) dog on her lap brings a smile to her face.

Figure 10.3: Ann Gilchrist Strong with household arts students in Baroda, India, 1917

Source: Courtesy of American Association of Family and Consumer Sciences records, #6578, Division of Rare and Manuscript Collections, Cornell University Library, https://digital.library.corn ell.edu/catalog/ss:549029

Strong's educational mission kept her busy, and so did remodelling the Maharaja's palaces and retraining his servants in Western ways. The complexity of the task is illustrated by one of the palaces, Laxmi Vilas Palace in Bharatpur. This had seven separate kitchens to cater for all religions and castes. Each kitchen had its own superintendent and staff of cooks, bakers, watermen, cleaners and sweepers, table boys and butlers, clerks and silver cleaners, sweet-makers, grinding women and cowherds, all of whom had to be retrained in properly hygienic ways. Strong bought fly screens, hoovers, floor-scrubbing machines and dishwashers and installed sawdust spittoons for betel-nut chewers who were subject to fines if they behaved improperly. Being research-minded, she undertook a survey of Indian diet and the local cost of living, concluding that 75 per cent of the population were semi-starved.[21]

To assist her work in India, Strong learnt how to fit her ideas about domestic science into Indian culture. Her book, *Domestic Science for High Schools in India* (1931) (co-written with a colleague, Mabel Needham), puts forward a carefully tailored case for scientific housework as being an extension of the moral training encoded in Indian sacred texts. Thus, cleanliness was simply a matter of adapting traditional practices: 'What orthodox Hindu', she asked, 'would enter a kitchen without first having bathed and changed her garments to those of silk? ... No one would enter ... with shoes on her feet'. 'We are told in the old Hindu law', she noted strategically, 'that those who prepare food must keep their hands and nails clean. They must bathe and put on clean clothes. ... Many of these laws are very wise. ... Their wisdom is borne out by the discoveries of science to-day'.[22]

Most of Strong's home economics students were men.[23] Domestic service, especially its higher echelons, was a male specialty in India, as it was in much of colonial Africa. When the social anthropologist Audrey Richards studied the Bemba tribe in Northern Rhodesia (now Zambia) in the early 1930s she found that laundry work, particularly ironing, was regarded as a fashionable employment for men. 'When the young man can acquire a bit of soap he likes to wash and iron in public outside his hut, surrounded by an admiring crowd of small boys.'[24] Perhaps this example might spur housework-allergic men in other cultures to greater efforts? Richards was unusual among anthropologists in finding domesticity interesting. Most of them have ignored the detailed study of everyday domestic lives.

We don't know what caused Ann Gilchrist Strong's change of heart, but she finally gave up her work in India and succumbed to John Studholme's entreaties. In 1920 she went to New Zealand to take over from the retiring Helen Rawson. There, in Otago, she continued Rawson's fight to maintain the high scientific standards of home science and to resist the Department of Education's attempts to turn the degree programme into a training course for technical and secondary school teachers. As an 'institution builder' of some stature, Strong deployed a number of strategies to advance the academic credibility of home science: she set up a postgraduate research programme; on a recruiting drive in the United States in 1924 she collected some exciting new teachers; she managed to secure three graduate fellowships from the Rockefeller Foundation and ten years' worth of grants from the Carnegie Corporation; and she developed a home economics extension programme. This professional networking was facilitated by the extensive visits Strong had paid in the years after her divorce to examine domestic science sites in England and other European countries.

Conclusion

The stories in this chapter demonstrate the extraordinary reach of the Euro-American movement to transform homes into citadels of science. Of course any nation will find the promotion of domestic science education for women an easier option than implementing social policies capable of tackling the inadequate resources and poverty that damage health in homes. The very existence of a vociferous international network of female household scientists who had already spent decades perfecting a scientific approach to housework was a golden opportunity for educators and policy makers everywhere. That's the cynical view. The less cynical one is that transferring new knowledge about germs and bacteria and nutritional science to other cultural contexts actually was of benefit, and did improve health. But the disparagingly named 'academic kitchens' that seeded themselves on the university campuses of different countries were, nonetheless, participants in a general process of colonisation and hegemony that is certainly not unique to the field of household science. The attitude behind the making of white sauce was thoroughly embedded in what was taught: the attitude that there's only one way of getting domestic products right, one that calls for an almost limitless programme of colonisation and that submits indigenous domestic cultures to a thick layer of germ-destroying bleach.

11

Legacies and meanings

Patent number 4,428,085 was lodged with the US Patent Office by an artist and inventor called Frances Grace Arnholz Bateson in 1980 and finally registered in January 1984. The patent was for an enterprise called 'Self-Cleaning Building Construction', and it consisted of 68 separate designs that together would enable houses and their contents to be cleaned automatically. Although this radical plan came many years after the zenith of the household science movement, it was inspired by the same principles: that cleanliness is essential, but it should be achieved as efficiently as possible. All the incumbent of the self-cleaning house had to do was press a button, wear waterproof clothes and hold an umbrella. In every room sprinklers housed in the ceiling and at the junction of wall and floor sprayed a mist of soap and water followed by drafts of warm air: the water could contain, as appropriate, germicides to counter communicable diseases, and bug repellents to deal with infestations of termites, carpenter ants, bedbugs, cockroaches, fleas and suchlike. The floors were coated in waterproof resin and were slanted so that gutters at the edges drained the water directly outdoors to the doghouse, giving the dog a good wash as well. Waterproof fabrics protected furniture, pictures and books. The whole process took under an hour. Particularly inventive was the method for laundering clothes. These were washed, dried and stored while hanging in a closet that was also a washing machine; they emerged from the wash on their hangers ready for wearing. The entire design was really quite like today's automatic car wash.[1]

Frances Bateson, known as Frances Gabe, who created this marvel, was the daughter of an architect and the wife of an electrical engineer. She was born in 1915, found school very boring, and spent 27 years inventing her self-cleaning house. Her eureka moment came when she confronted globules of fig jam her two young children had thrown at the wall. Gabe took the garden hose to the fig jam and the idea for her mechanised house was born. She converted her own house, which was up a dirt track in rural Oregon, and charged people to come and look at the results. With a portable model of the house (now on display in the Hagley Museum in Delaware, United States), she toured the country giving talks about its merits, and advocating the widespread adoption of self-cleaning building construction. Gabe thought women should spend less time doing housework and more time with their children. She thought, as other women had done before her, that architects should design houses so as to minimise housework. Her ideas and her model house got a lot of public attention from the 1980s to the early 2000s (they 'fascinated everyone from Harvard researchers to the media'[2]) but unfortunately she wasn't able to raise enough money to renew the patents, and then it didn't help when an earthquake ruined the house in 2001. Frances Gabe died in 2016 in a (non-self-cleaning) nursing home at the age of 101, both she and her invention largely forgotten. Her house, like the Bristol All-Electric House described in Chapter 9, still stands, although its new owner took out most of the self-cleaning features and uses it to keep bees and provide camping accommodation for travelling cyclists.

So does Gabe's clever invention and its sad fate stand as a kind of cipher, a summary, a sadly ironic memento, of the entire household science movement, especially that part of it with which this book has been concerned – its career as an academic subject? What did the movement really achieve? What, apart from a tired model of the self-cleaning house stored in a minor American museum, are its legacies today? This chapter summarises what the movement was about, proposes a few answers to the question of what it accomplished, and slips in a few extra stories to boast about the inventiveness, dedication to scientific method and unexpected legacies associated with the campaign to make housework the kind of subject that should be studied in universities around the world.

Change or revolution?

It was evident from the start that this campaign was about much more than the 'cabbages and King's' of the King's College for Women poem we remembered at the beginning of Chapter 7. Alice was right to stand there wondering what all the fuss about shining new technology in her cooking class was actually about. To simplify (always the goal of last chapters): the household science/sanitary science/domestic economy/home economics movement brought many individuals and groups in many nations and cultures together in an effort to make homes cleaner, food better and thus people healthier. The intellectual apex of this ambitious programme was the provision of undergraduate and postgraduate degrees in household science.

In order to count as movements, campaigns like the one *The Science of Housework* is about don't have to emerge as perfectly organised initiatives with names, official homes and their own sets of rules and regulations. They are, rather, collective and sustained efforts waged by individuals who are connected through informal/formal networks, and who share advocacy of a common goal. All these criteria for defining a social movement are amply met by the activities charted in previous chapters. The goals of such movements usually incorporate some alteration in social structures, systems or sets of values. Desired and achieved change can range from minor legislative or social initiatives to outright revolution.[3]

The household science movement didn't achieve any obvious revolution: that has to be admitted. Although its protagonists were clever, creative, well-connected and unbelievably diligent people, there was no mass adoption of efficiency schedules or scientific cooking: housework didn't rise in social value, and economists didn't raise their hands to a man in dismay at their collective failure to count housewives as contributors to the gross national product. Voices that argued for major architectural change or collective housekeeping were absorbed into the general chorus of conformity to the status quo. The hallowed masculine halls of academia did suffer a few blows when female professors of household science walked among them and refused to be consigned to campus cooking duties. Although the penetration of academia by household science proved to be temporary, its leaders did chalk up some spectacular successes on the way. Moments such as the granting of the BSc in household and social science at King's College of Household and Social Science (KCHSS) in 1920 or the one in 'domestic economics' at Cornell University in the United States in 1919 or the (four-year) bachelor of home science degree in New Zealand in 1922 would have been extremely gratifying to those who had worked so hard to get the subject up there on a par with other degree-worthy ones. To watch the wonderful new household science buildings rise from the ground in Kensington, or to catch a first sight of the sun streaming through the bright coloured windows of the Lillian Massey household science building in Toronto, must have been truly satisfying to those whose labours had made these triumphs possible.

Housework and the national health

There is, however, rather more to say on the topic of how scientific housework benefited the communities among which it lodged. Hidden under the layers of dust that have to be disturbed for this kind of history-telling were two major impacts. The first was the creation of opportunities for women who wanted to do science. With diplomas or degrees in household science and employed as demonstrators for the burgeoning household technology companies, the services of 'lady demons' who could brag in technical language about what the gleaming new domestic equipment would achieve made a difference to them and to the communities among which they worked. For them it was a way of learning science that could lead to other careers in that field. Other women might have chosen to be professors of chemistry or physics or physiology at Harvard or Cambridge, or anywhere really, but what they were offered, what was held out to them as within practicable reach, were academic appointments in some variant of the discipline that was household science. This was definitely better than nothing. It was how women inveigled their way (were seduced?) onto a path signposted 'to gender equality' – a destination that remains shrouded in mist.

Second, there was the undisputed effect on health. The early enthusiasts of scientific housework talked constantly in their lectures and textbooks about something called 'the laws of health'. This was an ill-defined phrase with great rhetorical power. Basically, the laws of health referred to those conditions that enable bodies to function well, conditions for which access to reliable science-based information is required. Let's just return for a moment to the kind of messages that were transmitted in community domestic education classes in the later 19th century. 'Remember that sanitary laws & legislation are only useful as they are applied individually in the home', instructed British sanitary lecturer Margaret Pillow.[4] The health campaigner Catherine Buckton (one of her attentive audiences is depicted in Chapter 3) gave classes to schoolgirls, 'working girls' and mothers in Leeds in the 1870s. Her first course of 'sanitary lectures' began with the observation that 1,538 people in Leeds, two-thirds of them children, had lost their lives in the past year through diseases that could have been prevented by sanitary housework. Buckton explained, in non-technical language, how cleanliness in food preparation and attention to hygiene could save lives. One of the examples she gave in her little book *Two Winters' Experience in Giving Lectures to my Fellow Townswomen of the Working Classes on Physiology and Hygiene* (1873) was of using a small steam kettle to show how hot air ascends: thus on washing day the window should be opened at the top rather than the bottom. A young mother told her that since she learnt this her son didn't have bronchitis any more. Buckton's talks ended with the admonition, about 150 years before politicians chanted it during the 2020s COVID-19 epidemic, to 'wash your hands regularly with soap and water'.[5]

The notion that good nutrition is fundamental to good health is commonly understood today. But knowledge relevant to domestic life generated by scientists in their laboratories and offices from the later 19th century onwards wasn't accessible to the general public until the domestic science movement took on the mission of broadcasting it. This involved a dramatic revision of long-standing ideas and practices. 'The first and most difficult lesson', explained *The American Kitchen Magazine* in 1900, talking about just this topic, 'was to teach the class that the so-called kitchen was a laboratory where we performed scientific experiments and not a place where highly seasoned and indigestible compounds with high sounding names were thrown together without regard to nutrition or economy'.[6] The tradition of conveying up-to-date scientific information about food went all the way back to Catharine Beecher, the tasty contents of whose *Domestic Receipt Book* (1846) were informed by all the latest research on food constituents such as gluten, albumen, casein and fibrin (this was before vitamins had been invented).[7] The books, pamphlets, classes and lectures that accumulated as the campaign to bring science into the home gathered momentum delivered a thoroughly mixed diet of both nutritional and sanitary knowledge. The result was a unique role in health improvement for the household science movement as a whole. According to some of those who have studied this process, the result adds up to a transformation of social habits as great as that generated by the first Industrial Revolution.[8]

In countries such as the United Kingdom and the United States, mortality rates began a steady decline once the domestic science movement had gained some hold, and this was *before* most medical interventions (except for smallpox vaccination) could have had any notable effect. Infant and child mortality rates, highly sensitive to environmental conditions, experienced the steepest fall. These large declines in mortality rates between about 1890 and 1920 are strong circumstantial evidence that the new domestic science education did actually change household behaviour.[9] Public health reforms improved the infrastructure of the material environment but did nothing necessarily to alter attitudes and behaviour relating to hygiene and nutrition in the home. The list of diseases whose transmission is mitigated by domestic and personal hygiene is a long one: chicken pox, diphtheria, gastroenteritis, measles, meningitis, polio, rubella, scabies, typhoid and viral hepatitis are just some of them.[10] Households which adopted the new sanitary science messages about boiling water and milk, avoiding faecal contamination, and providing safer and more nutritious meals, would have increased their members' survival chances. Links between scientific/medical research and curricula for teaching greater domestic efficiency were nourished by the many social connections that existed between medical and household scientists. Britain's Alice Ravenhill, for example, met the biochemist Frederick Gowland Hopkins, a Nobel Prize-winner for his discovery of vitamins, in 1903. This encounter would only have strengthened her case that nutritional advances had somehow to be incorporated into the practices of women feeding their families.[11]

It was precisely because the new understandings of disease engineered by the discovery of germs were so obviously relevant to housecleaning and food preparation that so much space in the domestic science texts was devoted to these themes. As Nancy Tomes phrased it in her *The Gospel of Germs* – and I very much concur with her view – 'One of my goals in writing this book has been to challenge the implicitly gendered division of knowledge that regards as significant what Pasteur did in the laboratory but dismisses as inconsequential what a public health nurse or housewife did with his insights.'[12] The domestic sphere isn't external to scientific knowledge about health, but part of it.[13] The determination to translate scientific knowledge and the emissions of medical research into plain language and everyday domestic techniques was what made the difference.

Why is this really significant impact of the domestic science movement not generally understood? The ideological dismissal of education in, and about, housework as nothing more than a tool for the oppression of women is one reason. Another is that historians, epidemiologists and sociologists who have tried to explain changes in mortality rates have focused their attention on public spaces – on the water supply, sewage systems, public baths and so on. Domestic work behaviour has entered their explanatory models only in such general terms as 'rising living standards' or 'improved nutrition'. But who translated into household practice enhanced knowledge about food and domestic standards of living other than the women who were the target audiences of all those classes, lectures, pamphlets and admonitory books? The more the health implications of household behaviour are investigated, the clearer is the idiocy of dismissing domestic science as simply an ideology designed to keep women in their place.

Practically no one gets excited about health hygiene in the home these days, but some of housework's implications for health do hit the media headlines from time to time. Among these is the news that, since housework is a form of exercise it can benefit both physical and mental health. 'Housework could keep brain young, research suggests'; 'Scientific research confirms that the mortality rate of men doing housework is reduced by half!' 'Huffing and puffing "can cut cancer risk"'.[14] The last headline refers to a study of 22,398 UK adults with an average age of 62 in whom 4.5 daily minutes of vigorous housework (carrying shopping, vacuuming, scrubbing the bathroom) was enough to cut by 32 per cent (over a seven-year period) the risk of multiple cancers. The finding about halving the mortality rate of men is from a Chinese study and is somewhat perplexing, since no effect was found for women. This might be because not enough women died in the follow-up period, or because the men who volunteered for heavy housework were healthier anyway. 'The underlying mechanism needs further study' the researchers decided.[15] But as a call to increased male domesticity, the finding does have a certain appeal.

Where has household science gone to?

The subject of 'household science' or 'home economics' began a curricular vanishing act in the late 1950s. By 1963 at least ten US colleges had stopped using the name 'home economics': the University of Wisconsin renamed its faculty 'The School of Family Resources and Consumer Sciences'; Michigan State University chose 'The College of Human Ecology'. In Canada, Toronto's Faculty of Household Science, the brainchild of Lillian Massey Treble and the showcase for those amazing stained glass windows, became the 'Faculty of Food Sciences'. By 1990 the job title of 'home economist' had been dropped altogether from the US Bureau of Labor Statistics' list of occupations. New graduates of the renamed and revamped domestic science degrees called themselves 'family counsellors', 'nutritionists', 'commercial interior designers', 'fashion designers' or 'teachers' – anything but home economists. Commercial companies entirely lost their enthusiasm for hiring home economists to help sell their wares, instead taking on 'marketing consultants' or 'communication specialists'. Accordingly, too, organisations such as the American Home Economics Association, founded in 1908, relinquished their old identities: the American Home Economics Association became the 'American Association of Family and Consumer Sciences' in 1993. The UK Home Economics Federation, which came on the scene much later in 1954, followed suit by retitling itself the 'Institute for Consumer Sciences' in 2000.

'Family and consumer sciences' is probably the main disciplinary label used for home economics/domestic science today. As a branch of technical education, this is a distinctly different subject from the one established in such places as KCHSS in London and at the universities of Chicago, Illinois, California, Toronto, Tokyo and so on more than a century ago. In 2024, the nearest King's College, London, offers to its erstwhile household and social science degree is a three-year honours BSc in nutritional sciences. At the University of Illinois in Chicago a BSc in nutrition taught by the somewhat weirdly named Department of Kinesiology and Nutrition is on offer, but the University of Chicago itself contains no trace of the empire Marion Talbot and others founded on the squalid marshes of its beginnings in 1892.

Something of the underlying motives for these transitions can be gleaned from what happened at the University of West Virginia where the appointment of a new home-economics-sceptic president transformed the female-led home economics curriculum into 'Home and Family Studies' with a man at its head. According to Margaret Rossiter in her research on American women scientists, an insuperable problem in the decline of university home economics programmes was exactly those academic barriers that had earlier thwarted efforts to establish them as academic subjects: the hostility of ambitious male university presidents who wanted to get rid of home economics.[16] Transforming home economics into nutritional science, human development, human ecology, family studies, and so forth, created a rationale for turfing the women out and replacing them with younger and more malleable male faculty.

The movement to make housework more scientific evolved at the same time as women were gaining more ground in the fight for education and equal rights. There were many points of contact between the two movements, not least the doors that household science opened for women to gain a foothold in those scientific occupations the men would have preferred them not to enter. In the first decades of the 20th century when women's rights came to the fore as a public issue, it became more difficult for university men to shut the door on women who wanted academic jobs in household science (even if some of them would have preferred to work in non-household science). There had, perhaps, even been some kudos for men in being seen to adopt a pro-women stance. Not all the leading women household scientists by any means were advocates of enhanced rights for women. Some, for example Women's Institute founder Adeline Hoodless in Canada and efficiency expert Christine Frederick in the United States, were of the opinion that scientific domesticity should bind women more tightly to the home. Others favoured a more liberated future. Among the latter we must count the outspoken house-redesigner Paulette Bernège in France; the pacifist sanitarian Hideko Inoue in Japan; and, in Britain, the suffragist electrical engineer Caroline Haslett and Winifred Boys-Smith, who took the suffrage cause with her to New Zealand when she founded home science there in 1911.

From housework to nutritional science

Renaming was a crucial part of household science's vanishing act. KCHSS was itself reinvented in 1953 as Queen Elizabeth College (QEC; after Elizabeth the Queen Mother, in line with KCHSS's long tradition of royal patronage). In that year a BSc in nutrition was offered for the first time. Both the degree and the Department of Nutrition in which it was housed were spearheaded by John Yudkin, a doctor who went to KCHSS in 1944 as professor of physiology, and who became a well-known writer of accessible books on nutrition. *Pure, White and Deadly* (1972) is his best-known. It's a riveting and still-relevant exposé of sugar as the cause of multiple ills – obesity, heart disease, diabetes, liver disease, gout, cancer, dental decay, dermatitis, short- and long-sight, at least. This came as news at the time to both the general public and many medical doctors, and was heartily contested by some of them, as well as naturally by the sugar and food industries.

Yudkin's work at KCHSS/QEC building nutrition as an academic specialism benefited from many years of research and teaching carried out by KCHSS staff. Some of this was mentioned in Chapters 6 and 7. Margaret McKillop, one of the founders of the household and social science degree and a chemistry tutor at King's College for Women from 1898 to 1914, worked for the Ministry of Food during the First World War. Her services at King's had been dispensed with after the kind of arguments common in academia about underpayment and the privileging of male staff.[17] During the war, McKillop wrote a book on food values, for which work she was awarded an MBE in 1919. Her book was one of the first attempts to translate the findings of nutrition research into usable information for teachers, demonstrators, caterers, social workers and 'many modern housekeepers, who are now well aware that scientific results and scientific method can be used very extensively even in housekeeping on a small scale'.[18]

Training courses at KCHSS for dieticians, whose services were increasingly required in hospitals and other institutions, were launched in 1933 and 1936 by Vernon Mottram who took over from the vitamin researcher Edward Mellanby as professor of physiology. By this time, KCHSS had built up an international reputation for world-class research in nutrition, physiology and microbiology. A successor to Margaret McKillop's book, co-authored by a graduate of Mottram's new diploma, Elsie Widdowson, is a text known and still used today as *McCance and Widdowson's Composition of Foods*; it contains food tables on which countless nutritional studies throughout the world have been based.[19]

In 1961 the royal presence on Campden Hill was required to open a new set of laboratories, named after John Atkins, the doctor whose anxiety about maternal domestic ignorance had been a plank in the platform on which household science had itself been built. The Atkins laboratories, composed of six storeys of 'brown Buckinghamshire facing bricks, with panels of cream bricks between the lines of windows', had the capacity to accommodate the work of 54 students and 22 researchers.[20] This time (in contrast to the fate of Dr Mellanby's howling dogs [see Chapter 7]), the experimental animals were properly catered for in ten rooms of their own. QEC's work and status as an internationally renowned centre for research and teaching in nutritional science was what drove the final nail into the coffin of household science. The subject had been attracting fewer and fewer students; the teaching of household science courses was terminated in 1967, and the Department of Household Science followed the convention of other academic renamings in becoming the 'Department of Food and Management Science'.

Wages for housework?

It isn't the purpose of this book to suggest remedies for the enduring trivialisation of housework. However, one of housework's signature features, its exclusion as unwaged labour from economic accounting systems, was nearly as crucial as the laws of health to many proponents of academic household science. Charlotte Perkins Gilman, whose book on the man-made world gave its name to Chapter 5, proposed payment for housework to her husband, whose response was to suggest she give up all the reading she was doing since it was obviously not doing anyone any good.[21] Gilman, and the other women economists who contested the non-valuation of domestic labour and whose work we looked at in Chapter 5, knew that reconfiguring it as economically valuable was the only way forward.

The idea that women should be paid for doing housework in their own homes flits in and out of political history. When the proposal to pay housewives was debated in the Western Australian Parliament in 1921, a local newspaper printed some verses about it:

Father:-

I say! Come quick Maria!
Here's little baby Ted
He's fallen in the fire
And burned his pretty head.

Mother:-

I cannot help it, Father
It's after union time
Besides, I would much rather
Read Marx's work sublime.[22]

A Marxist/Marxian analysis of domestic labour (what did Marx *really* think about housework?) was brought into the Euro-American women's liberation movement of the 1970s by a group of women who launched a new Wages for Housework campaign. The most prominent member of this campaign in the United Kingdom was Selma James, a former New York factory worker who had been involved in the anti-colonial movement. Together with the Italian Marxist feminist Mariarosa Dalla Costa, James wrote a liberationist classic called *Power of Women and the Subversion of the Community* that linked the unwaged nature of housework with women's position under capitalism. In 1974 Selma James and I exchanged our positions on wages for housework in the pages of a new magazine called *Race Today*. My position was that '[t]here would be no better way of affirming our role as housewives than to be paid by the State for doing housework in our own homes'. Exploitation by the state was no solution, I said: a housewife's wage would interrupt the process of working towards gender equality in the home, and would 'intensify the obligation that many women feel to be psychologically involved in the cleanliness and tidiness of their homes'. Fifty years on I still agree with myself. James's riposte was that: 'If housewives were getting as much an hour as sociologists, she [AO] would not have such a crisis of identity. … Sociologists are a crucial section of the State and therefore crucial to the counter-revolution. We identify ourselves as revolutionary slaves, not as counter-revolutionary masters.'[23]

So there you have a reason for dismissing everything I've said in this book. Note that at the time of writing the tenacious and untiring Selma James is 93 and still campaigning from an office in North London quite close to where I live. She's one example of the longevity enjoyed by many women whose names are associated with housework campaigns of one sort or another. I live in hope.

Surprising legacies

The household science movement helped to save much death and illness and gave rise to many critical ideas and achievements. Without its penetration of higher education these results would have been less likely. There are many other legacies, coalescences and coalitions of people, ideas, events and organisations which are traceable back to the really rather elegantly simple notion that if housework weren't women's work it would be pure science. I shall end this book with three further unpredicted and interesting legacies uncovered by my archeological digging into the household science movement. One is a poem created as a result of a KCHSS diploma; one concerns the challenge of nutrition under conditions of zero gravity; and the third entertains us with the story of a long-running argument about the best way to make porridge.

'A subaltern's love-song'

'Miss Joan Hunter Dunn, Miss Joan Hunter Dunn,/ I can hear from the car park the dance has begun,/Oh! Surrey twilight! Importunate band!/ Oh strongly adorable tennis-girl's hand!' John Betjeman's poem 'A subaltern's love-song' has much more in that vein. He and the star of his poem, Joan Hunter Dunn, met in London University's Senate House during the Second World War. Betjeman was working on film scripts for the Ministry of Information; Dunn was helping to run the Senate House catering department after having acquired a diploma in household science from KCHSS. The result of the Betjeman–Dunn meeting was his much-celebrated poem, an ode to suburban femininity in which Joan Hunter Dunn, who has a nicely rhymnable name, drinks lots of gin-and-lime and plays lots of tennis. Dunn's *Guardian* Obituary mentions the eroticism of the white coat she wore at work and her 'clean, clinical, motherly look'.[24] Who said household science isn't sexy?

Eating in space

In her *The Secret History of Home Economics*, Danielle Dreilinger notes another unforeseen legacy of nutritional home science: its contribution to the space programme. Would man have taken that first step on the moon without it? Astronauts have to eat. But eating in the zero gravity of space is tricky, both with regard to getting the correct nutrients in and in dealing with the post-digestion effluents that inevitably follow (the early space suits had no room for defecation). A woman called Beatrice Finkelstein ran a rose-pink kitchen laboratory at the Air Force research headquarters in Dayton, Ohio, in the late 1950s and early 1960s. There she headed the Food Technology Section of the department responsible for 'life support systems' and experimented on blending strange mixtures of clinically antibacterial 'low residue' foods that could go into space with the astronauts. Before each Mercury mission Finkelstein travelled to Cape Canaveral, serving her recipes as pre-flight meals to the astronauts, whom she got to know well, donating, in addition to the food, emotional and psychological support (as the female feeders of men have generally tended to do). Excited journalists writing about the first astronauts mentioned that 'when it came to a question of what they will eat, they left it up to a little woman'. Finkelstein was apparently on the small side, but her work was not, nor was that of the other female scientists whose work has permitted astronauts to survive in space. One called Rita Rapp, a physiologist who worked for NASA in the early 1960s, is described patronisingly as 'the scientist who packed lunches for 230,000 miles' (what do female nutritional scientists do except make lunch-boxes? See Bonnie Garmus's best-selling 2022 novel *Lessons in Chemistry*). Nutritionist Doris Calloway, who also researched space-eating, discovered broccoli's anti-cancer properties. For this the US Army named her Man of the Year in 1959.[25]

Results of this trail-blazing work by women home scientists can be seen on the shelves of any supermarket today: freeze-dried meals; exotic stir fry sauces; an unbelievable range of pre-prepared rice ('Caribbean', 'tomato and basil', 'coconut, lime and coriander') and foods to tempt the tastebuds of infants ('sweet potatoes & beef meatballs', 'free-range chicken and spring veg casserole'), all in the flexible pouch-packaging created by women who were employed to further man's exploration of space.

The great Norwegian porridge feud

In the 19th century people in Norway ate a lot of porridge, often two or three times a day. Women would make it by taking flour, oats, barley or rice, and simmering the grain with water to make a gruel. Then at the end they would stir in some extra flour. This well-tested, traditional method had been used for generations. Then a man called Peter Christen Asbjørnsen, a collector of folklore, came along and published a cookery book in 1864 that drew heavily on the work of German and other European scientists to challenge the inefficiency of women in the kitchen and propose that Norway's path to modern nationhood would be secured only by educating women in domestic science. Among Asbjørnsen's claims was one that proved uniquely incendiary: he said that the addition of flour to porridge-making didn't only make porridge indigestible but was a pointless drain on the national economy, costing thousands of kroner every year.

A huge amount of argument that went on for decades ensued about porridge. Asbjørnsen's book, which was called *Sensible Cookery*, was immensely popular among those (mostly educated urban men) who wanted to turn their backs on tradition and welcome the new modern, scientific age. While some Norwegians approved the introduction of what appeared to be science into porridge-cooking, others considered it an insult to women and their valuable domestic wisdom, accrued over the centuries. One of the latter was Eilert Sundt, the founder of sociology in Norway and the man whose book *On Cleanliness in Norway* hasn't ever been considered important enough to be translated into English (see Chapter 3). Sundt argued that the accumulated experience of women in the kitchen should be trusted. Asbjørnsen and his like never actually cooked porridge, so how would they know anything about it? The problem was that *Sensible Cookery* was not sensible. In fact it was a compendium of prejudiced, idiosyncratic and health-damaging ideas. As well as recommending white flour rather than the wholegrain variety Norwegian women used in their porridge-making, the book promoted coffee as a good substitute for meat and sugar as an excellent source of nutrition (I wonder if John Yudkin knew about it?).[26]

The definitive answer as to who was right about porridge came from the experiments of modern laboratory scientists in the 1940s. The women knew what they were doing. Adding flour at the end of the cooking process resulted in greater, not less, digestibility and it added both texture and sweetness by releasing beneficial enzymes. All this is comprehensively laid out in an article published in 2022, in the *International Journal of Gastronomy and Food Science*.[27]

Women may not always have been ready to grasp the tools of science with both (clean) hands, but sometimes they knew more than the scientists said they did, although it took science to prove it.

Conclusion

While the self-cleaning house is one place where the wisdom of the household science movement seems to have completely washed away, some of us still fantasise about it every day. I'm quite sure that the household science campaigners of a century ago would be disappointed to learn that the 'smart house' of the 2020s is absolutely not, when it comes to housework. Smart homes use internet-connected devices to drive remote monitoring and management of systems like heating, lighting and security. Smart lighting systems 'know' when someone is in the room and will need light; smart thermostats can modify heating settings to suit individual bodies. Thus also may pets and houseplants be kept alive. Smart refrigerators make shopping lists and create recipes based on what's in there (I have yet to be convinced that any machine can do this better than I can). Smart houses, unlike self-cleaning ones, are a deeply masculine vision of a house designed with the technically interested man in mind; the interests of houseworkers are simply not catered for.[28] Everything that Paulette Bernège said about architects ignoring women's expertise remains true. While it all *sounds* very clever, houses still don't self-clean, cooking still requires a modicum of intelligence and science, and the washing and ironing of clothes remain tasks over which men and women can still waste time arguing (see Chapter 2).

Cleanability, so beloved of housework's scientific proselytisers a century ago, is nowhere in the advertising rhetoric and images of the housing and furnishing industries in 2024. Ledges, crevices, ornate handles, unwashable fabrics, unreachable lights – these clamour to adorn our homes so that we have to spend time removing dirt from them. The scientific benefits of household cleanliness are now mainly the province of private cleaning companies which continue to exploit the exaggerated dramas about germs and bacteria that were so popular in the early household science texts. 'Even if you keep your house well organised, deep cleaning is required to keep bacteria and germs away', advises an American outfit in Oklahoma City called 'Home Maid Better'. Watch out particularly for the 'tons of germs' lurking in the vegetable drawer of your refrigerator, on your kitchen counters, in your mattress and your curtains. Just pay someone else to do it.[29] But don't tell Selma. Paying someone else to do your housework is a sin of colonial proportions.

I have much enjoyed all the excavating of hidden territories and forgotten histories that it has taken to write this book. The hidden dangers of the home thus revealed have hugely impressed me, but have left me little time for my own housework. As Pat Mainardi said in her stimulating 1969 text *The Politics of Housework*, writing about housework is not a good excuse for not doing it. Neither activity ranks highly on any scale: both are trivial, even menial. 'Menial', meaning 'not requiring much skill and lacking prestige', comes from the word for 'house' (Anglo-French *meignial*, old French *mesnie*, Latin *mansionem*). 'Menial' is therefore a word we should use with care.

On the matter of terminology, there are two terms I've used sparingly in this book: 'separate spheres' and 'patriarchy'. 'Separate spheres' occurs three times in Chapter 8, and patriarchy/patriarchal also crops up only three times, in the early chapters. I didn't want to overload the text with academic concepts (yes, they *are* academic concepts) that might put readers off. But the history and sociology related in *The Science of Housework* make sense only when hung, like dripping laundry, on the scaffold (washing line) of these powerful explanatory ideas. 'Separate spheres' is shorthand for the ideology and matching social/material arrangements that split the industrialising world into two from the mid-18th century on. Women's place became the home, whether or not they were actually working outside it, which many of them were, thus undertaking the 'double shift' that has been the subject of many academic and non-academic books. In contrast, men were allowed their freedom outside the home to engage in labour that was often exhausting or downright degrading, but there were entertaining opportunities as well. As a consequence of this division, men's view of homes as havens in a generally heartless world prevailed. It did so because of patriarchy, which is also a term with a specific meaning, namely 'a system of society or government in which men hold the power'.

Into this gendered and unjust landscape strode scientific housework, full of claims to make life better for everyone, and determined to stretch its probing tools into those very crevices of dirt and dust where women laboured. The reconceptualisation of homes as risky places full of germs, dirt and hazards promulgated by household science destabilised the comfortable saga of men about the paradise of the home. But embedded in the educational efforts designed to spread this reworked notion of homes was a fault of volcanic proportions: it was aimed almost exclusively at the female population. There were exceptions – in some places the men and boys who worked at sea and who had to make do without the services of female caterers on ships were taught how to cook, and Catherine Buckton wasn't alone among the early pioneers of domestic science in giving her educational talks to both boys and girls. But the main audience, both envisaged and actual, for education in household science was women. Even at university degree level, few men signed up for an immersion in scientific housework. More than that, the movement never took on board the mission to confront the whole superstructure of gender inequalities in domestic responsibility and labour.

Household science posed some threat to separate spheres ideology by making private and public domains less separable: the new portrayal of homes as hazardous brought them into line with the world outside. Yet this wasn't a great enough threat to call into question traditional gender arrangements. Men didn't respond *en masse* to the revelation of domestic dangers to health and well-being by channelling their own energies into doing something about these (although some of them did turn to the profitable pursuit of household technology). The advance of household science into the higher echelons of the education system was a logical step, but in this context it was a step too far. It was vulnerable to the male control of higher education, which used it to legitimise the concept of unequal gender-differentiated academic work. The two sets of motives clashed: the women household scientists genuinely wanted to uphold the rights of their subject to professional university status; the male professors and administrators genuinely wanted (because they were liberal educators) to let the subject in, but they also knew that this would enable them to continue discriminating against women. By being confined to the 'academic kitchen' of household science, women could be excluded from other academic areas men preferred to keep for themselves.

There was a masculine interest, too, in reining in the ambitions of university household science because to do so would help to defend the fiction of the home as a private place. Its study couldn't conceivably, therefore, be considered eligible for any kind of public intellectual status. No, it's better to sweep it under the carpet, or subject it to Frances Gabe's drenching and sanitising jets, except that these never caught on for the same reason, that in the end the important people weren't interested enough. Perhaps it's better not to think about housework too much, just to keep on doing it. But let us please remember, permanently, not just for a little rebellious while, all the work, intelligence and passion that made up the movement to take science into the home, thus giving us all better domestic health and housework itself the respect it deserves.

Appendix: List of characters

Abbott, Edith (1876–1957) US
Abel, Mary Hinman (1850–1938) US
Addams, Jane (1860–1935) US
Atkins, John (1875–1963) UK
Atkinson, Mabel (married name Palmer) (1876–1958) UK
Atwater, Wilbur Owen (1844–1907) US
Baddeley, Florence (1858–1923) UK
Barnett, Henrietta (1851–1936) UK
Barry, Alfred (1826–1910) UK
Beecher, Catharine (1800–1878) US
Beeton, Isabella (1836–1865) UK
Bell, Vanessa (1879–1961) UK
Benson, Clara (1875–1964) Canada
Bernège, Paulette (1896–1973) France
Bevier, Isabel (1860–1942) US
Black, Clementina (1853–1922) UK
Booth, Hubert Cecil (1871–1955) UK
Bondfield, Margaret (1873–1953) UK
Boys-Smith, Winifred (1865–1939) UK and New Zealand
Breckinridge, Sophonisba (1866–1948) US
Brereton, Maud Cloudesley (1872–1946) UK
Buckmaster, John Charles (1820–1908) UK
Buckton, Catherine (1826–1904) UK
Burstall, Sara (1859–1939) UK
Calder, Fanny (1838–1923) UK
Calloway, Doris (1923–2001) US
Campbell, Helen Stuart (1839–1918) US
Creighton, Louise (1850–1936) UK
Dendy, Arthur (1865–1925) UK
Dewey, Annie Godfrey (1850–1922) US
Elliott, S. Maria (1854–1942) US
Esdaile, Philippa (1888–1989) UK
Eyles, Leonora (1889–1960) UK
Faithfull, Lilian (1865–1952) UK
Finkelstein, Beatrice, US
Frederick, Christine (1883–1970) US
Freund, Ida (1863–1914) Austria and UK
Gabe, Frances (1915–2016) US
Gaekwad, Maharaja of (Sayajirao Gaekwad III) (1863–1939) India

Gilbreth, Frank (1868–1924) US
Gilbreth, Lillian (1878–1972) US
Gilman, Charlotte Perkins (1860–1935) US
Gordon, Alice (1854–1929) UK
Gradwell, Cecil (1855–1942) UK
Greville, Daisy, Countess of Warwick (1861–1938) UK
Grey, Maria (1816–1906) UK
Hall, Radclyffe (1880–1943) UK
Haslett, Caroline (1895–1957) UK
Helgesen, Helga (1863–1935) Norway
Hewins, William (1865–1931) UK
Hoodless, Adelaide (1857–1910) Canada
Howes, Ethel Puffer (1872–1950) US
Hutchins, Bessie (E.L. Hutchins) (1858–1935) UK
Inoue, Hideko (1875–1963) Japan
Kedzie, Nellie (1858–1956) US
Kyrk, Hazel (1886–1967) US
Laird, Annie (1871–1939) US and New Zealand
Lancaster, Maud, UK (1870–1950)
Lane-Claypon, Janet (1877–1967)
Lathrop, Julia (1858–1932) US
Lawrence, Maude (1864–1933) UK
Lihotsky, Grete (Margarete Schütte-Lihotsky) (1897–2000) Austria
Macarthur, Mary (1880–1921) UK
MacDonald, Ishbel (1903–82) UK
Matheson, Cécile (1874–1950) UK
Matheson, Helen (1876–1936) UK
Matthews, Mabel (1879–1970) UK
McKillop, Margaret (1864–1929) UK
Mellanby, Edward (1884–1955) UK
Mellanby, May (1882–1978) UK
Meyer, Adele (1855–1930) UK
Meyer, Erna (1890–1975) Germany
Miyakawa, Sumi (1875–1948) Japan
Morgan, Agnes Fay (1884–1968) US
Morley, Edith (1875–1964) UK
Mottram, Vernon (1882–1976) UK
Nightingale, Florence (1820–1910) UK
Norton, Alice Peloubet (1860–1928) US
Oakeley, Hilda (1867–1950) UK
Palmer, Alice Freeman (1885–1902) US
Parloa, Maria (1843–1909) US
Partridge, Margaret (1891–1967) UK

Pattison, Mary (1869–1951) US
Peel, Constance (1868–1934) UK
Peet, Louise (1885–1983) US
Pillow, Margaret (formerly Scott) (1859–1929) UK
Plunkett, Harriette (1826–1894) US
Prudden, Theophil Mitchell (1849–1924) US
Rapp, Rita (1928–1989) US
Ravenhill, Alice (1859–1954) UK
Rawson, Helen (1886–1964) UK and New Zealand
Reid, Margaret (1896–1991) US
Reynard, Helen (1875–1947) UK
Richards, Ellen Swallow (1842–1911) US
Rücker, Arthur (1845–1915) UK
Rücker, Thereza (1863–1941) UK
Salmon, Lucy (1853–1927) US
Sater, Lenore (1897–1966) US
Schmitz, Cornelia (1843–1925) UK
Smithells, Arthur (1860–1939) UK
Spurgeon, Caroline (1869–1942) UK
Stowe, Harriet Beecher (1811–1896) US
Strong, Ann Munroe Gilchrist (1875–1957) New Zealand
Studholme, John (1829–1903) New Zealand
Sundt, Eilert (1817–1875) Norway
Talbot, Marion (1858–1948) US
Taylor, Frederick (1856–1956) US
Taylor, Maud (1869–1941) UK
Thompson, Benjamin (Count Rumford) (1753–1814) US
Treble, Lillian Massey (1854–1915) Canada
Urwick, Edward (1867–1945) UK
Wallas, Ada (1859–1934) UK
Walls, Graham (1858–1932) UK
Webb, Beatrice (formerly Potter) (1858–1943) UK
Woolf, Virginia (1882–1941) UK
Youmans, Edward (1821–1887) US
Youmans, Eliza (1826–1914) US
Yudkin, John (1910–1995) UK

Notes

Prologue
1. The Connected Histories of the BBC: Zena Skinner Interview, p 6, https://connectedhistoriesofthebbc.org/.
2. Burstall, S.A. and Douglas, M.A. (eds) (1911) *Public Schools for Girls*, London: Longmans & Co., p 155.
3. *Woman's Own*, 3 October 2022; *Woman*, 5 October 2022.
4. Novy, P. (1945) ('Foreword' by Lady Beveridge) *Housework Without Tears*, London: Pilot Press, p 36.
5. Mainardi, P. (1970, first published 1969) 'The politics of housework', in R. Morgan (ed) *Sisterhood is Powerful*, New York: Vintage Books, pp 447–53, p 450.

Chapter 1
1. Bourke, J. (1993) *Husbandry to Housewifery: Women, Economic Change, and Housework in Ireland, 1890–1914*, Oxford: Clarendon Press, p 14.
2. Kedzie, N. cited in Holt, M.I. (1995) *Linoleum, Better Babies & the Modern Farm Woman 1890–1930*, Albuquerque: University of New Mexico Press, p 46.
3. Oakley, A. (2019 [1974]) *The Sociology of Housework*, Oxford: Basil Blackwell, pp 41–3.
4. Rawnsley, D. (2022) 'It's in the detail: changes to census definitions and concepts over fifty years', https://blog.ukdataservice.ac.uk/changes-census-definitions/.
5. Office of National Statistics (2022) 'Story of the Census', https://www.ons.gov.uk/visualisations/storyofthecensus/.
6. Pettitt, A.K. (nd) 'Five steps to becoming a better housewife', https://www.thedarlingacademy.com/articles/five-steps-to-becoming-a-better-housewife/.
7. Hopkins, S. (2023) 'I'm a traditional housewife and love spending hours cooking and cleaning for my husband', https://www.joe.co.uk/life/im-a-traditional-housewife-378855.
8. Ravenhill, A. (1951) *The Memoirs of an Educational Pioneer*, Toronto and Vancouver: J.M. Dent and Sons, pp 77–8.
9. Attar, D. (1990) *Wasting Girls' Time: The History and Politics of Home Economics*, London: Virago, p 2.
10. Ehrenreich, B. and English, D. (1979) *For Her Own Good: 150 Years of the Experts' Advice to Women*, London: Pluto Press, p 151, emphasis in original.
11. 'What Robin Morgan said at Denver' (1973) *Journal of Home Economics*, January, p 13; Dreilinger, D. (2021) *The Secret History of Home Economics*, New York: W.W. Norton & Company, p 247.
12. Akiyama, Y. (2008) *Feeding the Nation: Nutrition and Health in Britain before World War One*, London: Bloomsbury Academic.
13. Sheard, S. (2000) 'Profit is a dirty word: the development of public baths and wash-houses in Britain 1847–1915', *Social History of Medicine*, 13(1): 63–85.
14. Douglas, M. (1966) *Purity and Danger: An Analysis of the Concepts of Pollution and Taboo*, London: Routledge and Kegan Paul, p 35, p 69.
15. Fardon, R. (1998) *Mary Douglas: An Intellectual Biography*, London: Routledge, p 80.
16. Ger, G. and Yenicioglu, B. (2004) 'Clean and dirty: playing with boundaries of consumer's safe havens', *Advances in Consumer Research*, 31: 462–7, p 464.
17. Tomes, N. (1998) *The Gospel of Germs: Men, Women, and the Microbe in American Life*, Cambridge, MA: Harvard University Press, p 17.

[18] Pillow, M. (1897) 'Domestic economy teaching in England', *Parliamentary Papers*, 25: 157–86, p 158.
[19] Ask the Scientists (2023) 'The science of house work: find your uncommon ways to unwind', https://askthescientists.com/ways-to-unwind/.
[20] Adjei, N.K. and Brand, T. (2018) 'Investigating the associations between productive housework activities, sleep hours and self-reported health among elderly men and women in western industrialised countries', *BMC Public Health*, 18: 110.
[21] *National Standards of Healthcare Cleanliness 2021*, London: NHS.
[22] Ackerley, L. (2019) 'Guest editorial', *Perspectives in Public Health*, 139(6): 275–6, p 275.
[23] Dreilinger, p xv.
[24] Rossiter, M.W. (1982) *Women Scientists in America: Vol. 1 Struggles and Strategies to 1940*, Baltimore and London: The Johns Hopkins University Press, p xv.

Chapter 2

[1] Schulte, B. and Swenson, H. (2020) 'An unexpected upside to lockdown: men have discovered housework', *The Guardian*, 17 June; Topping, A. and Duncan, P. (2020) 'Lockdown-fuelled novelty of domestic chores wanes for men', *The Guardian*, 9 December.
[2] Sparks, H. (2020) 'Why singing "Happy Birthday" handwashing song can spread COVID-19: study', *New York Post*, 8 September.
[3] Kimmitt, P.T. and Redway, K.F. (2016) 'Evaluation of the potential for virus dispersal during hand drying: a comparison of three methods', *Journal of Applied Microbiology*, 120(2): 478–86.
[4] Reynolds, K.A., Verhougstraete, M.P., Mena, K.D., Sattar, S.A., Scott, E.A. and Gerba, C.P. (2022) 'Quantifying pathogen infection risks from household laundry practices', *Journal of Applied Microbiology*, 132(2): 1435–48.
[5] 'Hospital pillows found to harbor millions of life-threatening germs' (2011) https://www.buildingbetterhealthcare.com/news/article_page/Hospital_pillows_found_to_harbour_millions_of_life-threatening_germs/71644.
[6] Kõljalg, S., Mändar, R., Sõber, T., Rööp, T. and Mändar, R. (2017) 'High level bacterial contamination of secondary school students' mobile phones', *GERMS*, 7(2): 73–7.
[7] Pritchard, C. (2012) 'Is the toilet seat really the dirtiest place in the home?', *BBC News*, 17 November, https://www.bbc.co.uk/news/magazine-20324304.
[8] Freeman, M.C., Stocks, M.E., Cumming, O., Jeandron, A., Higgins, I.P.T., Wolf, J., Prüss-Üstün, A., Bonjour, S., Hunter, P.R., Fewtrell, L. and Curtis, V. (2014) 'Systematic review: hygiene and health: systematic review of handwashing practices worldwide and update of health effects', *Tropical Medicine & International Health*, 19(8): 906–16.
[9] Møretrø, T., Nguyen-The, C., Didier, P., Maître, I., Izsó, T., Kasza, G., Skuland, S. E., Cardoso, M.J., Ferreira, V.B., Teixeira, P., Borda, D., Dumitrascu, L., Neagu, C., Nicolau, A.I., Anfruns-Estrada, E., Foden, M., Voysey, P. and Langsrud, S. (2021) 'Consumer practices and prevalence of *Campylobacter*, *Salmonella* and norovirus in kitchens from six European countries', *International Journal of Food Microbiology*, 347: 109172.
[10] Simonnes, K. (2017) 'People feel safe in their own kitchen', https://www.sv.uio.no/tik/english/research/news-and-events/news/2017/kitchen-jacobsen.html.
[11] Chase, E.H. (1897) 'Sanitary precautions', *The American Kitchen Magazine*, 7(May): 56–9, p 56.
[12] Gillies, E. (2021) 'Determining the most effective common household disinfection method to reduce the microbial load on domestic dishcloths: a pilot study', *Environmental Health Review*, 63(4): 101–6.
[13] Woodford, C. (2015) *Atoms under the Floorboards: The Surprising Science Hidden in Your Home*, London: Bloomsbury Sigma, p 266.
[14] Møretrø et al.

15. Royal Society for the Prevention of Accidents, 'Accidents don't have to happen: facts and figures', https://www.rospa.com/home-safety/advice/general/facts-and-figures.
16. Van Bronswijk, J.E.M.H. (1981) *House Dust Biology for Allergists, Acarologists and Mycologists*, Zoelmond: Author.
17. Van Bronswijk, p 172.
18. Dhar, D. (2019) 'Women's unpaid care work has been unmeasured and undervalued for too long', *Essays on Equality*, The Global Institute for Women's Leadership, London: King's College, pp 30–33, p 30.
19. Ferrant, G., Pesando, L.M. and Nowacka, K. (2014) 'Unpaid care work: the missing link in the analysis of gender gaps in labour outcomes', OECD Development Centre, December, https://www.oecd.org/dev/development-gender/Unpaid_care_work.pdf.
20. Rentokil Initial (2015) 'Initial launches HygieneConnect', https://www.rentokil-initial.com/media/news-releases/news-2015/initial-launches-hygiene-connect-27-2-15.aspx.
21. Kinnison, A., Cottrell, R.R. and King, K.A. (2004) 'Proper hand-washing techniques in public restrooms: differences in gender, race, signage, and time of day', *American Journal of Health Education*, 35(2): 86–9, p 87.
22. Klepp, I.G. (2007) 'Patched, louse-ridden, tattered: clean and dirty clothes', *Textile: Cloth and Culture*, 5(3): 254–75.
23. Ibbetson, C. (2020) 'Do men do their fair share of housework?', https://yougov.co.uk/topics/society/articles-reports/2020/02/07/do-british-men-do-their-fair-share-housework.
24. Sullivan, O. (2000) 'The division of domestic labour: twenty years of change?', *Sociology*, 34(3): 437–56.
25. Ibbetson, C. (2022) 'Men and women disagree on how much they contribute to the housework', https://yougov.co.uk/topics/society/articles-reports/2022/08/31/men-and-women-disagree-how-much-they-contribute-ho.
26. Kaufmann, J.-C. (1998) *Dirty Linen: Couples and their Laundry*, London: Middlesex University Press, p 120.
27. Myrstad, A.M. (2005) 'Thrift and traces of work: on housewife films and sales talk', in G. Hagemann and H. Roll-Hansen (eds) *Twentieth-century Housewives: Meanings and Implications of Unpaid Work*, Oslo: Unipub forlag, Oslo Academic Press.

Chapter 3

1. Matheson, C. (1907) *Board of Education Special Reports on Educational Subjects Vol. 19, School Training for the Home Duties of Women Part III, the Domestic Training of Girls in Germany and Austria*, London: HMSO, pp 33–5.
2. Beecher, C.E. (1854 edition, first published 1841) *A Treatise on Domestic Economy for the Use of Young Ladies at Home and at School*, New York: Harper and Bros, pp i–iv, emphasis in original.
3. Board of Education (1906) *Special Reports on Educational Subjects Vol. 16, School Training for the Home Duties of Women Part II Belgium, Sweden, Norway, Denmark, Switzerland and France*, London: HMSO, p 19.
4. Board of Education, p 336.
5. Dyhouse, C. (1977) 'Good wives and little mothers: social anxieties and the schoolgirl's curriculum, 1890–1920', *Oxford Review of Education*, 3(1): 21–35, p 21.
6. Ehrenreich, B. and English, D. (1979) *For Her Own Good: 150 Years of the Experts' Advice to Women*, London: Pluto Press, p 142.
7. Board of Education, pp 83–4.
8. Board of Education, p 336.
9. Pillow, M. (1897) 'Domestic economy teaching in England', *Parliamentary Papers*, 25: 157–86, p 161.

Notes

[10] Board of Education, p 121.
[11] Board of Education, p 173.
[12] Burstall, S.A. (1907) *English High Schools for Girls: Their Aims, Organization and Management*, London: Longmans & Co, pp 194–6.
[13] Dowdall, D. (2014) *Educating for Femininity? Reform of Working and Middle Class Girls' Education in Victorian England*, BA thesis, Department of History, Wellesley College, p 29.
[14] Akiyama, Y. (2008) *Feeding the Nation: Nutrition and Health in Britain before World War One*, London: Bloomsbury Academic, pp 27–9; Mäenpää, S. (2001) 'From pea soup to hors d'oeuvres: the status of the cook on British merchant ships', *The Northern Mariner/Le Marin du nord*, 11(2): 39–55.
[15] Pycroft, Miss (1897) 'History of training schools for teachers of domestic economy in England', *Journal of the Royal Society of Arts*, 45(2333) 966–71, p 966.
[16] Buckmaster, J.C. (1874) *Buckmaster's Cookery being an Abridgement of some of the Lectures Delivered in the Cookery School at the International Exhibition for 1873 and 1874 together with a Collection of Approved Recipes and Menus*, London: G. Routledge and Sons, p 143.
[17] 'National Training School of Cookery', *Wikipedia*. https://en.wikipedia.org/wiki/The_National_Training_School_of_Cookery
[18] Hoodless, A. (1898) *Public School Domestic Science*, Toronto: Copp, Clark Co, p 103.
[19] Purvis, J. (1991) *A History of Women's Education in England*, Milton Keynes: Open University Press, p 26.
[20] Akiyama, p 54.
[21] Turnbull, A. (2004) 'Calder, Fanny Louisa (1838–1923, promoter of education in domestic subjects', *Oxford Dictionary of National Biography*.
[22] Delamont, S. (2004) 'Burstall, Sara Annie (1859–1939), headmistress', *Oxford Dictionary of National Biography*.
[23] Crick, D.E. (1912) 'Teaching of domestic economy in secondary schools', *Journal of the Royal Sanitary Institute*, 33(12): 611–17, p 611.
[24] Ravenhill, A. (1905) 'The teaching of "domestic science" in the United States of America', *Special Reports on Educational Subjects Vol 15*, London: HMSO, p 25.
[25] Oram, R. (2020) *Useful for Life: Women, Girls, and Vocational School Reform in Chicago, 1880–1930*, PhD thesis, Loyola University, p 92.
[26] Richards, E. and Butler, N.M. (1889) 'Domestic economy as a factor in public education', *Educational Monographs*, 2(4): 115–42, p 122.
[27] Calder, F.A. and Mann, E.E. (1892) *A Teachers' Manual of Elementary Laundry Work*, London: Longmans, Green & Co, p vii.
[28] Barnett, H.O.W. (1895) *The Making of the Home. A Reading-book of Domestic Economy*, London: Cassell & Co, p 21.
[29] Newsholme, A. and Scott, M.E. (1893) *Domestic Economy: Comprising the Laws of Health in their Application to Home Life and Work*, London: Swan Sonnenschein & Co, p 1.
[30] Newsholme and Scott, p 37.
[31] Mjelde, L. (2006) *The Magical Properties of Workshop Learning*, Bern: Peter Lang AG, International Academic Publishers; 'Helga Helgesen', *Wikipedia*. https://en.wikipedia.org/wiki/Helga_Helgesen
[32] Board of Education, pp 177–8.
[33] Oram, p 97.
[34] Daniels, C.E.J. and Bayliss, R.A. (1985) 'Alice Ravenhill, home economist, 1859–1954', *Westminster Studies in Education*, 8(1): 21–36, p 32.
[35] Ravenhill, A. (1951) *The Memoirs of an Educational Pioneer*, Toronto and Vancouver: J.M. Dent and Sons, p 111, emphasis in original.
[36] Ravenhill (1905), p 50, p 73.

37 'H.M.S.' (1905) 'Review of Alice Ravenhill's book on *The Teaching of Domestic Science in America*', *The Manchester Guardian*, 20 June.
38 Scott, M.E. (1967) *The History of the F. L. Calder College of Domestic Science 1875–1965*, Liverpool: Wetteren printed, p 13.
39 Editorial (1899) 'Public school instruction in cooking', *Journal of the American Medical Association*, 32: 1183.
40 Board of Education, p 127.
41 [no author] (1906) 'The teaching of hygiene and temperance in elementary schools', *British Medical Journal*, 17 November, 1412–14.
42 Ravenhill, A. (1907) *Lessons in Practical Hygiene for Use in Schools*, Leeds: E. J. Arnold & Son, p 5, pp 153–4.
43 *Report of Interdepartmental Committee on Physical Deterioration Vol. III, Appendix and Index, Parliamentary Papers*, 1904, XXXII, pp 153–4. Cited in Dyhouse, p 23.
44 Purvis, p 28.
45 Board of Education, p 86.
46 [no author] (1906) 'Special report on school training for the home duties of women', *The Practical Teacher*, 27(1): 9–12, p 11.
47 Smithells, A. (1907) 'School training for home duties of women', *Report of the Seventy-Sixth Meeting of the British Association for the Advancement of Science, York, August 1906*, London: John Murray, pp 781–4, pp 782–3.

Chapter 4

1 Paulley, J.W. (1993) 'The death of Albert Prince Consort: the case against typhoid fever', *QJ An International Journal of Medicine*, 86(12): 837–41; [no author] (1871) 'The illness of HRH The Prince of Wales', *The British Medical Journal*, 2(571): 671–3; McHugh, J. and Mackowiak, P.A. (2014) 'Death in the White House: President William Henry Harrison's atypical pneumonia', *Clinical Infectious Diseases*, 59(4): 990–5.
2 National Health Society leaflet, 'How to keep fever out of houses', Margaret Eleanor Pillow Papers, Women's Library Archives, London School of Economics, 7MEP/2/2.
3 Pillow, M.E. (1896) 'Drains and drainage', *Our Paper: The Monthly Organ of the Women's Help Society*, 4(55): 920; Margaret Eleanor Pillow Papers, Women's Library Archives, London School of Economics, 7MEP/2/5.
4 Plunkett, Mrs H.M. (1885) *Women, Plumbers, and Doctors; or, Household Sanitation*, New York: D. Appleton and Company, p 11.
5 Scott, M.E. (1891) 'Woman's work in promoting the cause of hygiene', *International Congress of Hygiene & Demography held in London August 10th to 17th*, p 7, Margaret Eleanor Pillow Papers, Women's Library Archives, London School of Economics, 7MEP/2/4.
6 MacDonald, C. (1986) *Adelaide Hoodless: Domestic Crusader*, Toronto: Dundurn Press.
7 Plunkett, p 239.
8 Plunkett, Mrs H.M. (1885) 'Great-grandmother's year', *The New England Kitchen Magazine*, 111(2): 61–3; 'Great-grandmother's year: second paper', *The New England Kitchen Magazine*, 111(4): 149–53.
9 Cited in Strasser, S. (1982) *Never Done: A History of American Housework*, New York: Pantheon Books, p 105; Beecher, C.E. (1854, first published 1841) *A Treatise on Domestic Economy for the Use of Young Ladies at Home and at School*, New York: Harper and Bros; Campbell, H. (1881) *The Easiest Way in Housekeeping and Cooking*, New York: Fords, Howard & Hulbert.
10 Roberts, E. (1984) *A Woman's Place: An Oral History of Working-class Women 1890–1940*, Oxford: Basil Blackwell.
11 Read, S. (2008) '"Thy righteousness is but a menstrual clout": sanitary practices and prejudice in Early Modern England', *Early Modern Women*, 3: 1–25; Delaney, J., Lupton,

Notes

M.J. and Toth, E. (1977) *The Curse: A Cultural History of Menstruation*, New York: The New American Library, Inc; Vostrak, S.L. (2008) *Under Wraps: A History of Menstrual Hygiene Technology*, Lanham: Lexington Books.

12 Adams, A. (2001) *Architecture in the Family Way: Doctors, Houses, and Women, 1870–1900*, Montreal and Kingston: McGill-Queen's University Press, chapter 2.

13 Roberts, p 134.

14 Plunkett, *Women, Plumbers, and Doctors*, p 132.

15 Mokyr, J. (2000) 'Why "more work for mother?" Knowledge and household behavior, 1870–1946', *The Journal of Economic History*, 60(1): 1–41, p 16.

16 Tomes, N. (1998) *The Gospel of Germs: Men, Women, and the Microbe in American Life*, Cambridge, MA: Harvard University Press, p 7.

17 Adams, p 91.

18 Mokyr, p 25.

19 Beeton, I.M. (1879, first published 1861) *The Book of Household Management*, London: Ward, Lock & Co, p 23.

20 Hughes, K. (2005) *The Short Life and Long Times of Mrs Beeton*, London: Fourth Estate.

21 Elliott, S.M. (1914, first published 1905) *Household Bacteriology*, Boston and Chicago: American School of Home Economics, p 5, p 3.

22 Elliott, p 12.

23 Prudden, T.M. (1910) *Dust and its Dangers*, New York and London: G.P. Putnam's Sons, p 2, p 25.

24 Tomes, p 163.

25 Tomes, p 167.

26 [no author] (1891) 'Interview with Miss Margaret Eleanor Scott the first woman to pass the examination in sanitary science and law established by the Council of the Sanitary Institute', *Woman's Herald*, 28 March, p 353.

27 Mumford, M.E. (1894) 'The place of women in municipal reform', *The Outlook*, 31 March, 587–8, p 587.

28 Charlton, C. (nd) 'Miscellany: the National Health Society Almanack, 1883', http://www.localpopulationstudies.org.uk/PDF/LPS32/LPS32_1984_54-57.pdf, p 55.

29 [no author] (1889) 'Lenten lectures for ladies at the Sanitary Institute', *Public Health*, May 1888–April 1889, p 371.

30 Martin, T. (1951) 'The experimental researches of Benjamin Thompson, Count Rumford', *Bulletin of the British Society for the History of Science*, 1(6): 144–58, p 144; Knight, D. (2004) 'Thompson, Sir Benjamin, Count Rumford in the nobility of the Holy Roman Empire', *Oxford Dictionary of National Biography*.

31 Levenstein, H. (1980) 'The New England kitchen and the origins of modern American eating habits', *American Quarterly*, 32(4): 369–86.

32 Davidson, C. (1982) *Woman's Work is Never Done: A History of Housework in the British Isles 1650–1950*, London: Chatto & Windus, p 165.

33 Pattison, M. (1915) *The Business of Home Management (The Principles of Domestic Engineering)*, New York: Robert M. McBride & Co, pp 87–90.

34 Kane, K. (2012) 'A regency bicentennial: the servant tax', https://recordoffice.wordpress.com/2017/01/06/treasure-42-a-licence-to-employ-a-servant-1878/; 'Male servants tax 1777–1852', https://www.familysearch.org/en/wiki/England_Eighteenth_Century_Taxation_-_International_Institute.

35 Salmon, L.M. (1897) *Domestic Service*, New York: Macmillan Co; Carruyo, L. (2022) 'Gender, race, and the status of household labour in Lucy Maynard Salmon's *Domestic Service* (1897)', *Women's History Review*, 31(7): 1127–48.

36 Frederick, C. (1913) *The New Housekeeping: Efficiency Studies in Home Management*, Garden City: Doubleday, Page & Company, pp 7–8.
37 [no author] (1909) 'Lake Placid Conference on Home Economics 1899–1908', *Journal of Home Economics*, 1(1): 3–21.
38 Ravenhill, A. (1901) 'Women as sanitary inspectors' and 'Practical hygienic teaching in England', *Lake Placid Conference on Home Economics: Proceedings of First, Second and Third Conferences*, American Home Economics Association.
39 Fields, A.M. and Connell, T.H. (2004) 'Classification and the definition of a discipline: the Dewey Decimal Classification and home economics', *Libraries & Culture*, 39(3): 245–59.
40 *Lake Placid Conference on Home Economics*, p 4.
41 Richards, E.H. (1900) *Air, Water and Food, From a Sanitary Standpoint*, New York: J. Wiley & Sons, p 1.
42 Swallows, P.C. (2014) *The Remarkable Life and Career of Ellen Swallow Richards*, Hoboken: John Wiley & Sons, p 57.
43 Richards, E.H.S. (1910) *Euthenics: The Science of Controllable Environment*, Boston: Whitcomb & Barrow, p vii.
44 Richards, E.H. (1897) 'The place of science in woman's education', *The American Kitchen Magazine*, 7(6): 224–7, p 226.
45 Thompson, P.J. (1994) 'Ellen Swallow Richards (1842–1911): ecological foremother', paper presented at the Annual Meeting of the American Educational Research Association, 5–8 April.

Chapter 5

1 Gilman, C.P. (1911) *The Man-made World or Our Androcentric Culture*, New York: Charlton Company.
2 Peel, C.D. (1917) *The Labour-saving House*, London: John Lane.
3 Eyles, M.L. (1922) *The Woman in the Little House*, London: Grant Richards, p 38.
4 Candee, H.C. (1900) 'Architecture and interiors', *The American Kitchen Magazine*, 13(11[2]): 52–4, pp 52–3.
5 Millar, J. (2010) 'The first women architect', *Architects' Journal*, 11 November, https://www.architectsjournal.co.uk/. Not everyone agrees with this view; see Merrick, J. (2011) 'Elizabeth Wilbraham: the first lady of architecture', *The Independent*, 16 February, https://www.independent.co.uk/arts-entertainment/architecture/elizabeth-wilbraham-the-first-lady-of-architecture-2215936.html.
6 Black, C. (1918) 'Domestic idiocies', *The Contemporary Review*, 115: 67–75, p 72, p 68.
7 Black, C. (1918) *A New Way of Housekeeping*, London: W. Collins, Sons & Co.
8 Bernège, P. (1928) *De la méthode ménagère*, Orléans: Tessier.
9 Bernège, P. (1928) *Si les femmes faisaient les maisons*, Paris: à Mon chez moi.
10 Richards, E.H. (1905) *The Cost of Shelter*, New York: John Wiley & Sons, p 72, pp 75–6.
11 Peet, L.J. and Sater, L.E. (1940, first published 1934) *Household Equipment*, New York: John Wiley & Sons, Inc., p xi.
12 Taylor, F. (1915) 'Foreword', in M. Pattison, *The Business of Home Management (The Principles of Domestic Engineering)*, New York: Robert M. McBride & Co, p 17.
13 Campbell, H. (1881) *The Easiest Way in Housekeeping and Cooking*, New York: Fords, Howard & Hulbert, pp 17–18.
14 Frederick, C. (1915) *Efficient Housekeeping or Household Engineering*, London: George Routledge, p 14. (Table 5.1 is from a different edition, *Household Engineering: Scientific Management in the Home* (1923) Chicago: American School of Home Economics.)

Notes

15. Rutherford, J.W. (1996) *'Only a Girl': Christine Frederick, Efficiency, Consumerism, and Woman's Sphere*, PhD thesis, Louisiana State University and Agricultural & Mechanical College, pp 176–7.
16. Frederick, p 78.
17. Rutherford, p 165, p 168.
18. Belliveau, A.R. (2012) 'Psychology's first forays into film', American Psychological Association, https://www.apa.org/monitor/2012/05/film.
19. Wharton, E. (1927) *Twilight Sleep*, New York: D. Appleton & Co.
20. Steiner, S. (2006) 'Radical and chic', *The Guardian*, 1 April, https://www.theguardian.com/lifeandstyle/2006/apr/01/homes1.
21. Hochhäusl, S. (2013) 'From Vienna to Frankfurt Inside Core-House Type 7: a history of scarcity through the modern kitchen', *Architectural Histories*, 1(1): 24, pp 1–19, http://doi.org/10.5334/ah.aq; 'Margarete Schütte-Lihotzky', *Wikipedia*. https://en.wikipedia.org/wiki/Margarete_Sch%C3%BCtte-Lihotzky
22. Henderson, S.R. (2013) 'The new woman's home', excerpt from *Building Culture: Ernst May and the New Frankfurt Initiative, 1926–1931*, Bern, Frankfurt, London and New York: Peter Lang, p 154.
23. Hagemann, K. (1996) 'Of "old" and "new" housewives: everyday housework and the limits of household rationalization in the urban working-class milieu of the Weimar Republic', *International Review of Social History*, 41: 305–30.
24. Nolan, M. (1990) '"Housework made easy": the Taylorized housewife in Weimar Germany's rationalized economy', *Feminist Studies*, 16(3): 549–77.
25. Beecher, C.E. and Stowe, H.B. (2002 edition, first published 1869) *The American Woman's Home*, New Brunswick: Rutgers University Press, p 34.
26. Gilman, C.P. (1913) 'The waste of private housekeeping', *The Annals of the American Academy of Political and Social Science*, 48: 91–5.
27. Gilman, C.P. (1912) *What Diantha Did*, London: T. Fisher Unwin.
28. Stephenson, C.T. (1992) '"Integrating the Carol Kennicotts": Ethel Puffer Howes and the Institute for the Coordination of Women's Interests', *Journal of Women's History*, 4(1): 89–113.
29. Black, *A New Way of Housekeeping*, p 128.
30. Folbre, N. (1991) 'The unproductive housewife: her evolution in nineteenth century economic thought', *Signs*, 16(3): 463–84.
31. Marshall, A. (1920) *Principles of Economics*, London: Macmillan and Co; McGourty, A. (2020) 'Unequal equilibrium: the historical foundations of gender inequality in neo-classical economics', *The Knowles Review of Economic History*, 1(1): 59–70.
32. McKillop, M. and Atkinson, M. (1911) *Economics, Descriptive and Theoretical*, London: Allman & Son, p 93.
33. Atkinson, M. (1911) 'The economic relations of the household', in A. Ravenhill and C.J. Schiff (eds) *Household Administration: Its Place in the Higher Education of Women*, New York: H. Holt and Company, p 123, p 130.
34. 'Valuation of nonmarket housework', *Wikipedia*. https://en.wikipedia.org/wiki/Valuation_of_nonmarket_housework#:~:text=The%20valuation%20of%20nonmarket%20housework,with%20child%20care%20and%20nurturing; van de Ven, P. (2018) 'Including unpaid household activities: an estimate of its impact on macro-economic indicators in the G7 economies and the way forward', *Working Paper no. 91*, OECD.
35. Kyrk, H. (1933, first published 1929) *Economic Problems of the Family*, New York: Harper & Bros.
36. Le Tollec, A. (2020) *Finding a New Home (Economics): Toward a Science of the Rational Family, 1924–1981*, PhD thesis, Université de Paris-Saclay, France.

37. See Dimand, R.W., Dimand, N.A. and Forget, E.L. (eds) (2000) *A Biographical Dictionary of Women Economists*, Aldershot and Lyme: Edward Elgar.
38. Reid, M.G. (1934) *Economics of Household Production*, New York: John Wiley & Sons.
39. Forget, E.L. (2000) 'Margaret Gilpin Reid' in Dimand et al, pp 357–62, p 358. Reid's work fed directly into economist Gary Becker's much better-known 'new home economics', although Becker makes no acknowledgement of this debt.

Chapter 6

1. There are two notable exceptions: Blakestad, N.L. (1994) *King's College of Household & Social Science and the Household Science Movement in English Higher Education c. 1908–1939*, DPhil, University of Oxford; Marsh, N. (1986) *The History of Queen Elizabeth College*, London: King's College.
2. Marsh, pp 6–7.
3. Hearnshaw, F.J.C. (1929) *The Centenary History of King's College London 1928–1928*, London: George G. Harrap & Company, p 377.
4. KCHSS Archives, KW/EPH1, 'Historical sketch King's College, Ladies' Department' (nd), p 4.
5. KCHSS Archives, KW/SYL1, King's College, London, 'Lectures to Ladies at Kensington, Syllabus of Lectures, Easter Term 1878', p 4.
6. KCHSS Archives, KWA/RAD1, Students' address & courses 1894–5.
7. Morley, E. (2016, first published 1944) *Before and After: Reminiscences of a Working Life*, Reading: Two Rivers Press, pp 47–8.
8. King's College London (2021) 'Celebrating LGBT History', https://www.kcl.ac.uk/news/celebrating-kings-lgbt-history1v.
9. Jones, C.K. and Snaith, A. (2010) '"Tilting at universities": Woolf at King's College London', *Woolf Studies Annual*, 16: 1–44.
10. Jones and Snaith, p 31.
11. KCHSS Archives, KW/SYL5 1895–1896.
12. KCHSS Archives, KW/SYL7 1898–99, p 36.
13. KCHSS Archives, KW/SYL8 1899–1900, p 50.
14. KCHSS Archives, KW/EPH/1, *KCW Magazine*, 1(1), Michaelmas Term 1896, p 13.
15. Rawson, Mrs S. (1899) 'Where London girls may study. II.- King's College, Kensington Square', *The Girls' Realm Annual*, November 1899–October 1899, pp 1201–7, p 1206.
16. Faithfull, L.M. (1924) *In the House of my Pilgrimage*, London: Chatto & Windus, p 105.
17. Faithfull, p 110.
18. Cited in Oakeley, H.D. (1939) *My Adventures in Education*, London: Williams & Norgate, p 141.
19. Faithfull, p 121.
20. KCHSS Archives, KAS/ACII/F3, 'Statement on the work of King's College for Women and the place it fills in the educational system of London', Memorandum by Lady Rücker.
21. KCHSS Archives, KW/M3, King's College Ladies' Department, Meeting of Committee, 26 March 1897.
22. KCHSS Archives, KW/SYL8 1899–1900.
23. KCHSS Archives, KAS/ACII F3–7, 'Memorandum on the history of the Home Science Department of King's College for Women' (nd).
24. KCHSS Archives, KAS/ACII/F3.
25. Ravenhill, A. (1951) *The Memoirs of an Educational Pioneer*, Toronto and Vancouver: J.M. Dent and Sons, pp 139–40.
26. 'Lizzie B.' (2022) 'Cecil Gradwell (1885–1942) – women who meant business', https://womenwhomeantbusiness.com/2021/02/10/cecil-gradwell-1855-1942/.

27 KCHSS Archives, KWA/SCR3, Prospectus King's College, University of London, Women's Department, Course of lectures on General Hygiene Miss Alice Ravenhill.
28 KCHSS Archives, KW/SYL15 1907–8, Annual Report, p 76.
29 KCHSS Archives, KW/M5a/6/7, King's College for Women Board of Studies for Home Science and Economics, Minutes of Meetings 28 February, 6 March, 12 March, 19 March, 1908.
30 KCHSS Archives, KAS/ACII/F3, 'Statement on the work of King's College for Women and the place it fills in the educational system of London'.
31 KCHSS Archives, Q/EPH/SYL/1-56, SYL 1, King's College for Women, University of London, Special Courses for the Higher Education of Women in Home Science and Household Economics, Session 1909–10, p 2.
32 KCHSS Archives, Q/EPH/SER 1/12-23; Cowper, N. (1948) 'King's College for Women in 1908', *KCHSS Magazine*, May, pp 13–14.
33 Smithells, A. (1921) 'The university and women's work. Address delivered at the inauguration of the King's College (London University) Courses for the Higher Education of Women in Home Science and Household Economics, October 2, 1908', in A. Smithells, *From a Modern University: Some Aims and Aspirations of Science*, Oxford: Oxford University Press, pp 66–78, p 73.
34 KCHSS Archives KW/PC.
35 KCHSS Archives KW/PC, *Leeds Mercury*, 3 October 1908; *The Manchester Guardian*, 19 November 1908.
36 KCHSS Archives, KW/EPH3a, 'A model market' (poster); KW/M5, Meeting 24 January 1911.
37 Hearnshaw, p 440.
38 Marsh, pp 38–9.
39 Marsh has a table showing 'The royal connection' at the back of his book (no page number).
40 *The Calendar of King's College 1909–1910*, London: Richard Clay and Sons, 1909, pp 425–43.
41 KCHSS Archives, Q/EPH/SYL/1-56, SYL1, King's College for Women, University of London, Special Courses for the Higher Education of Women in Home Science and Household Economics, Session 1909–10, pp 9–10, p 14.
42 KCHSS Archives, KWA/REC4, Record Books 1910-11-12-13.
43 KCHSS Archives, KWA/GPF/11, 'Speech at the opening of the extension of the Gloucester School of Domestic Science, October 7, 1911', p 1, pp 4–5.
44 'A college for women', *The Times of India*, 19 April 1919, p 12.

Chapter 7

1 Croak, L. (1929) 'Alice through the cooking class', *King's Minstrel*, March, p 15.
2 Marsh, N. (1986) *The History of Queen Elizabeth College*, London: King's College, pp 143–4.
3 See, for example, Marsh, p. 41 and Hawgood, B.J. (2010) 'Sir Edward Mellanby (1884–1955) GBE KCB FRCP FRS: nutrition scientist and medical research mandarin', *Journal of Medical Biography*, 18: 150–7.
4 Freund, I. (1911) 'Domestic science – a protest', *The Englishwoman*, 29: 147–63, p 150, p 156.
5 Freund, I. (1905) 'Invitation to the periodic table' in A. Phillips (ed) *A Newnham Anthology*, Cambridge: Newnham College, pp 72–3; Palmer, B. (2007) 'Ida Freund: teacher, educator, feminist, and chemistry textbook writer', *Transactions on Internet Research*, pp 49–54, https://web.archive.org/web/20131015164524/http://internetjournals.net/journals/tir/2007/July/Paper%2012.pdf; Ogilvie, M.B. (2004) 'Freund, Ida, (1863–1914), chemist', *Oxford Dictionary of National Biography*.

6. Robinson, R. (1912) 'King's College for Women', *The Freewoman*, 15 February, pp 255–7, p 256.
7. KCHSS Archives, KW/EPH4a, 'A reply to a Paper sent by Miss Freund to the Conference on Domestic Science Teaching, held at Gloucester, February 18th, 1911' by Sir Arthur Rucker.
8. Freund, I. (1911) 'Domestic science – a protest II', *The Englishwoman*, 30: 279–96, p 282.
9. Blakestad, N.L. (1994) *King's College of Household & Social Science and the Household Science Movement in English Higher Education c. 1908–1939*, DPhil, University of Oxford, p 145.
10. Stewart, L. (1989) 'The politics of women's education: establishing home economics at the University of British Columbia, 1914–1949', *Historical Studies in Education*, 261–81.
11. KCHSS Archives, Q/EPH/SER 1/1-4, *The Magazine of the Household and Social Science Department, King's College for Women*, May, 1920, p 35.
12. KCHSS Archives, Q/EPH/SYL17, *Report of Session 1914–15*, p 8; Blakestad, p 182.
13. Cited in Marsh, p 81.
14. KCHSS Archives, Q/EPH/SYL17, *Report of Session 1914–15*, p 9.
15. *Royal Commission on University Education in London* (the Haldane Commission), *Final Report of the Commissioners* (1913), London: HMSO.
16. KCHSS Archives, KWA/GPF16, Meyer, L.B., Kimpton, N.A. and Carruthers, M.D. (1913) Letter headed 'The Old Students' Association', *The Journal of Education*, December, p 88.
17. KCHSS Archives, KWA/GPF16, Letter to H. Oakeley from E. Plumer, 7 April 1914.
18. *The Haldane Commission, Second Report (1911) Minutes of Evidence with Appendices and Index*, Appendix 11 (b) 'Memorandum on the University Education of Women in London by Miss Hilda D. Oakeley', pp 102–4.
19. KCHSS Archives, QA/C/M1, Executive Committee Minutes 12 November 1918, p 3.
20. KHHSS Archives, KW/SYL, SYL17.
21. Lane-Claypon, J.E. (1921) *Hygiene of Women and Children*, London: Henry Frowde and Hodder & Stoughton, p 5.
22. Lane-Claypon, J.E. (1919) 'Adventures in higher education: the science of housewifery', *The Graphic*, 20 December, 100(2612): 940.
23. Lane-Claypon, J.E. (1922) 'Household science as a university course', *The Sphere*, 9 December, p 256.
24. KCHSS Archives, Q/EPH/RPT3, 1921–22, 'Household & Social Science Department King's College for Women, Dean's Report for the Session 1921–22'.
25. KCHSS Archives, Q/EPH/RPT3, 1918–19.
26. Dale, H.D. (1955) 'Edward Mellanby, 1884–1955', *Biographical Memoirs of Fellows of the Royal Society*, 1(1): 193–222.
27. Parascandola, J. and Ihde, A.J. (1977) 'Edward Mellanby and the antirachitic factor', *Bulletin of the History of Medicine*, 51(4): 507–15.
28. Maternowski, C. (2017) 'Lady Mellanby's dental utopia', https://nursingclio.org/2017/05/31/lady-mellanbys-dental-utopia/.
29. Platt, B.S. (2004) 'Mellanby, Sir Edward (1884–1955), medical scientist and administrator', *Oxford Dictionary of National Biography*.
30. KCHSS Archives, Q/EPH/RPT3, Household & Social Science Department King's College for Women, Dean's Report for the Session 1917–18.
31. *The Times Educational Supplement*, 10 June 1920, p 312.
32. Haldane Commission, 3rd Report, 1911, p xiv.
33. KCHSS Archives, Q/EPH/RPT3, 'Household & Social Science Department King's College for Women, Dean's Report for the Session 1917–18', p 2.
34. KCHSS Archives, QA/C/M2, Executive Committee Minutes, 10 February 1920.

Notes

35. KCHSS Archives, QA/C/M3, Executive Committee Minutes, 11 May 1926, appended document, 'University of London King's College for Women – Household and Social Science Department Visitation under Statute 76'.
36. Winkelstein, W. (2004) 'Claypon, Janet Elizabeth Lane [married name Janet Elizabeth Forber, Lady Forber] (1877–1967), physiologist and epidemiologist', *Oxford Dictionary of National Biography*.
37. KCHSS Archives, Q/EPH/PRG2/1, commemoration dinner, 3 March 1927.
38. KCHSS Archives, Q/EPH/SER1/12-23, Magazine of KCHSS, November 1950, 'Professor Mottram's Address to the Old Students' Association'.
39. KCHSS Archives, Q/EPH/SER1/12-23, Magazine of KCHSS, June 1951, p 11.

Chapter 8

1. Napoleoni, L. (2020) 'On the covert role of knitting during the French Revolution and World War II', *Literary Hub*, 4 November, https://lithub.com/on-the-covert-role-of-knitting-during-the-french-revolution-and-world-war-ii/.
2. Although I did visit the University of Chicago Archives for the writing of my book *Women, Peace and Welfare* (2018) and read some relevant papers then.
3. Cited in Angstman, C.S. (1898) 'College women and the new science', *Popular Science Monthly*, 53: 674–90, p 683.
4. Gavazzi, S.M. and Low, J.N. (2020) 'Confronting the wealth transfer from tribal nations that established land-grant universities', American Association of University Professors, Spring, Beyond Town and Gown, https://www.aaup.org/article/confronting-wealth-transfer-tribal-nations-established-land-grant-universities; 'Land-grant university', *Wikipedia*. https://en.wikipedia.org/wiki/Land-grant_university
5. Talbot, M. (1936) *More Than Lore: Reminiscences of Marion Talbot, Dean of Women, The University of Chicago, 1892–1925*, Chicago: University of Chicago Press, p 97.
6. Talbot, M. and Richards, E.R. (1887) *Home Sanitation: A Manual for Housekeepers*, Boston: Ticknor and Company, pp 29, 34, 69.
7. Talbot, M. (1896) 'Sanitation and sociology', *American Journal of Sociology*, 2(1): 74–81, p 81.
8. Talbot, M. (1910) *The Education of Women*, Chicago: University of Chicago Press, p 14.
9. Bordin, R. (1993) *Alice Freeman Palmer: The Evolution of a New Woman*, Ann Arbor: The University of Michigan Press, p 4.
10. Talbot, *More Than Lore*, p 99.
11. Cited in Gray, H.H. (2015) Foreword to new edition of Talbot (1936) *More Than Lore*, pp vii–xx, p x.
12. *The American Kitchen Magazine* (1897), 6(4): 185.
13. Talbot, *More Than Lore*, pp 99–100.
14. Bulmer, M. (1984) *The Chicago School of Sociology: Institutionalization, Diversity and the Rise of Sociological Research*, Chicago: University of Chicago Press, p 8. See Deegan, M.J. (2015) 'A twisted path: Park, gender and praxis', in P. Kivisto (ed) *The Anthem Companion to Robert Park*, London: Anthem Press, pp 17–36, p 20 for other references.
15. 'On equal terms: educating women at the university of Chicago', The University of Chicago Library, www.lib/uchicago.edu/collex/exhibits/exoet/marion-talbot.
16. Hammond, C.H. (2000) 'Sophonisba Breckinridge (1866–1948)', in R.W. Dimand, M.A. Dimand and E.L. Forget (eds) *A Biographical Dictionary of Women Economists*, Cheltenham: Edward Elgar, pp 81–9, p 83.
17. Bordin, p 4.
18. Talbot, Foreword, *More Than Lore*, p xvi.
19. Talbot, M. and Breckinridge, S.P. (1912) *The Modern Household*, Boston, MA: Whitcomb & Barrows, preface (np) and pp 86–8.

20. Norton, A.P. (1916) *Food and Dietetics*, Chicago: American School of Home Economics, p 32, pp 52–3.
21. Thomas, W.I. (1897) 'On a difference in the metabolism of the sexes', *American Journal of Sociology*, 3: 31–63.
22. Deegan, p 26.
23. Park, R.E. and Burgess, E.W. (1921) *Introduction to the Science of Sociology*, Chicago: University of Chicago Press; Harvey, L. (1987) *Myths of the Chicago School*, Farnborough: Avebury, p 31.
24. Park, R.E. (1918) 'Education and its relation to the conflict and fusion of cultures: with special reference to the problems of the Negro and Missions', *Publications of the American Sociological Society*, December, p 59.
25. Delamont, S. (1992) 'Old fogies and intellectual women: an episode in academic history', *Women's History Review*, 1(1): 39–61.
26. Deegan, M.J. (2006) 'The human drama behind the study of people as potato bugs: the curious marriage of Robert E. Park and Clara Cahill Park', *Journal of Classical Sociology*, 6(1): 101–22.
27. Robbins, S. and Tippen, C.H. (2018) 'Gathering around Hull-House dining tables', *American Studies*, 57(3): 11–38.
28. Bartow, B. (1979) 'Isabel Bevier at the University of Illinois and the home economics movement', *Journal of the Illinois State Historical Society*, 72(1): 21–38, p 29.
29. Bevier, I. (1904) *The House: Its Plan, Decoration and Care*, American School of Household Economics, p 163; Bevier, I. (1901) 'Household science in a State University', *American Kitchen Magazine*, 15: 203–5, p 203.
30. Bevier, I. (1913) 'Some points in the making and judging of bread', *University of Illinois Bulletin*, 25, 17 March.
31. Department of Household Science University of Illinois 1916–17, 'Circular of Information and Announcement of Courses 1916–7', *University of Illinois Bulletin*, 13(38), 22 May 1916, p 9, p 21.
32. Department of Household Science, p 48.
33. Miller, E. (2004) *In the Name of the Home: Women, Domestic Science, and American Higher Education, 1865–1930*, PhD thesis, University of Illinois at Urbana-Champaign, p 182.
34. Okey, R., Johnson, B.K. and Macinney, G. (nd) 'Agnes Fay Morgan, Home Economics', Berkeley College of Chemistry, https://chemistry.berkeley.edu/news/agnes-fay-morgan-home-economics-berkeley.
35. Rossiter, M.W. (1982) *Women Scientists in America, Vol. 1, Struggles and Strategies to 1940*, Baltimore and London: The Johns Hopkins University Press, p 200; 'Agnes Fay Morgan', *Wikipedia*. https://en.wikipedia.org/wiki/Agnes_Fay_Morgan
36. Leinaweaver, J.B. (2013) 'Practice mothers', *Signs*, 38(2): 405–30.
37. Christman, J. (2014) *Borrowed Babies*, New York: Shebooks (spellings as in original).
38. See, for example, Bulmer; Chapoulie, J.-M. (2020) *Chicago Sociology*, New York: Columbia University Press.
39. Lengermann, P.M. and Niebrugge-Brantley, J. (1998) 'Women and the birth of sociology', in P.M. Lengermann and J. Niebrugge-Brantley, *The Women Founders: Sociology and Social Theory, 1830–1930*, New York: McGraw-Hill, Inc., pp 14–18, p 14.
40. Delamont, p 41.
41. Abbott, A. (1999) *Department and Discipline: Chicago Sociology at One Hundred*, Chicago: University of Chicago Press, p 14.
42. Bulmer, p 25, pp 25–6, p 33, p 39.
43. Diner, S.J. (1975) 'Department and discipline: the Department of Sociology at the University of Chicago, 1892–1920', *Minerva*, 13(4): 514–53.

Notes

44 Platt, J. (1983) 'The development of the "participant observation" method in sociology: origin myth and history', *Journal of the History of the Behavioral Sciences*, 19(4): 379–93.
45 Ehrenreich, B. and English, D. (1979) *For Her Own Good: 150 Years of the Experts' Advice to Women*, London: Pluto Press, p 135.

Chapter 9

1 Bose, C.E., Bereano, P.L. and Malloy, M. (1984) 'Household technology and the social construction of housework', *Technology and Culture*, 25(1): 53–82, p 56.
2 Fox, J. (1990) 'Selling the mechanized household: 70 years of ads in Ladies Home Journal', *Gender and Society*, 4(1): 25–40.
3 Davidson, C. (1982) *Woman's Work is Never Done: A History of Housework in the British Isles 1650–1950*, London: Chatto & Windus.
4 Edwards, E.E. (1935) *Report on Electricity in Working Class Homes*, London: Electrical Association for Women.
5 Campbell, H. (1881) *The Easiest Way in Housekeeping and Cooking*, New York: Fords, Howard & Hulbert.
6 Gordon, Mrs J.E.H. (1891) *Decorative Electricity*, London: Sampson Low, Marston, Searle, & Rivington, Limited.
7 Lancaster, M. (ed Lancaster, E.W.) (1914) *Electric Cooking Heating Cleaning etc Being a Manual of Electricity in the Service of the Home by 'Housewife' (Maud Lancaster)*, London: Constable & Company, p 2.
8 'Hair dryer', *Wikipedia*. https://en.wikipedia.org/wiki/Hair_dryer
9 Lancaster, p 8, emphasis in original.
10 *The Electrical Age for Women* (1928) 1(10): 398.
11 *The Electrical Age for Women* (1926) 1(1): 4–5.
12 Bowden, S. and Offer, A. (1994|) 'Household appliances and the use of time: the US and Britain since the 1920s', *The Economic History Review*, 47(4): 725–48.
13 Davidson, p 38.
14 Symons, L. (1993) 'The Electrical Association for Women, 1924–1986', *IEE Proceedings-A*, 140(3): 215–20, p 215.
15 Messenger, R. (1967) *The Doors of Opportunity: A Biography of Dame Caroline Haslett*, London: Femina Books, p 18.
16 Heald, H. (2019) *Magnificent Women and their Revolutionary Machines*, London: Unbound, pp 126–7; see also Symons.
17 Messenger, pp 101–2.
18 Cited in Symons, p 217.
19 Haslett, C.H. (ed) (1934) *The Electrical Handbook for Women*, London: Hodder & Stoughton Limited, p 40, p 73.
20 KCHSS Archives, QAP/GPF 7/64.
21 Haslett, C.H. (1938) 'Caroline Haslett CBE' in The Countess of Oxford and Asquith (ed) *Myself When Young by Famous Women of Today*, London: Frederick Muller, pp 97–116, p 113.
22 'E is for Electricity & the Electrical Association for Women', https://specialcollections universityofsouthampton.wordpress.com/2022/06/29/e-is-for-electricity-the-electrical-association-for-women/.
23 Brereton, M.A.C. (ed) (nd [1903?]) *Cooking by Gas*, London: The British Commercial Gas Association, p 166.
24 Brereton, M.A.C. (1913) 'Domestic service as a career for educated women', in *A Conference on the Economics of the Home held at the National Gas Congress & Exhibition*, London: Sir Joseph Causton & Sons, pp 6–20, p 7.

25. Tomes, N. (1998) *The Gospel of Germs: Men, Women, and the Microbe in American Life*, Cambridge, MA: Harvard University Press, pp 167–8.
26. Peters, E. (2022) '"On the fringe of the Technical World": female electrical appliance demonstrators in interwar Scotland', *Women's History Review*, 31(2): 230–54, p 244.
27. Haslett, C. (1939) *Household Electricity*, London: The English Universities Press, p 75.
28. Davidson, p 113.
29. Caroline Haslett cited in *The Leeds Mercury*, 28 January 1928, West Yorkshire Archives, Leeds, Electrical Association for Women branch records for Wetherby, Morley and Leeds, WYL1362.
30. Davidson, pp 127–8.
31. 'Goblin Teasmade', https://www.teasmade.uk/goblin/.
32. Hoy, S. (1995) *Chasing Dirt: The American Pursuit of Cleanliness*, New York: Oxford University Press, p 152; Science Museum Group, 'British Vacuum Cleaner Company, 1901', https://collection.sciencemuseumgroup.org.uk/people/ap26719/british-vacuum-cleaner-company-limited.
33. Clendinning, A. (1999) *Demons and Domesticity: A History of Women and the London Gas Industry, 1889–1939*, PhD thesis, McMaster University, Hamilton, p 77.
34. Cited in Peters, p 1.
35. Dover, H.L. (1930) 'A possible career for girl guides: saleswomen in electrical showrooms', *The Electrical Age for Women*, 1(16): 635–6, p 636.
36. 'Mary Berry', *Wikipedia*. https://en.wikipedia.org/wiki/Mary_Berry
37. Levy, P. (2004) 'Cradock, Phyllis Nan Sortain [Fanny], (1909–1994), television chef', *Oxford Dictionary of National Biography*.
38. Levy, P. (2004) 'Patten [née Brown], (Hilda Elsie) Marguerite, (1915–2015), cookery writer and broadcaster', *Oxford Dictionary of National Biography*.
39. Jaine, T. (2018) 'Zena Skinner Obituary', *The Guardian*, 20 March; The Connected Histories of the BBC, https://chbbc.sussex.ac.uk/.
40. *Kensington News and West London Times*, 16 August 1935.
41. Dismore, V. (1930) '"Tell us more about Electricity" says Mrs Housewife and Miss Bachelor Girl', *The Electrical Age for Women*, 2(2): 69–71, p 71.
42. 'The Electric Lullaby' (1926) *The Electrical Age for Women*, 1(1): 33.
43. Lawson, Mrs W. (1928) 'Electricity at the zoo', *The Electrical Age for Women*, 1(8): 304–5.
44. Cited in Messenger, p 42.
45. Holmes, H. (1931) 'The Bachelor Girls' Electrical Home as shown at the Bachelor Girls' Exhibition, London', *The Electrical Age for Women*, 2(3): 106–8, p 106; see 'The Bachelor Girls' Exhibition', Institution of Engineering and Technology Archives blog, https://ietarchiveblog.org/2017/08/01/the-bachelor-girls-exhibition-london-1930/.
46. 'The EAW house at Bristol: how the enterprise was received by the public' (1936) *The Electrical Age*, 3(1): 19–22; Hankin, E. (2012) *Buying Modernity? The Consumer Experience of Domestic Electricity in the Era of the Grid*, PhD thesis, University of Manchester, pp 89–90; Reece, S.H. and Roberts, G.K. (1998) '"This electric age is woman's opportunity": the Electrical Association for Women and its All-Electric House in Bristol, 1935', *The Local Historian*, 28(2): 94–107.
47. 'Margaret Partridge – electrical engineer and "wicked adventuress"', Institution of Engineering and Technology Archives blog, https://ietarchivesblog.org/2019/12/12/margaret-partridge-electric-engineer-and-wicked-adventuress/; Institution of Engineering and Technology Archives blog 'Lizzie B.' 'Women who meant business: Margaret Partridge (1891–1967)', https://womenwhomeantbusiness.com/2022/02/28/Margaret-partridge-1891-1967/.
48. 'Margaret Partridge', Institution of Engineering and Technology Archives blog.

49 Cited in Bix, A.S. (2002) 'Equipped for life: gendered technical training and consumerism in home economics, 1920–1980', *Technology and Culture*, 43(4): 728–54, p 751.
50 Lupton, E. and Miller, J.A. (1992) *The Bathroom, the Kitchen and the Aesthetics of Waste: A Process of Elimination*, Dalton: Studley Press, p 1.
51 Cited in *The Electrical Age*, 1934, 2(16): 653.

Chapter 10

1 Turnbull, A. (1994) 'An isolated missionary: the domestic subjects teacher in England, 1870–1914', *Women's History Review*, 3(1): 81–100, p 82.
2 De Zwart, M.L. (2003) *Home Economics Education in British Columbia 1913–36: Through Postcolonial Eyes*, PhD thesis, University of British Columbia, Canada, p 1, emphasis in original.
3 De Zwart, p 2.
4 Cox, R. (2011) 'Dishing the dirt: dirt in the home', in R. Cox (ed) *Dirt: The Filthy Reality of Everyday Life*, London: Profile Books, pp 8–73, p 39.
5 Educational Systems of the Chief Crown Colonies and Possessions of the British Empire, including Reports on the Training of Native Races Part II West Africa; Basutoland; Southern Rhodesia; East Africa Protectorate; Uganda; Mauritius; Seychelles (1905) *Board of Education Special Reports on Educational Subjects*, Vol 13, London: HMSO, p 301.
6 Griggs, M. (1988) 'A minority perspective on curriculum theory and practice', in H.V. Williams (ed) *Empowerment through Difference*, Peoria: Glencoe, pp 87–104. Cited in de Zwart, p 27.
7 Ishii, K. and Jarkey, N. (2002) 'The housewife is born: the establishment of the notion and identity of the *shufu* in modern Japan', *Japanese Studies*, 22(1): 35–47, p 37.
8 The transcription of Japanese names varies. I follow the usage in Tatsumi, Y. (2011) *Constructing Home Economics in Imperial Japan*, PhD thesis, University of Maryland. This is the source of much of my information on household science in Japan.
9 Tatsumi, p 85.
10 Cited in Tatsumi, pp 127–8.
11 Cited in Tatsumi, p 104.
12 Tatsumi, p 139.
13 Ravenhill, A. (1913) 'The art of right living', Department of Agriculture (Women's Institutes), *Province of British Columbia Bulletin no 50*, Victoria, British Columbia, pp 13–14.
14 Roberts, D. (2003) 'Massey, Lillian Frances (Treble), 1854–1915', *Dictionary of Canadian Biography*, Vol 14.
15 Durand, L.B. (1915) 'The latest science – housecraft', *MacLean's*, 1 April, https://archive.macleans.ca/article/1915/4/1/the-latest-science-housecraft/.
16 Heap, R. (1999) 'From the science of housekeeping to the science of nutrition: pioneers in Canadian nutrition and dietetics at the University of Toronto's Faculty of Household Science, 1900–1950', in E. Smyth, S. Acker, P. Bourne and A. Prentice (eds) *Challenging Professions: Historical and Contemporary Perspectives on Women's Professional Work*, Toronto: University of Toronto Press, pp 141–170, p 148.
17 Heap, p 155.
18 Studholme, J. (1909) 'Report to Chancellor', 19 May, cited in T. Fitzgerald and J. Collins (2011) *Historical Portraits of Women Home Scientists: The University of New Zealand, 1911–1947*, Amherst: Cambria Press, p 35.
19 McDonald, H. (1996) 'Boys-Smith, Winifed Lily', *Dictionary of New Zealand Biography*.
20 McDonald.
21 Thomson, H. and Thomson, S. (1963) *Ann Gilchrist Strong: Scientist in the Home*, Christchurch: Pegasus Press, p 80.

22. Needham, M.A. and Strong, A.C. (1929) *Domestic Science for High Schools in India*, Bombay: Oxford University Press, p 399.
23. Turner, M.E. (1923) 'Home economics venture upon "India's Coral Strand"', *The Iowa Homemaker*, 3(8).
24. Richards, A.L. (1951, first published 1939) *Land, Labour and Diet in Northern Rhodesia: An Economic Study of the Bemba Tribe*, Oxford: Oxford University Press, p 101.

Chapter 11

1. On Gabe, see Hopkins, A. (2017) 'Feminist inventor created the world's first "self-cleaning house" because she was sick of housework', https://www.dailymail.co.uk/news/article-4728482/Frances-Gabe-self-cleaning-house-sick-housework.html; Palahniuk, C. (2004) *Fugitives and Refugees: A Walk in Portland, Oregon*, London: Vintage Books, pp 29–33; Zimmerman, J. (ed) (1983) *The Technological Woman: Interfacing with Tomorrow*, New York: Praeger, pp 75–82.
2. Keeling, B. (2017) 'A peek inside the world's first and only self-cleaning house', https://sf.curbed.com/2017/7/18/15994034/self-cleaning-house.
3. Diani, M. (1992) 'The concept of social movement', *The Sociological Review*, 40(1): 1–25.
4. Lecture notes, Margaret Eleanor Pillow Papers, Women's Library Archives, London School of Economics, 7/MEP/1/3.
5. Buckton, C.M. (1873) *Two Winters' Experience in Giving Lectures to My Fellow Townswomen of the Working Classes on Physiology and Hygiene*, Leeds: William Wood, p 6.
6. [no author] (1900) 'News from the field', *The American Kitchen Magazine*, 13(1): 33–4, p 33.
7. Beecher, C.E. (1846) *Miss Beecher's Domestic Receipt Book: Designed as a Supplement to her Treatise on Domestic Economy*, New York: Harper and Bros.
8. Mokyr, J. (2000) 'Why "more work for mother?" Knowledge and household behavior, 1870–1946', *The Journal of Economic History*, 60(1): 1–41, p 35.
9. See Tomes, N. (1998) *The Gospel of Germs: Men, Women, and the Microbe in American Life*, Cambridge, MA: Harvard University Press; Garwin, A.J. (2000) *Coming Clean: The Health Revolution of 1890–1920 and its Impact on Infant Mortality*, Master's thesis, University of Tennessee.
10. Greene, V.W. (1984) *Cleanliness and the Health Revolution*, New York: Soap and Detergent Association, p 32.
11. Blakestad, N.L. (1997) 'King's College of Household and Social Science and the origins of dietetics education', in D.F. Smith (ed) *Nutrition in Britain: Science, Scientists and Politics in the Twentieth Century*, London: Routledge, pp 75–98, pp 83–4.
12. Tomes, p 16.
13. On a related point, the importance of the home in the development of modern science, see Opitz, D., Berwik, S. and Van Tiggelen, B. (2016) *Domesticity in the Making of Modern Science*, Houndmills: Palgrave Macmillan.
14. Davis, N. (2019) 'Housework could keep brain young, research suggests', *The Guardian*, 19 April; [no author] 'Scientific research confirms that the mortality rate of men doing housework is reduced by half!', https://inf.news/en/health/e636a58578333eabfad89721ba3d1c63.html; Hayward, E. (2023) 'Huffing and puffing "can cut cancer risk"', *The Times*, 28 July.
15. Yu, R., Leung, J. and Woo, J. (2013) 'Housework reduces all-cause and cancer mortality in Chinese men', *PLOS ONE* 8(11).
16. Rossiter, M.W. (1997) 'The men move in: home economics, 1950–1970', in S. Stage and V.B. Vincenti (eds) *Rethinking Home Economics: Women and the History of a Profession*, Ithaca and London: Cornell University Press, pp 96–117.

Notes

17 Rayner-Canham, M. and Rayner-Canham, G. (2008) *Chemistry was Their Life: Pioneer British Women Chemists, 1880–1949*, London: Imperial College Press, pp 106–7.

18 McKillop, M. (1916) *Food Values: What They Are and How to Calculate Them*, London: George Routledge & Sons, Limited, p iii.

19 Whitehead, R. (2015) 'Widdowson, Elsie May (1906–2000), nutritionist', *Oxford Dictionary of National Biography*; McCance, R.A. and Widdowson, E.M. (2002) *McCance and Widdowson's Composition of Foods*, Cambridge: Royal Society of Chemistry.

20 [no author] (1961) 'Queen Elizabeth College, London, Sir John Atkins Laboratories', *Nature*, 20 May, pp 684–5, p 684.

21 Hill, M.A. (1980) *Charlotte Perkins Gilman: The Making of a Radical Feminist, 1860–1896*, Philadelphia: Temple University Press.

22 Cited in Traikovski, L. (2003) 'The housewives' wages debate in the 1920s', *Journal of Australian Studies*, 78, https://caringlabor.wordpress.com/2011/01/25/louie-traikovski-the-housewives%E2%80%99-wages-debate-in-the-1920s/, pp 11–12.

23 James, S., 'Sex, race and working class power' and Oakley, A., letter, *Race Today*, January 1974; S. James 'Response', *Race Today*, March 1974.

24 Hawtree, C. (2008) 'Obituary: Joan Jackson: born Joan Hunter Dunn', *The Guardian*, 18 April, p 39; Betjeman, J. (1978) 'A Subaltern's Love-song', *Collected Poems*, London: John Murray.

25 Dreilinger, D. (2021) *The Secret History of Home Economics*, New York: W.W. Norton & Company, chapter 12; Gurstelle, W. (2021) 'Beatrice Finkelstein, the woman who fed the astronauts', *Scientific American*, 10 March, https://www.scientificameican.com/article/beatice-finkelsteimn-the-woman-who-fed-the-astronanuts/; Sanders, W. (2018) 'The woman who got real food to space', National Air and Space Museum, https://airandspace.si.edu/stories/editorial/woman-who-got-real-food-space; 'Doris Calloway', *Wikipedia*. https://en.wikipedia.org/wiki/Doris_Calloway

26 Asbjørnsen, P.C. (1864) *Fornuftig Madstel* ['Sensible Cookery']; Birkedal, T. (2021) 'The great Norwegian porridge feud', *Norwegian American*, 16 June, https://www.norwegianamerican.com/the-great-norwegian-porridge-feud/; Prichep, D. (2018) 'The great Norwegian porridge debate, or tradition vs. science', https://www.npr.org/sections/thesalt/2018/03/09/591957289/the-great-norwegian-porridge-debate-or-tradition-vs-science; Allwood, M.S. (1957) *Eilert Sundt: A Pioneer in Sociology and Social Anthropology*, Oslo: Olaf Norlis Forlag.

27 Fooladi, E.C. and Hopia, A. (2022) 'Revisiting the "porridge feud" in 19th century Norway: how knowledge and methods from multiple disciplines may reveal new clues to historical cooking practices', *International Journal of Gastronomy and Food Science*, 27: 100475 [online].

28 Berg, A.-J. (1998) 'A gendered scientific-technical construction: the smart house', in D. MacKenzie and J. Wajcman (eds) *The Social Shaping of Technology*, Buckingham: Open University Press, pp 301–13, p 273.

29 https://homemaidbetter.com/recurring-cleaning-service/.

Additional sources

Prologue

Berthold-Bond, A. (1999) *Better Basics for the Home*, New York: Three Rivers Press.
Engle, V. (2010) *Women* [documentary for BBC Television].
Griggs, B. (1993) *The Green Witch: A Modern Woman's Herbal*, London: Vermilion.
Hunt, S. (2002) *Making Competition Work in Electricity*, New York: John Wiley & Sons.
March, M. and Smith, M.R. (1897) 'Household labor as exercise', *The American Kitchen Magazine*, 6(5): 197–200.
Oakley, A. (1974) *Housewife*, London: Allen Lane.
Oakley, A. (1974) *The Sociology of Housework*, London: Martin Robertson.
Oakley, A.R. (1974) *Work Attitudes and Work Satisfaction of Housewives*, PhD thesis, University of London.
Oakley, A. (2011) *A Critical Woman: Barbara Wootton, Social Science and Public Policy in the Twentieth Century*, London: Bloomsbury Academic.
Quigg, M.R. (1994) *1001 Country Household Hints*, Devizes: Selectabook.
Rayner, C. (1967) *Housework the Easy Way*, London: Corgi Mini-Books.
Steinfeld, C. (2004) *Liquid Gold: The Lore and Logic of Using Urine to Grow Plants*, Totnes: Green Books.

Chapter 1

Campbell, H. (1897) *Household Economics*, New York: G.P. Putnam's Sons.
Davidson, C. (1982) *Woman's Work is Never Done: A History of Housework in the British Isles 1650–1950*, London: Chatto & Windus.
Friedan, B. (1963) *The Feminine Mystique*, London: Victor Gollancz.
Gavron, H. (1966) *The Captive Wife: Conflicts of Housebound Mothers*, London: Routledge & Kegan Paul.
Hardyment, C. (1988) *From Mangle to Microwave: The Mechanization of Household Work*, Oxford: Basil Blackwell.
Horsefield, M. (1997) *Biting the Dust: The Joys of Housework*, London: Fourth Estate.
Hoy, S. (1995) *Chasing Dirt: The American Pursuit of Cleanliness*, Bridgewater: Replica Books.
Lopata, H.Z. (1971) *Occupation Housewife*, New York: Oxford University Press.
Oakley, A. (1972) *Sex, Gender and Society*, London: Maurice Temple Smith (revised edition with new introduction, Farnham: Ashgate, 2015).
Oakley, A. (1974) *Housewife*, London: Allen Lane.

Oakley, A. (1974) *The Sociology of Housework*, London: Martin Robertson (new edition with new introduction, Bristol: Policy Press, 2019).

Oakley, A. (2018) *Women, Peace and Welfare: A Suppressed History of Social Reform, 1880–1920*, Bristol: Policy Press.

Stage, S. and Vincenti, V.B. (eds) (1997) *Rethinking Home Economics: Women and the History of a Profession*, Ithaca and London: Cornell University Press.

Strasser, S. (1982) *Never Done: A History of American Housework*, New York: Pantheon Books.

'Unpaid care and domestic work', https://www.actionaid.org.uk/our-work/womens-economic-rights/unpaid-care-and-domestic-work

You, X. (2020) 'Working with husband? "Occupation's wife" and married women's employment in the Censuses in England and Wales between 1851 and 1911', *Social Science History*, 44(4): 585–613.

Chapter 2

Alzywood, M., Jackson, D., Aveyard, H. and Brooke, J. (2020) 'COVID-19 reinforces the importance of handwashing', *Journal of Clinical Nursing*, 29(15–16): 2760–1.

Atlas, R. (2019) 'What is the role of design and architecture in slip, trip, and fall accidents?', *Proceedings of the Human Factors and Ergonomics Society 2019 Annual Meeting*, 531–6, https://journals.sagepub.com/doi/pdf/10.1177/1071181319631093

Bee, P. (2015) 'An incredibly filthy story you must read', *The Times*, 19 May.

Best, E.L and Redway, K. (2015) 'Comparison of different hand-drying methods: the potential for airborne microbe dispersal and contamination', *Journal of Hospital Infection*, 89(3): 215–17.

Breen, R. and Cooke, L.P. (2005) 'The persistence of the gendered division of labour', *European Sociological Review*, 21(1): 43–57.

Egert, M., Schmidt, I., Bussey, K. and Breves, R. (2010) 'A glimpse under the rim: the composition of microbial biofilm communities in domestic toilets', *Journal of Applied Microbiology*, 108(4): 1167–74.

Finch, J.E., Prince, J. and Hawksworth, M. (1978) 'A bacteriological survey of the domestic environment', *Journal of Applied Bacteriology*, 45(3): 357–64.

Global Hygiene Council, *Handwashing Fact Sheet*, https://www.hygienecouncil.org/media/3/factsheet-handwashing.pdf

Hateley, P.M. and Jurnaa, P.A. (1999) 'Hand washing is more common among healthcare workers than the public', *British Medical Journal*, 319: 518–21.

Miranda, V. (2011) 'Cooking, caring and volunteering: unpaid work around the world', *OECD, Social, Employment and Migration Working Papers* No.116, Paris: OECD Publishing.

Møretrø, T., Moen, B., Almli, V.L., Teixeira, P., Ferreira, V.B., Åsli, A.W., Nilsen, C. and Langsrud, S. (2021) 'Dishwashing sponges and brushes: consumer practices and bacterial growth and survival', *International Journal of Food Microbiology*, 337: 108928, https://doi.org/10.1016/j.ijfoodmicro.2020.108928

Morubagal, R.R., Shivappa, S.G., Mahale, R.P. and Neelambike, S.M. (2017) 'Study of bacterial flora associated with mobile phones of healthcare workers and non-healthcare workers', *Iranian Journal of Microbiology*, 9(3): 143–51.

National Safety Council (2023) 'Deaths in the home: introduction – injury facts', https://injuryfacts.nsc.org/home-and-community/deaths-in-the-home/introduction/

Pfefferle, P.I., Keber. C.U., Cohen, R.M. and Garn, H. (2021) 'The hygiene hypothesis: learning from but not living in the past', *Frontiers in Immunology*, 21, https://doi.org/10.3389/fimmu.2021.635935

Pilcher, J. (2000) 'Domestic divisions of labour in the twentieth century: "change slow a-coming"', *Work, Employment & Society*, 14(4): 771–80.

Pittet, D. and Allegranzi, B. (2018) 'Preventing sepsis in healthcare: 200 years after the birth of Ignaz Semmelweis', *Eurosurveillance*, 23(18): 18–00222, doi: 10.2807/1560-7917.ES.2018.23.18.18-00222

Royal Society for the Prevention of Accidents, *Safer by Design: A Framework to Reduce Serious Accidental Injury in New-build Homes*, https://www.rospa.com/home-safety/advice/safer-by-design

Royal Society for Public Health (2019) *Too Clean or Not Too Clean? Making the Case for Targeted Hygiene in the Home and Everyday Life*, https://www.rsph.org.uk/static/uploaded/06b37f30-2241-4e98-aba93fc15346e7a5.pdf

Stone, A. (2003) 'Audit of soap usage by a primary care team', *British Medical Journal*, 327: 1453–4.

WHO/UNICEF (2021) *State of the World's Hand Hygiene: A Global Call to Action to Make Hand Hygiene a Priority in Policy and Practice*, New York: UNICEF and WHO.

Chapter 3

Anon (1899) 'Importance of teaching domestic science', *The British Medical Journal*, 21 October, 1123–4.

Bayliss, R. (1975) 'Home economics and the special reports', *Journal of Educational Administration and History*, 7(1): 18–27.

Bayliss, R. and Daniels, C. (1988) 'The Physical Deterioration Report of 1904 and education in home economics', *History of Education Society Bulletin*, 4: 29–39.

Bird, E. (1998) '"High class cookery": gender, status and domestic subjects, 1890–1930', *Gender and Education*, 10(2): 117–31.

Booth, C. (ed) (1889–1903) *Life and Labour of the People in London*, London: Macmillan & Co.

Brewis, G. (2004) 'Matheson, (Marie) Cécile (1874–1950), settlement warden and social worker', *Oxford Dictionary of National Biography*.

Buckton, C.M. (1879) *Food and Home Cookery*, London: Longmans, Green.

Burstall, S.A. (1894) *The Education of Girls in the United States*, New York: Swan Sonnenschein & Co and London: Macmillan & Co.

Burstall, S.A. (1909) *Impressions of American Education in 1908*, London: Longmans, Green and Co.

Hunt, F. (ed) (1987) *Lessons for Life: The Schooling of Girls and Women 1850–1950*, Oxford: Basil Blackwell.

Klungseth, N.J. and Olsson, N.O.E. (2013) 'Norwegian cleaning research: an overview and categorization', *Facilities*, 31(7/8): 290–313.

Parloa, M. (1879) *First Principles of Household Management and Cookery: A Text-Book for Schools and Families*, Boston: Houghton, Mifflin & Co.

Randolph, E. (1942) *A Brief History of the Teaching of Home Economics in the Public Schools of the United States*, MSc thesis, Indianapolis College of Education, Butler University.

Ravenhill, A. (1910) *Household Foes: A Book for Boys and Girls*, London: Sidgwick & Jackson.

Ravenhill, A. and Heap, E. (1905) 'The present position assigned to hygiene teaching in primary & secondary schools', *Journal of the Royal Sanitary Institute*, 26(1–3): 173–5.

Sillitoe, H. (1933) *A History of the Teaching of Domestic Subjects*, London: Methuen & Co.

Smithells, A. (1901) 'Science teaching in relation to domestic economy', *The American Kitchen Magazine*, 14(4): 125–8.

Sundt, E. (1869) *Om renligheds-stellet i Norge* [On Cleanliness in Norway], Christiania: Abelsted.

Thompson, F. (1945) *Lark Rise to Candleford: A Trilogy*, London: Oxford University Press.

Turnbull, A. (1994) 'An isolated missionary: the domestic subjects teacher in England, 1870–1914', *Women's History Review*, 3(1): 81–100.

Wild, P.T. (nd) 'The mysterious early life of Maria Parloa', *The Bethel Grapevine*, https://www.bethelgrapevine.com/articles/the-mysterious-early-life-of-maria-parloa

Chapter 4

Iozzio, C. (2022) 'Who was Eliza Youmans?', https://www.popsci.com/science/eliza-youmans-profile/

Nutting, M.A. (1923) 'Annie Godfrey Dewey', *Journal of Home Economics*, 15(7): 357–69.

'Woman of the century/Harriette M. Plunket', https://en.wikisource.org/wiki/Woman_of_the_Century/Harriette_M._Plunket

Youmans, E.A., Chambers, T.K. and Cole, R.O. (1879) *Lessons in Cookery: Hand-book of the National Training School for Cookery (South Kensington, London)*, New York: D. Appleton.

Youmans, E.L. (1857) *The Hand-book of Household Science*, New York.

Chapter 5

Berry, F. (2017) 'Housewife writ large: Marie Méchanique, Paulette Bernège and new feminist domesticity in interwar France', *Oxford Art Journal*, 40(1): 7–26.

Davis, M.M. (2007) *Feminist Applepieville: Architecture as Social Reform in Charlotte Perkins Gilman's Fiction*, MA thesis, University of Missouri-Columbia.

DeRock, D. (2021) 'Hidden in plain sight: unpaid household services and the politics of GDP measurement', *New Political Economy*, 26(1): 20–35.

'The Frankfurt kitchen', *Wikipedia*. https://en.wikipedia.org/wiki/Frankfurt_kitchen

Frederick, C. (1929) *Selling Mrs. Consumer*, New York: The Business Bourse.

Gilbreth, F.B. and Carey, E.G. (1949, first published 1948) *Cheaper by the Dozen*, London: William Heinemann.

Gilbreth, F.B. and Carey, E.G. (1954, first published 1950) *Belles on Their Toes*, London: William Heinemann.

Graham, L.D. (1999) 'Domesticating efficiency: Lillian Gilbreth's scientific management of homemakers', *Signs*, 24(3): 633–75.

Hackney, F. (2016) 'Getting a living, getting a life: Leonora Eyles, employment and agony, 1925–1930', in S. Hawkins, N. Phillips, R. Ritchie and S.J. Kleinberg (eds) *Women in Magazines: Research, Representation, Production and Consumption*, London: Routledge, pp 107–24.

Joannou, M. (2004) 'Eyles [née Pitcairn; *other married name* Murray], (Margaret), novelist and journalist', *Oxford Dictionary of National Biography*.

Lichtenstein, D. (2013) 'Domestic novels of the 1920s: regulation and efficiency in *The Home-maker, Twilight Sleep,* and *Too Much Efficiency*', *American Studies*, 52(2): 65–88.

Llewellyn, M. (2004) 'Designed by women and designing women: gender, planning and the geographies of the kitchen in Britain 1917–1946', *Cultural Geographies*, 11(1): 42–60.

Midal, A. (2021) 'Death of women: the dark side of modern design history', *Design History Society Annual Conference 2–4 September*, Basel, Switzerland.

Paris, I. (2019) 'Between efficiency and comfort: the organization of domestic work and space from home economics to scientific management, 1841–1913', *History and Technology*, 35(1): 81–104.

'Paulette Bernège', *Wikipedia*. https://en.wikipedia.org/wiki/Paulette_Bern%C3%A8ge

Ryan, D. S. (2004) 'Peel [née Bayliff], Constance Dorothy Evelyn (1868–1934), journalist and writer on household management', *Oxford Dictionary of National Biography*.

Veblen, T. (1899) *The Theory of the Leisure Class: An Economic Study in the Evolution of Institutions*, New York: Macmillan.

Walker, L. (2002) 'Home making: an architectural perspective', *Signs*, 27(3): 823–35.

Winterson, G. (nd) Women's Pioneer Housing – a history', https://womenspioneer.co.uk/a-history-of-wph/#:~:text=On%204th%20October%201920,individual%20homes%20at%20moderate%20rents

Yun-Ae, Y. (1996) 'Margaret G. Reid: life and achievements', *Feminist Economics*, 2(3): 17–36.

Chapter 7

Creighton, L. (1907) *The Economics of the Household*, London: Longmans, Green & Co.

Creighton, L. (1909) *The Art of Living and Other Addresses to Girls*, London: Longmans, Green & Co.

Esdaile, P. (1927 and 1931) *Economic Biology for Students of Social Science*, London: University of London Press.

Evans, B. (2017) 'The national kitchen in Britain, 1917–1919', *Journal of War & Culture Studies*, 10(2): 115–29.

Gould, P. (1997) 'Women and the culture of university physics in late 19th-century Cambridge', *The British Journal for the History of Science*, 30(2): 127–49.

Hartwell, G.A. (1926) 'Yeast extract as a supplement to gelatin', *Biochemistry Journal*, 20(6): 1279–81.

Hutton, C. (2004) 'Holden, Charles (1875–1960), architect', *Oxford Dictionary of National Biography*.

Lane-Claypon, J.E. (1916) *Milk and its Hygienic Relations*, London: Medical Research Council.

Morabia, A. (2010) 'Janet Lane-Claypon-Interphase Epitome', *Epidemiology*, 21(4): 573–6.

Rayner-Canham, M. and Rayner-Canham, G. (2011) 'The rise and fall of domestic chemistry in higher education in England during the early 20th century', *Bulletin of the History of Chemistry*, 36(1): 35–42.

Reynolds, K.D. (2004) 'Greville [*née* Maynard], Frances Evelyn [Daisy], countess of Warwick (1861–1938)', *Oxford Dictionary of National Biography*.

Tinkler, C.K. and Masters, H. (1920 and 1925) *Applied Chemistry: A Practical Handbook for Students of Household Science and Public Health*, vols 1 and 2, London: Crosby Lockwood & Son.

Wallas, A. (1929) *Before the Bluestockings*, London: Allen & Unwin.

Winkelstein, W. (2006) 'Janet Elizabeth Lane-Claypon, a forgotten epidemiologic pioneer', *Epidemiology*, 17(6): 705.

Chapter 8
Bane, L. (1955) *The Story of Isabel Bevier*, Peoria: Chas. A. Bennett Co., Inc.

Coghlan, C.L. (2005) '"Please don't think of me as a sociologist": Sophonisba Preston Breckinridge and the early Chicago School', *The American Sociologist*, Spring: 1–22.

Deegan, M. (1988) *Jane Addams and the Men of the Chicago School, 1892–1918*, New York: Transaction Books.

Fact Source, 'How universities borrowed orphans to teach parenting', https://thefactsource.com/practice-babies-how-universities-borrowed-orphans-to-teach-parenting/

Fitzpatrick, E. (1990) *Endless Crusade: Women Social Scientists and Progressive Reform*, New York: Oxford University Press.

Jabour, A. (2012) 'Relationship and leadership: Sophonisba Breckinridge and women in social work', *Affilia*, 27(1): 22–37.

Smith, D. (1988) *The Chicago School: A Liberal Critique of Capitalism*, Houndmills: Macmillan Education.

Spain, D. (2011)'The Chicago of Jane Addams and Ernest Burgess: same city, different visions', in D.R. Judd and D. Simpson (eds) *The City, Revisited: Urban Theory from Chicago, Los Angeles and New York*, Minneapolis: University of Minnesota Prees, pp 51–64.

Talbot, M. (1917) 'Housekeeping and the public health', *American Journal of Public Health*, 7(12): 1026–30.

Chapter 9
Baker, N. (2020) 'The three energetic sisters: the women's organisations promoting electricity, gas and coal in the home', https://electrifyingwomen.org/the-three-energetic-sisters/

Bowden, S. and Offer, A. (1996) 'The revolution that never was: gender, class and the diffusion of household appliances in interwar England', in V. De Grazia with E. Furlough (eds) *The Sex of Things: Gender and Consumption in Historical Perspective*, Berkeley: University of California Press, pp 244–74.

Busch, J. (1983) 'Cooking competition: technology on the domestic market in the 1930s', *Technology and Culture*, 24(2): 222–45.

'The electrifying life of Caroline Haslett' (2020) Institute of Engineering and Technology Archives blog, https://ietarchivesblog.org/2020/12/24/the-electrifying-life-of-caroline-haslett/

Goodall, F. (1999) *Burning to Serve: Selling Gas in Competitive Markets*, Ashbourne: Landmark Publishing.

Gooday, G.J.N. (2004) 'Gordon [née Brandreth; *other married name* Butcher], Alice Mary, Lady Danesfort, (1854–1928), author and promoter of domestic electricity', *Oxford Dictionary of National Biography*.

Gooday, G. (2021) 'Women in energy engineering: changing roles and gender contexts in Britain, 1890–1934', in A.H. Moore and R.W. Sandwell (eds) *In a New Light: Histories of Women and Energy*, Montreal and Kingston: McGill-Queen's University Press, pp 114–33.

Locker, A. (2004) 'Partridge, Margaret Mary, (1891–1967), electrical engineer', *Oxford Dictionary of National Biography*.

'M. A. Cloudesley Brereton', *Wikipedia*. https://en.wikipedia.org/wiki/Cloudesley_Brereton

McConnell, A. (2004) 'Booth, Hubert Cecil, (1871–1955), civil engineer', *Oxford Dictionary of National Biography*.

Moore, A.H. and Sandwell, R. (eds) (2021) *In a New Light: Histories of Women and Energy*, Montreal and Kingston: McGill-Queen's University Press.

Peet, L.J. and Sater, L.E. (1934) *Household Equipment*, New York: John Wiley & Sons.

Pursell, C. (1993) '"Am I a lady or an engineer?" The origins of the Women's Engineering Society in Britain, 1918–1940', *Technology and Culture*, 34(1): 78–97.

Pursell, C. (1999) 'Domesticating modernity: the Electrical Association for Women, 1924–86', *The British Journal for the History of Science*, 32(1): 47–67.

Sprenger, E. and Webb, P. (1993) 'Persuading the housewife to use electricity? An interpretation of material in the Electricity Council Archives', *The British Journal for the History of Science*, 26(1): 55–65.

Chapter 10

'Benson, Clara', *Wikipedia*. https://en.wikipedia.org/wiki/Clara_Benson

Campbell, J.D. (1998) 'Benson, Gertrude Helen and Benson, William Noel', *Dictionary of New Zealand Biography*.

Fitzgerald, T (2007) 'An absent presence: women professors at the University of New Zealand 1911–1961', *Journal of Educational Administration and History*, 39(3): 239–53.

Hancock, M. (2001) 'Home science and the nationalization of domesticity in colonial India', *Modern Asian Studies*, 35(4): 871–903.

Hansen, K.T. (ed) (1992) *African Encounters with Domesticity*, New Brunswick: Rutgers University Press.

The Japan-British Exhibition, https://www.gardenhistorygirl.co.uk/post/the-japan-british-exhibition-of-1910/

Moxon, M.C. (1936) 'The development of home economics in Canada', *Journal of Home Economics*, 28(3): 148–50.

Sand, J. (2003) *House and Home in Modern Japan: Architecture, Domestic Space and Bourgeois Culture 1880–1930*, Cambridge, MA: Harvard University Press.

Sasaki, K., Uchiyama, Y. and Nakagomi, S. (2020) 'Study abroad and the transnational experience of Japanese women from 1860s–1920s: four stages of female study abroad, Sumi Miyakawa and Tamo Jōdai', *Espacio, Tiempo y Educación*, 7(2): 5–28.

Sparks, L. (2017) 'Too many cooks spoil the soup: conflicting British nutrition education policy approaches and African responses', *Journal of World History*, 28(3 & 4): 525–50.

Taylor, L. (1998) 'Strong, Ann Monroe Gilchrist', *Dictionary of New Zealand Biography*.

Thenilescribes (2017) 'Looking through Egyptian glass: the stained glass windows at U of T's Lillian Massey Building', 21 October, https://nilescribes.org/2017/10/21/stained-egyptian-glass-windows-at-lillian-massey-building/

Tipton, E.K. (2009) 'How to manage a household: creating middle class housewives in modern Japan', *Japanese Studies*, 29(1): 95–110.

Tomida, H. (1994) 'Ōe Sumi (1875–1948) and domestic science in Japan', in H. Cortazzi (ed) *Britain & Japan: Biographical Portraits*, Folkestone: Japan Library, pp 331–43.

Toronto Reference Library blog (2014) '100 years of light! Explanation of the stained glass windows in the Lillian Massey Building, University of Toronto', 27 February, https://torontopubliclibrary.typepad.com/trl/2014/02/100-years-of-light-the-stained-glass-story-at-the-lillian-massey-building.html

Vanleek Hill Stories 'A history of racism and stereotyping in Vankleek Hill's past', https://vankleekhillstories.wordpress.com/2021/02/26/black-history-month/#more-1080

Chapter 11

Bruckdorfer, R. (2004) 'Yudkin, John (1910–1995), nutritionist', *Oxford Dictionary of National Biography*.

Dalla Costa, M. and James, S. (1973) *Power of Women and the Subversion of the Community*, London: Falling Wall Press.

Garmus, B. (2022) *Lessons in Chemistry*, New York: Doubleday.

Toupin, L. (2018) *Wages for Housework: A History of an International Feminist Movement, 1972–77*, London: Pluto Press.

Yudkin, J. (1972) *Pure, White and Deadly: The Problem of Sugar*, London: Davis-Poynter.

Index

References to figures appear in *italic* type; those in **bold** type refer to tables.

A

Abbott, A. 149
Abbott, E. 131, 140–1, 143, 149
Adams, P. 112–13
Addams, J. 142, 149
advertisements 152, 154–6, 163–4, 174, *175*
African Gold Coast 174
AIDS epidemic 9
Akiyama, Y. 8
all-electric homes 168–70, *171*
American Home Economics Association (AHEA) 8, 187, 197
American Kitchen Magazine 67
American Woman's Home, The (Beecher) 80–1
Applecroft Experiment Station 74–5
Applied Chemistry (Tinkler & Masters) 120
architecture *see* house design
army 29
Asbjørnsen, P.C. 202–3
Asquith, E. 109
Association of Collegiate Alumnae (ACA) 132
Association of Teachers of Domestic Science 31
astronauts 201–2
Atkins, J. 108–9, 110
Atkinson, M. 7, 83–4, 85, 87, 96, 98, 104
attachment theory 148
Atwater, W. 57, 60, 140, 144
Austin, A. 81

B

babies xvi, xvii, 2, 74, 122, 147–8
bacteria 13–15, 19, *52*
  see also germs; microbes
bacteriology 45, 51–2, 63, 103–4
Baddeley, F. 98, 105
Balfour, A. 109
Barnett, H. 33
Baroda College of Science 188–9
Barrows, A. 60
Barry, A. 88
Batchelor, F. 185
Bateson, F. 191–2
Beale, P. 96
Bedford College 90, 180–1
beds 17
Beecher, C. 24–5, 49, 65, 80, 194

Beeton, I. 51, 54
Belgium 13, 26, 27, 35, 77, 177
Bell, V. 91
Bemba tribe 189
Benson, C. 184, 185
Bernège, P. 68–9, *70*, 77, 198
Berry, M. 167
Betjeman, J. 201
Beveridge, W. 127
Bevier, I. 144–5, 146, *147*
Black, C. 67–8, 82, 87, 94
Blackwell, E. 55
Blakestad, N. 93
Bondfield, M. 97
Bonham Carter, Hilary 108
Bonham Carter, Hugh 108
Book of Household Management (Beeton) 51, 54–5
Booth, C. 39, 40
Booth, H.C. 165, 166
Borrowed Babies (Christman) 148
Bourke, J. 1
boys 19, 28, 29, 32
Boys-Smith, W. 185, 186–7, 198
bread 145
Breckinridge, S. 131, 137–8, 139, 140, *141*, 143, 147, 149
Brereton, C. 126
Brereton, M.A.C. 126, 161–2, 164, 171
Bristol All-Electric House 169, *170*
British Commercial Gas Association (BCGA) 161, 162
British Vacuum Cleaner Company 165, 166
Buckley, B. 109
Buckmaster, J.C. 29–30
Buckton, C. 194
Bulmer, M. 149
Burgess, E. 141, 142
Burrows, R. 126
Burstall, S. 28, 31–2, 34–5
Business of Home Management, The (Pattison) 58, 72

C

Calder, F. 31, 33
Calorimeter 139–40
Campbell, H. 7, 49, 72–3, 153
Canada 173–4, 182–4
Candee, H.C. 67

Captive Wife, The (Gavron) 5
care work 18, 84
Cartesian principle 68–9
Chicago School of Civics and Philanthropy (CSCP) 143
Chicago School of Sociology, The (Bulmer) 149
Chicago School, The (Smith) 149
children *see* babies
citizenship 137–8
cleanability 69–71, 204
cleaning xxi
cleaning products xxi
  see also household products
cleaning utensils 15, *16*
cleanliness 3, 9, 10, 14–15, 18–20, 27, 189, 194
  see also food hygiene; hand hygiene; hygiene
cleanliness project 18
clothes washing *see* laundry
co-operative housekeeping 82
coal 153
colonialism 174–5
  see also Canada; India; New Zealand
Columbia University 178–9
cookers 166
  see also stoves
cookery xxi, 8, 25, *26*, 27, 29–31, 47–8
  see also food hygiene
cookery books 54–5
Cooking by Gas (Brereton) 161–2, 164
Cornell University 148, 193
Cost of Shelter, The (Richards) 70
COVID-19 pandemic 12–13, 131
Cradock, F. 167
Creighton, L. 117
Crick, D.E. 32
Cutler, J. 91

D

daily schedule (Frederick) **75**
Davidson, C. 152
De la méthode ménagère (Bernège) 68–9
de Zwart, M.L. 173–4, 175
Decorative Electricity (Gordon) 154
Deegan, M.J. 142, 149
Delamont, S. 149
Dendy, A. 96
'Department and discipline' (Diner) 149
Descartes, R. 68–9
Dewey, M. & A. 60–1
Dewey, T. 109
Dillon, T. 116
Diner, S. 149
Dingman's Electric soap 174
Dingman's Electric soap advertisement *175*

dirt 9
  see also germs
Dirty Linen (Kaufmann) 12, 21
disease 195
  miasma theory of 44–5
  see also health
dishwashing 15, *16*, 30
division of labour xvi–xvii, 20–1
Domecon, D. 147–8
domestic accidents 15–16
Domestic Economy as a Factor of Public Education (Richards) 33
Domestic Economy (Newsholme & Scott) 34
Domestic Receipt Book (Beecher) 194
domestic science *see* household science
domestic science education xiii–xiv, 23, 25–9
  and colonialism 174–6, 182–90
  cookery 29–31
  hygiene and health 38–41, 194
  international exchanges 34–6
  Japan 176, 177 *(see also* Inoue, H.; Miyakawa, S.)
  London School of Electrical Domestic Science 167–8
  reputation 31–3
  resistance to 42
  textbooks 33–4
  A Treatise on Domestic Economy (Beecher) 24–5
  and whiteness 173–4
  see also household science; household science courses; Ravenhill, A.
Domestic Science for High Schools in India (Strong) 189
domestic science movement 56, 64, 66, 68, 77, 173, 194–5
  see also household science movement
domestic servants 58–9
Domestic Service (Salmon) 59
domestic technologies 54, 71, 75, 151–2, 158, 161
  all-electric homes 168–70, 171
  and housework hours 171
  Japan 177, 182
  lady demonstrators 166–8
  see also Electrical Housecraft; electricity; gas; hairdryers; vacuum cleaners
Dover, H. 167
drains 44–7
Draper, A. 146
Dreilinger, D. 201
Dunn, J.H. 201
Durkheim, É. xvii
dust 17–18
Dust and Its Dangers (Prudden) 53–4
dust-garden methodology 52, *53*
Dyer, M. 185

Index

E

Easiest Way in Housekeeping, The (Campbell) 72–3, 153
Economic Biology for Students of Social Science (Esdaile) 120
Economic Problems of the Family (Kyrk) 84
economic theory 82–6
economics 104
Economics: Descriptive and Theoretical (McKillop & Atkinson) 83–4
Economics of Household Production (Reid) 85
Edison, T. 153
Education of Women, The (Talbot) 134
Edwards, E. 153, 171
efficiency 73–7, 80, 176
Efficient Housekeeping or Household Engineering (Frederick) 74
Ehrenreich, B. 8, 150
'Electric Flat for Bachelor Girls' 168–9
electric lighting 153–4, 164
electric soap 174
electric soap advertisement *175*
Electrical Association for Women (EAW) 152, 159–61, 166, 167
Electrical Development Association (EDA) 159, 161
Electrical Handbook for Women, The (EAW) 160–1, 164, *165*
Electrical Housecraft 160–1
electricity 151, 152, 154–8
all-electric homes 168–70, 171
and health 162–6
English, D. 8, 150
Environmental Health Review (journal) 15
Esdaile, P. 120
euthenics 63
Eyles, L. 66–7

F

Faithfull, E. 92
Faithfull, L. 92–3, 94, *95*, 96, 97, 98
family and consumer sciences 197
family wage 83
'female redomestication' 80
feminism 7–8
Finkelstein, B. 202
Finland 26
First World War 125
food xxi
see also cookery
Food and Dietetics (Norton) 139
Food and Home Cookery (Buckton) 25, *26*
food hygiene 14–15, 54, 194
For Her Own Good (Ehrenreich & English) 8, 150
France 14, 26, 27, 35, 68–9, 130, 177, 179
Frankfurt Kitchen 77–81

Frederick, C. 3, 72, 73–5, 77, 82, 176, 198
Freund, I. 110–12

G

Gabe, F. 191–2
Garton, R. 109
gas 151, 152, 161–2, 177
and health 162–6
gas cookers 166
gas lighting 153
gas meter 72
gender
and cleanliness 19–20
and educational opportunities 28–9, 37
(see also domestic science education)
and house design 66–9
and housework 18–19, 20–1, 27–8, 29, 76, 172
and 'seperate spheres' 204–5
see also boys; girls; women
germ theory 44–5, 50, 132
Germany 23, 26, 35, 57, 77, 80, 177, 179
Frankfurt Kitchen 77–81
Women's Engineering Society 160
germs 13–15, 195
see also bacteria; microbes
GERMS (journal) 14
Ghana 174
Gilbreth, L. 49, 72, 73–4, 76, 159
Gilliland, M. xiv
Gilman, C.P. 65, 81, 199
girls 19, 176
see also domestic science education; gender
Girls' Realm Annual 92
Gloucester School of Domestic Science 105
Gordon, A. 154
Gospel of Germs, The (Tomes) 9, 195
Gradwell, C. 96–7, 104
Grand Domestic Revolution, The (Hayden) 81
Grey, M. 88
Griggs, M.B. 175
gross domestic product (GDP) 84

H

Hagemann, K. 79–80
hairdryers 154, *155*
Haldane Commission 116–18, 127
hand hygiene 12–14
Handbook of Household Science, The (Youmans) 56
handwashing 19
Harper, W.R. 134, 137
Haslett, C. 158–9, 159–60, 161, 164, 167, 168, 171, 198
Hayden, D. 81
Headlam, A. 109

health 38–41, 162–6, 194–6
  see also disease
Heath, F. 96
Helgesen, H. 35
Henderson, C. 134
Hierta-Retzius, A. 35
Hinduism 189
Hinman Abel, M. 57
Hobhouse, L. 127
Holden, C. 112–13
Holiday, H. 183
home economics *see* household science
Home Sanitation (Talbot & Richards) 132, *133*
Hoodless, A. 30–1, 46, 198
Hopkins, F.G. 195
house design
  all-electric homes 168–70, 171
  and cleanability 69–71
  Frankfurt Kitchen 77–81
  and gender 66–9
  kitchenless homes 81–2
  Rumford Kitchen 56–7, 143
  self-cleaning house 191–2
  smart houses 203–4
House, The (Bevier) 144–5
Household Administration (Inoue) 179
Household Administration (Ravenhill) 84
household appliances *see* domestic technologies
Household Bacteriology (Elliott) 51–2
Household Electricity (Haslett) 164
Household Equipment (Peet) 171
Household Equipment (Peet & Sater) 71
Household Foes (Ravenhill) 28
household production 84, 85
household products xxi, 21–2
household science 7–9, 10–11, 131–2, 149–50, 205–6
household science courses 161, 196–8
  King's College for Women (KCW) 101–2, 103–5, 118–22
  criticism 110–12
  King's College Women's Department 98–100
  see also domestic science education; King's College of Household and Social Science (KHSS)
household science movement 2, 3, 7, 8, 10, 42
  criticism 110
  legacies 192–6, 201–3
  see also domestic science movement
housewife, definition 6
housewife films 21–2
housewifery 27, 28–9, 31–2
housework
  before 20th century 47–50
  author's academic interest in 4–5
  author's adult experience of x, xv–xvi, xvii–xx
  author's childhood memories of x–xiii, xiv–xv
  co-operative 82
  definitions 1, 2
  and economic theory 82–6
  and gender 18–19, 20–1, 27–8, 29, 76, 172
  Japan 176–7
  and patriarchy xvii
  practical aids xxi–xxii
  practical tips xx–xxi, *121*
  scientific 2, 71–6, 205 (*see also* domestic science education; household science)
  daily schedule (Frederick) **75**
  Frankfurt Kitchen 77–81
  satire about 76–7
  wages for 199–201
  women's lack of enthusiasm for 38–9
  working hours 170–1
Housework the Easy Way (Rayner) xviii
housing 39, 66
Howes, E.P. 81–2
Hull-House Settlement 36, 142–3
Hutchins, B. 97
hygiene 36–7, 39–40, 49–50, 97, 119, 194
  see also cleanliness; food hygiene; hand hygiene
hygiene hypothesis 18
Hygiene of Women and Children (Lane-Claypon) 122–3

I

If Women Made Houses (Bernège) 69
India 188–9
infant mortality 39, 54
Inoue, H. 177–80, 198
Institute for the Coordination of Women's Interests 81–2
Institute of Domestic Science, Japan 181–2
International Health Exhibition 1884 49–50
International Journal of Applied Microbiology 13
Introduction to the Science of Sociology (Park and Burgess) 142
Iowa State College 161
Ireland 153
ironing xx–xxi, 153, 156–7, 189
irons 158
Irwin, M. 178

J

James, S. 200
Japan 174–5, 176–7
Japan Women's University 180
Japanese educators 177–82
Jenkins, M. 186
Johnson, B. 13

Index

K

Kaufmann, J.-C. 12, 21
Kedzie, N. 2–3
King, F. 185
King's College
  Lectures for Ladies 88–92
  nutritional sciences 197
  Women's Department
    development of household science 92–7
    household science courses 98–100
King's College for Women (KCW)
  Campden Hill building 112–16
  college magazine 107
  criticism 110–12
  first students 100–1
  fund-raising and publicity 102–3, 108–10
  graduate jobs 115, 125–6
  Haldane Commission 116–18, 127
  household science courses 101–2, 103–5, 118–22
  nutrition research 123–5
  practice house 147
  social science courses 126–7
  staff and students *106, 118*
King's College of Household and Social Science (KCHSS) 87, 108, 116, 127, 128–9, 161, 193, 198–9
King's Minstrel (magazine) 107
kitchens 14–15, 30–1, 194
  All-Electric House 169
  Frankfurt Kitchen 77–81
  kitchenless homes 81–2
  National Kitchen 125
  Rumford Kitchen 56–7, 143
Klepp, I. 20
knitting 130
Koch, R. 51
Kyrk, H. 84–5, 144

L

labour, division of xvi–xvii, 20–1
Labour-saving House, The (Peel) 66
Ladies' College, Edinburgh 32
Laird, A. 184–5
Lake Placid convention 44, 59–63, 179
Lancaster, M. 154–5
Lane-Claypon, J. 122–3, 125, 126, 127
Langworthy, C. 60
Lark Rise to Candleford (Thompson) 28
Lathrop, J. 143
laundry xx–xxi, 12, 19–20, 21, 33, 49, 153, 189, 191
  see also washing machines
laundry detergent 174, *175*
Lawrence, M. 126
'laws of health' 194

Lectures for Ladies 88–92
Life and Labour of the People in London (Booth) 39
lighting 153–4
Lihotzky, G. 77–81
Lillian Massey School of Household Science 184, 185
Lindsay, J. 126
Liverpool Cookery School 31
London School of Economics (LSE) 96, 126–7
London School of Electrical Domestic Science 167–8

M

MacArthur, M. 97
MacDonald, I. 108
MacDonald, R. 108
Maclean's (magazine) 184
Maharaja Sayajirao University 188
Mainardi, P. 204
Making of the Home (Barnett) 33–4
Malawi 175
Man-made World, The (Gilman) 65
manual training 32
Marshall, A. 83
Massey, L. 184
Masters, H. 120
Matheson, C. 23
Matheson, H. 27
Matthews, M. 159
McKillop, M. 83–4, 87, 91, 94, 98, 161, 198
Meiji era, Japan 176
Mellanby, E. 123–4, 127
Mellanby, M. 123, 124–5
Memoirs of an Educational Pioneer (Ravenhill) 37
menstruation 49
Merchant Shipping Act 1906 29
Meyer, A. 94, *95*, 96, 108, 109
Meyer, C. 94
miasma theory of disease 44–5
microbe-hunters 51
microbes 50–5
  see also bacteria; germs
Miers, H. 109
Milk and its Hygienic Relations (Lane-Claypon) 122
mission schools 174–5
Miyakawa, S. 177, 180–2
mobile phones 14, 19
Modern Household, The (Talbot & Breckinridge) 139
Modern Utopia, A (Wells) 70–1
More Than Lore (Talbot) 132
Morgan, A.F. 146–7
Morgan, R. 8
Morley, E. 90–1, 93

Morrill Land Grant Act 1862, US 131
mortality rates 195
Mosley, E. 168
motherhood 2
  see also babies
Mottram, V. 125, 128–9, 199
Mount Holyoke system 132

N

National Association of Teachers of Home Economics 31
National Health Service 10, 15
National Health Society 37, 45, 55–6
National Kitchen 125
National Training School of Cookery 30, 31
Nautical Cookery Schools 29
navy 29
needlework 26, 27, 174
Never Done (Strasser) 48–9
New England Kitchen 56–7
New Housekeeping, The (Frederick) 77
New Way of Housekeeping, A (Black) 68, 82
'New World' stove 151
New Zealand 185–7, 189–90
Newman, D. 169
Northern Union of Training Schools of Cookery 31
Norton, A.P. 139
Norton, M.P. 60
Norway 14, 21–2, 26, 35, 41, 202–3
nutrition 194–5
nutrition research 123–5, 145, 146–7, 185, 201–2
nutritional sciences 197, 198–9

O

Oakeley, H. 97, 98, 100, 105, 109, 112, 116, 117, 121–2, 126, 130
Occupation Housewife (Lopata) 5
Old Maids (Gray) 88
On Cleanliness in Norway (Sundt) 41
Otago University 185–7, 189–90

P

Palmer, A.F. 97, 130, 134, 137, 138, 147, 149
Park, C.C. 142
Park, R. 141, 142
Parloa, M. 35, 60
Partridge, M. 168, 169–70
Pasteur, L. 51
pathogens *see* germs
patriarchy xvii, 41
Pattern, M. 167
Peel, C. 66
Peet, L. 71, 171
periodic table cupcakes *111*
Pettitt, A.K. 6

Physical Deterioration Report 1904 40–1
Pillow, M. 10, 39, 46–7, 55
plumbing 45–7
Plumer, E. 117
Plunkett, H. 44, 45, 47, 50
poetry 201
Politics of Housework, The (Mainardi) xx, 204
porridge feud, Norway 202–3
Portugal 14
practice houses 147–8
Prudden, T.M. 52–4
public baths 8
Public School Domestic Science (Hoodless) 30–1
Pure, White and Deadly (Yudkin) 198
Purity and Danger (Douglas) 9, 10

Q

Queen Elizabeth College 198–9

R

racism *see* whiteness
Radclyffe Hall, M. 91
Rapp, R. 202
Ravenhill, A. 7, 28, 32, 36–8, 40, 60, 87, 93, *95*, 96, 97, 98, 102, 182–3, 195
Rawson, H. 185, 187
refrigerators 158, 163–4
Reid, M. 85, 86
Rentokil 19
Report of the Interdepartmental Committee on Physical Deterioration 1904 40–1
research *see* nutrition research; Respiration Calorimeter
Respiration Calorimeter *140*
Richards, A. 189
Richards, E. 7, 33, 37, 57, 61–3, *62*, 70, 131, 132, 135, 144, 147
Richardson, O. 97
Richardson, R.B. 46
Richmond, E. 166
rickets research 124
Roberts, E. 50
Robinson, R. 111
Rockefeller, J.D. 132
Roosevelt, T. 103
Rossiter, M. 197
Royal Society for the Prevention of Accidents (RoSPA) 15–16
Rücker, A. 94, 111–12
Rücker, T. 94, *95*, 96, 98, 102, 109, 164
Rumford Kitchen 56–7, 143
Russia 179

S

Sanitary Institute 56
sanitary reform 55–6
sanitation 133–4
Sater, L. 71
Sayajirao Gaekwad (Maharaja) 188

Index

Schmitz, C. 88, 90, 92
Schütte-Lihotzky, M. *see* Lihotzky, G.
science 50, 160
scientific housework 2, 7, 71–6, 205
   daily schedule (Frederick) **75**
   Frankfurt Kitchen 77–81
   satire about 76–7
   see also domestic science education;
      household science
Scott, M. 34
   see also Pillow, M.
Second World War 130
Secret History of Home Economics
   (Dreilinger) 201
self-cleaning house 191–2
Selling Mrs Consumer (Frederick) 82–3
Semmelweis, I. 19
Sensible Cookery (Asbjørnsen) 203
'seperate spheres' 204
servants 58–9
settlement sociology 7, 142–3
sewing machines 166
sexism 142, 149
Shaw, P.A. 57
Sheard, S. 8
Sherman, H. 60
Shields, R. 122
Si les femmes faisaient les maisons (Bernège) 69
silverfish 17, *18*
Singer, I. 166
Skinner, Z. xi, 167
Small, A. 134, 140, 141
smart houses 203–4
Smith, A. 84
Smith, D. 149
Smithells, A. 42, 87, 101, 103, 112
social science courses 126–7
sociology 133–4, 137, 148–9
   and sanitary science 141–4
   settlement sociology 7
Sociology of Housework, The (Oakley) 4–6
Some Points in the Making and Judging of Bread (Bevier) 145
space programme 201–2
Spurgeon, C. 93
Starr, F. 134
Stephen, L. 91
stoves 151
   see also cookers
Strong, A.G. 187–90
Studholme, J. 185–6, 188
'subaltern's love-song, A' (Betjeman) 201
Sundt, E. 203
Swan, J. 153
Sweden 13, 26, 28, 35–6

T

Talbot, M. 130, 131, 132–7, 138–9, 147, 149, 179
Tale of Two Cities, A (Dickens) 130
Taylor, F. 71–2
Taylor, M. 98, 102
Teacher's Manual of Elementary Laundry Work
   (Calder & Mann) 33
technology *see* domestic technologies
televisions 158
Theory of the Leisure Class (Veblen) 82
Thomas, W.I. 141, 142
Thompson, F. 28
Tinkler, C. 120
Tomes, N. 195
Treatise on Domestic Economy
   (Beecher) 24–5
Trinidad and Tobago 174–5
Twilight Sleep (Wharton) 77

U

United Kingdom (UK) 14–15, 26–7, 31, 39–40, 158, 179, 180–1
United Nations 18–19
United States 26, 27, 32–3, 35, 131–2, 178–9
University of Chicago 130, 132, 136–7, 179, 197
   Department of Household Administration 138–41, 149
   Department of Social Science and Anthropology 134–5, 141–4
   Dicky Domecon 147–8
   nutrition research 146–7
   School of Social Service Administration (SSA) 143
University of Illinois 144–6, 175, 197
University of Toronto 182–4, 196
University of West Virginia 197
Urwick, E.J. 127

V

vacuum cleaners 17, *156*, 158, 165–6
van Bronswijk, J. 17, 18
Vassar, M. 135
Veblen, T. 82
Vestry Hall, Kensington *89*
Vincent, G. 179

W

Wade Park School, Cleveland 32
wages for housework movement 1, 199–201
Wallas, A. 126
Wallas, G. 126
Warr, G. 88, 91
washing *see* laundry
washing machines 158, 182
washing-up aids 15, *16*
Wasting Girls' Time (Attar) 7–8
Webb, S. 127
Well of Loneliness, The (Radclyffe Hall) 91
Westminster School of Business Training for Women 97

Wharrie, M.W. 109
Wharton, E. 76–7
What Diantha Did (Gilman) 81
white sauce 174
whiteness 172, 173–5
Wilkinson, E. 172
Williams, E. 6
Woman in the Little House, The (Eyles) 66–7
Woman (magazine) xviii
Woman's Own (magazine) xviii
women
  cleanliness 19–20
  employment 58–9, 166–8
  housework 18–19, 38–9, 170
  and sanitary reform 55–6
  University of Chicago 138
  working hours 170
  see also gender
Women, Peace and Welfare (Oakley) 6–7

Women, Plumbers, and Doctors (Plunkett) 44, 45, *46*, 47
Women Scientists in America (Rossiter) 10
Women's Advisory Council on Solid Fuel 152
Women's Congress 102
Women's Engineering Society (WES) 159
Women's Gas Council (WGC) 152
Women's Industrial Council 67, 97
women's liberation movement 200
women's movement 1
Women's Pioneer Housing 66
women's rights 197–8
Women's Work is Never Done (Davidson) 152
Woolf, V. 91
World War I 125
World War II 130

Y

Yudkin, J. 198

www.ingramcontent.com/pod-product-compliance
Lightning Source LLC
Chambersburg PA
CBHW051533020426
42333CB00016B/1911